KT-439-411

Orde
Class: 781.285 ESC
Accession No: 136107
Type: 3 Weeks

'I really know very little about the technology of these instruments . . . but I do know what their buttons do. I have a lot of analog instruments in my setup still, and I know if I turn this little button it gives me a little more brightness, for instance. So, when I sit down to play – which I do almost every day – the first thing I do is find me a sound. The moment I have a sound, I have some music.' *Josef Zawinul, keyboardist and band leader for Weather Report.* (**Mandel, 1996**)

Tower Hamlets College
Learning Centre

136107

WITHDRAWN FROM ~~~~~~~~ COLLEGES
SIXTH FORM LIBRARY

£17.99

Cambridge Introductions to Music

Music Technology

Emphasising the creative aspect of music technology, this *Introduction* sets out an overview of the field for music students in a non-scientific and straightforward way. Engaging and user-friendly, the book covers studio concepts: basic audio and the studio workflow, including audio and MIDI recording. It explores synthesisers, samplers and drum machines as well as basic concepts for electronic performance. In considering the role of the DJ, the book addresses remixing and production, drawing upon many examples from the popular music repertoire as well as looking at the studio as an experimental laboratory. The creative workflow involved in music for media is discussed, as well as controllers for performance and the basics of hacking electronics for music. The *Introduction* as a whole reflects the many exciting areas found today in music technology, and aims to set aspiring musicians off on a journey of discovery in electronic music.

JULIO D'ESCRIVÁN is Reader in Creative Music Technology at Anglia Ruskin University, Cambridge.

Cambridge Introductions to Music

'Cambridge University Press is to be congratulated for formulating the idea of an "Introductions to Music" series.' Nicholas Jones, *The Musical Times*

Each book in this series focuses on a topic fundamental to the study of music at undergraduate and graduate level. The introductions will also appeal to readers who want to broaden their understanding of the music they enjoy.

- Contain textboxes which highlight and summarise key information
- Provide helpful guidance on specialised musical terminology
- Thorough guides to further reading assist the reader in investigating the topic in more depth

Books in the series

Gregorian Chant   David Hiley

Music Technology   Julio d'Escriván

Serialism   Arnold Whittall

The Sonata   Thomas Schmidt-Beste

The Song Cycle   Laura Tunbridge

Cambridge Introductions to Music

Music Technology

JULIO D'ESCRIVÁN

THE LEARNING CENTRE
TOWER HAMLETS COLLEGE
ARBOUR SQUARE
LONDON E1 0PS

CAMBRIDGE
UNIVERSITY PRESS

CAMBRIDGE
UNIVERSITY PRESS

University Printing House, Cambridge CB2 8BS, United Kingdom

Published in the United States of America by Cambridge University Press, New York

Cambridge University Press is part of the University of Cambridge.

It furthers the University's mission by disseminating knowledge in the pursuit of education, learning and research at the highest international levels of excellence.

www.cambridge.org
Information on this title: www.cambridge.org/9780521170420

© Julio d'Escriván 2012

This publication is in copyright. Subject to statutory exception and to the provisions of relevant collective licensing agreements, no reproduction of any part may take place without the written permission of Cambridge University Press.

First published 2011, 2012
Second Edition 2012
Reprinted 2013

A catalogue record for this publication is available from the British Library

Library of Congress Cataloguing in Publication data
Escriván Rincón, Julio d', 1957–
Music technology / Julio d'Escriván.
    p.   cm. – (Cambridge introductions to music)
Includes bibliographical references and index.
ISBN 978-1-107-00080-3 (hardback) – ISBN 978-0-521-17042-0 (paperback)
1. Music – Data processing.   2. Sound – Recording and reproducing –
Digital techniques.   I. Title.   II. Series.
ML74.E83   2011
786.7 – dc23   2011033056

ISBN 978-1-107-00080-3 Hardback
ISBN 978-0-521-17042-0 Paperback

Cambridge University Press has no responsibility for the persistence or accuracy of URLs for external or third-party internet websites referred to in this publication, and does not guarantee that any content on such websites is, or will remain, accurate or appropriate.

Contents

Preface

It is difficult to know exactly when electronic music became part of university curricula, but it was probably as early as the 1960s, at least at graduate level. However, we can safely say that 'music technology' as a subject, or as the title of a course, is a fairly recent development. The term probably began to be used in the late 1990s and has only become a standard feature of the higher education on offer in the 2000s. There are a great number of music technology courses all over the world. In Great Britain alone there are, at the time of writing, around eighty-three higher education institutions that offer BA Honours degrees in some aspect of music technology: creative music technology, sound technology, music production, music and sonic arts, and many other variations. The subject is popular and encompasses a wide variety of topics, including sound synthesis, composition, sonic art, electronic music, music for media, computer music and many others.

The problem is, in a sense, how wide ranging the choices are. It is a problem for students, since under a similar heading they can expect very different courses from different institutions. It is a problem for universities, because there are many types of candidates with different but useful skill-sets that are suitable for the course (two of my best students did not have any music background, but had foundation studies in art and design).

But how is music technology different from audio technology? Audio technology only becomes music technology when it is applied to music-making. This sounds obvious to begin with, but it isn't. From an old-school perspective, anyone who is 'twirling the knobs' or programming is a technician and not a musician. And, indeed, this is how it all began. The reality of it is that as technical facilities have become more accessible, musicians have become empowered. They no longer have to rely on a specialist to make the machines work, as was the case up to the early 1980s. MIDI and hard-disk recording have firmly put the musician in the driving seat. Technology is now also at the service of composing, arranging, writing and orchestrating music, as much as in the past it has been at the service of recording and synthesis. This is not to say that we don't need audio technologists. Audio scientists are indispensable, as they calculate necessary stuff like more natural-sounding reverbs, digital-signal processing plugins, new synthesis algorithms, software abstractions, and develop the informatics of sound management and storage. Yet without a doubt, these pursuits remain firmly in the field of science, sometimes without enough contribution from artists looking to use and misuse the tools. Yet there is probably more science in everyday music-making than there ever was before. This signals a change in education curricula which is only happening gradually, so it is not uncommon to have first-year students balk at the idea of learning to code or calculate (or even be aware of) an acoustic measurement; they didn't think they had signed up for that!

This book will help you explore current trends in music technology while introducing some key concepts and techniques: it aims to give you an overall view of the field. It probably isn't deep enough or comprehensive enough so, beware, this is only the tip of the iceberg. There is a lot of follow-up work you need to do. Simply reading it is not enough. Try and verify the ideas presented here regarding microphones, production and mastering, for instance, in your own music-making. Think about the experimental possibilities of your studio, dream up weird and wonderful controllers, get ready to hack your younger siblings' (or children's) toys. Follow the threads of information provided by the references and you will discover a rich world of musical experience, much more than I can include in fewer than 75,000 words. It will enable you to embark on what could be a lifelong journey of creative interaction with technology for the sake of making beautiful sound.

I have organised the book into four areas. Broadly speaking, Chapters 1, 2 and 3 review the basics of sound and consider the process of recording and creativity in the studio. Chapters 4 and 5 are more focused on DJ and laptop performance issues. Chapters 6 and 7 are aimed at the working musician: it is probable your work as a professional in the near future may strongly involve production or making music for media. Chapters 8, 9 and 10 are dedicated to creative music technology, where we will look at The 'X-Files' of music technology: dreamt-up musical instruments coming to life; making musical sounds with unthinkable objects and generally pushing our gear to the limits for the elusive prize – a sound that will give us some music.

Acknowledgements

Although I am certain I will forget somebody, I will try to mention everyone I am in debt to. So . . . for making it happen, the editors, without whom I wouldn't even have thought of writing this book: Vicki Cooper who had the idea of commissioning a title like this for the *Introductions* series, and Becky Taylor who, together with Vicki, gave me the support, encouragement and guidance I needed during the writing process. Also to my Production Editor Christina Sarigiannidou who helped me navigate the intricacy of the final stage with kindness and good humour. For generously supporting me through a sabbatical for most of the period of writing I am grateful to Anglia Ruskin University and in particular to my Head of Department Paul Jackson, whose friendship and collegiate spirit have helped me through this project. For kindly reviewing chapters for me: Nick Collins (the English one, the younger, who is always a mentor to me in these things); Justin 'Dr Hip Hop' Williams; film composer and fellow scholar, Miguel Mera; film composer Roger Jackson; *compadre* Gareth Stuart; and admired creative music programmer, Thor Magnusson. For being part of the Twitter and Facebook crowdsource that I bounced ideas back and forth with: fellow author Bob Gluck; fellow composer and SuperColliderrer Jason Dixon; fellow composer Miguel Noya; my former students and friends Paul Jones, Jack Ashley, Natasha Roberts and Daniel Smith; and all those who poked me with their comments, likes and tweets as I shared my book-writing pains! And, for giving me helpful comments in class as I tried my explanations and graphics on them, my students of Laptop Musicianship at Anglia Ruskin University.

Finally, Milly, my wife and partner, who supports me unconditionally and my beautiful artistic daughters, Isabel, Mariela, Emilia and Ana Teresa. *Music Technology* is dedicated to them.

Figures

Every effort has been made to trace the copyright holders for all images used. In the event of any query please contact the publisher.

Chapter 1

Representing and storing sound

In this chapter we will describe the basic physics of sound and what an audio signal is. We will look at how we work out sound levels and, in simple terms, some of the maths behind that. We also discuss digital recording and therefore sampling. We describe different ways of representing sound and the way we perceive different frequencies. Finally, we discuss the capture and storage of sound as computer data and the most common standards for carrying digital audio.

Physics of sound: the audio signal

What is sound?

First, a problem: to study sound properly, it would be really useful to be able to represent it visually. But sound is, well . . . sound, a sensation for the ears. When we are able to see sound, what we see is how sound affects other things: the mythical soprano who breaks a wine-glass with a high-pitched warble, or the rippling wave patterns on the surface of a metal plate on top of a loudspeaker. In the same way, to represent sound graphically we need to show how one or more of its characteristics can be visualised. It may be how its amplitude changes over time, or how the different frequencies present in the sound change over time, or, to complicate things slightly, it can be to show how loud those different frequencies are in comparison to one another.

Although this is not a book on acoustics, let's for a minute look at what sound contains that may be useful to represent visually for our purposes. Sound is a phenomenon. This means it is something we perceive, in this case, through our sense of hearing and, in fact, through our whole body (which you will know if you have been to any concerts of drone electronica!). Sound is, in fact, what we call the sensation produced by changes in air pressure as they are perceived through our whole body and more specifically through our ears. These changes are in turn generated by the interaction between a number of objects that excite each other into motion. For instance, if we strike a large metallic sheet with a stone, we will get a loud **noise** with some accompanying resonant sound. The loud noise is produced

HOW SOUND PROPAGATES

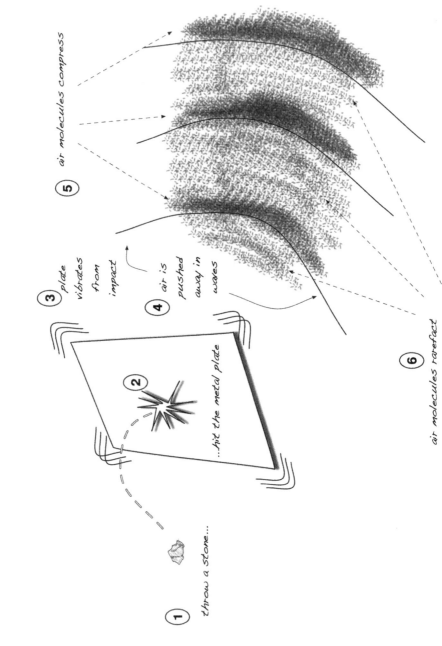

Figure 1.1 How sound propagates

by the sudden impact between stone and metal, and as the metal sheet is made to vibrate by the energy of the impact, it creates strong and sudden, but gradually decreasing, changes in air pressure as it finally comes to rest again. The molecules of air are compressed as the metal sheet bends out (called compression because the air pressure is greater as it is being pushed) and then as it bends in they are rarefied (**rarefaction** is a decrease in air pressure); see Figure 1.1.

The strength of those air-pressure changes at every instant you measure them is called *amplitude*. Our perception, with our ears, of that magnitude is called *loudness* (this is measured in *phons*, but more of that later). The speed with which those changes occur is called *frequency*. The number of changes in pressure per second, or rather *periods* of the pressure waves – the time it takes for the wave to complete its cycle – is measured in cycles per second, a unit known as the Hertz.[1] The kind or quality of the sound is called *timbre*. When the changes in air pressure are steady, regular, predictable, they are perceived as pitches we can identify: E, A, D, G, B, etc. When the changes are not regular, as in the example given in Figure 1.1, we perceive *noise* (which is a subject unto itself![2] But for now, let's just be practical and call it noise).

To model the way the air compresses and rarefacts we use a sine wave. It is the simplest sound wave possible: it represents a simple and smooth repetitive oscillation. We describe its amplitude as positive to represent compression and as negative to represent rarefaction. Figure 1.2 illustrates the different aspects we can measure in a sound wave (using a sine for simplicity).

How do we measure sound?

To represent sound, we first need to measure its characteristics in some way. Before we start we need a scale that can represent pretty large numbers within a few measurements; this is due to the way we perceive frequency and amplitude of sound. What we perceive as 'equal changes' when we measure frequencies are not in fact separated by equal magnitudes. For instance, if we play the note *middle C* (*MIDI* note 60, or C3)[3] on the piano and go up in *octave intervals* to the following Cs for a few octaves, we believe we perceive a regular progression where the distance between consecutive Cs is simply one octave, each time, to our ears. But in fact, where the ear perceives the following linear increments – 'one octave above C', 'two octaves above C', 'three octaves above C', 'four octaves above C', 'five octaves above C', etc. – the actual physical measurements are 261.62 Hz, 523.25 Hz, 1046.50 Hz, 2093 Hz, 4186 Hz, 8372 Hz, etc. . . . which means that where our brain tells us we have simply jumped one similar interval higher (an octave), the physical measurement tells us that we have doubled the previous number of frequencies each time. In our

MEASURING A SOUND WAVE

(a sine wave is used herein showing how we measure waves)

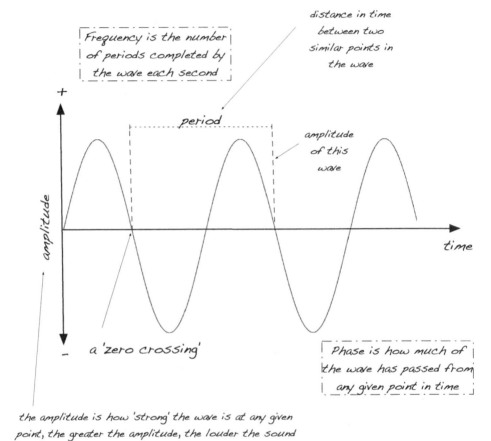

Frequency is the number of periods completed by the wave each second

distance in time between two similar points in the wave

period

amplitude of this wave

+

amplitude

time

a 'zero crossing'

−

Phase is how much of the wave has passed from any given point in time

the amplitude is how 'strong' the wave is at any given point, the greater the amplitude, the louder the sound

Figure 1.2 Measuring a sound wave

example, jumping up three octaves is actually multiplying the original frequency almost by 10! To cut a long story short, we will need to use *exponential* scales to measure sound. This doesn't only apply to pitch. It applies to amplitude as well, so that something which is twice as loud as something else to our ears is, in fact, ten units of amplitude larger; *loudness* is a physiological impression of how intense a sound is to our ears. Just imagine: if you have two guitarists playing, for you to perceive their amplitude as being twice as loud you need twenty guitarists! (there's a thought . . .)

So how can we represent a series of numbers that grow exponentially to be able to measure frequency and amplitude? We are going to need a mathematical concept:

the logarithm.[4] At this point you may want to make yourself a coffee because the following is a little involved. OK, here it goes...

If you take a series of numbers like:

1, 10, 100, 1000, 10000, 100000

you could find a different way to represent them by observing that they are powers of 10. So, as shorthand, you could represent them by writing down what power of 10 is needed to make each number. The sequence above then becomes:

0, 1, 2, 3, 4, 5

which is quite compact! And to get the original number you simply elevate 10 to the number found in that simpler and compact series:

$10^0 = 1, 10^1 = 10, 10^2 = 100, 10^3 = 1000, 10^4 = 10000$, etc.

These exponents are logarithms in base 10:

$\log(1) = 0, \log(10) = 1, \log(100) = 2, \log(1000) = 3$, etc.

In summary, we have a series of numbers which looks linear:

0, 1, 2, 3, 4, 5

actually representing an exponential one:

1, 10, 100, 1000, 10000, 100000

Very useful, don't you agree? Getting back to our measurements of sound, remember that amplitude grows exponentially, as we said earlier. And, our measurements of loudness start with very small numbers. For instance, we can hear a change in air pressure of 0.00002 Pascals, but as we consider other things we normally hear, we will see that the numbers grow quite rapidly. (By the way, a Pascal, or Pa, is a measure of force exerted over an area, so it can be used to measure the pressure of the atmosphere upon the earth, and sound results from changes in air pressure, so you get the idea!)

Your bedroom,[5] if it is reasonably quiet at night, will have average changes in air pressure of about 0.00063 Pa. If somebody speaks to you in a normal voice from one metre away, that exerts upon your ears around 0.02 Pa. If you stand about ten metres away from a diesel truck, the measurement would be about 0.63 Pa. One metre away from a chainsaw, 6.3 Pa. Sounds will be painfully loud at 63.2 Pa, and a jet plane, fifty metres away, will produce 200 Pa.[6] Let's put these numbers in a list:

0.00002, 0.00063, 0.02, 0.63, 6.3, 63.2, 200

They don't look very memorable, do they? So, if we apply some maths we mentioned earlier (and some we have not mentioned yet!) we can represent our loudness differences above like this:

0, 30, 60, 90, 110, 130, 140

which immediately looks simpler and more memorable.[7] So how did we arrive at the latter numbers? Sound-pressure levels and loudness are measured in a logarithmic scale with units called decibels. A decibel, loosely defined, is the logarithm of a ratio between a certain quantity and a reference level. If this confuses you, just think that we are measuring ratios, that is, relationships between two numbers, to see how much bigger or smaller one is than the other. Then think that the resulting ratios will grow very rapidly, so we need our trusty logarithms to represent those numbers more compactly. The first ratio should be 1, meaning that the numbers being compared are equal. Given our measurements of loudness, then we would have:

$$0.00002/0.00002 = 1 \quad \text{and} \quad \log(1) = 0$$

So, if two sounds have the same level, the difference between them is 0 decibels, or 0 dB. This is why in the last series of numbers we started with 0. All other changes will be expressed in reference to that one. 0 dB is, then, the reference level meaning that there is no difference between the two loudnesses being compared. To show that we are measuring sound-pressure levels we notate this as:

0 dB SPL

At this point, know that we can use the decibel for measuring any ratios, so if our decibels are used to measure power, say for amplification of the sound, then the reference would be to milliwatts and the unit would be dBm.

The formula for calculating decibels of sound-pressure level is:

$$LeveldB = 20\log\left(\frac{measured\ amplitude}{reference\ amplitude}\right)$$

So, now we can find where the other numbers in the simpler list above came from.

Your quiet bedroom (0.00063 Pa) in relation to the smallest change in sound-pressure level you can detect (0.00002 Pa) would be 30 dB, because:

$$LeveldB = 20\log\left(\frac{0.00063}{0.00002}\right) = 29.9662$$

which is near enough to 30 dB. The voice, one metre away (0.02 Pa), in relation to the smallest change in sound-pressure level you can detect (0.00002 Pa) would be 60 dB, because:

$$LeveldB = 20\log\left(\frac{0.02}{0.00002}\right) = 60$$

And now if you keep plugging the pressure levels of the diesel truck, the chainsaw, the painful sound and the jet plane, you will get the other values we arrived at earlier.

What does this mean for people working in a studio? For a start, mixer-channel strip faders should make a little more sense to you now. Notice that they have a marking for 0 dB right at the top of the fader. This means that you can set your recording reference level (0 dB) as the loudest that you can get without unwanted distortion of the audio signal. Meaning: nothing should go above the reference. Once you have established this through trial and error by getting the musicians to play as loud as they will play in the song (not as loud as they *can* play!), you then measure all other levels in relation to that as a reference, making sure they are below 0 dB and that all of them combined do not go beyond 0 dB.

The audio signal

At this point, let's briefly review the process of how you capture an audio signal. Earlier we said that sound is made of changes in air pressure that are perceived through our ears. To model that and be able to store sound, engineers have replicated that process by designing very sensitive membranes that simulate the way our eardrums work. Simply put, the membranes vibrate mechanically and are attached to *transducers* (devices to convert one form of energy into another) that create electric current at intensities that are higher or weaker depending on how strongly or weakly the membrane is affected by the changes in air pressure (see Figure 1.1).

Once sound has been converted to electrical impulses, we refer to it as an *audio signal*. A signal being simply that: something which represents something else, in this case audio. Note that the behaviour of the electrical current mimics the sound-pressure levels picked up by the microphone membrane (also known as a *diaphragm*). This is to say that there will be fluctuations in current for each fluctuation in air pressure; actually, this is what is known as an *analogue* process: one thing affects another so efficiently that the second one can be used to represent the first (chew on that for a moment, it is a simple but key statement). By the same logic, if we take an electrical current and make it stronger (i.e. amplify it), then feed it into loudspeakers, we will hear the sound again, but potentially louder. Before the digital era, the two main (though not exclusive) recording methods of the twentieth century consisted

ANALOGUE TO DIGITAL

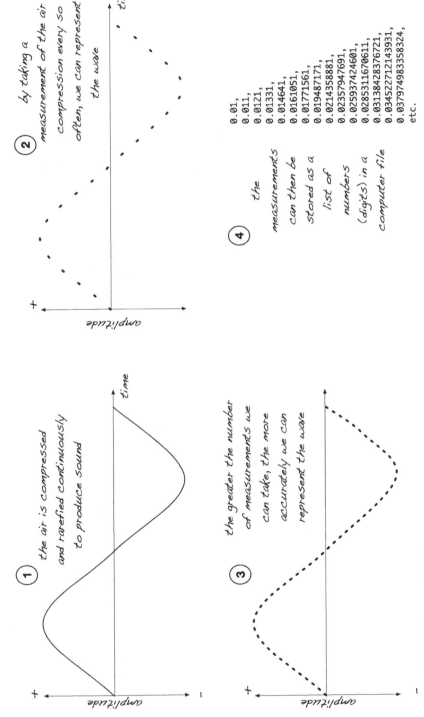

① the air is compressed and rarefied continuously to produce sound

② by taking a measurement of the air compression every so often, we can represent the wave

③ the greater the number of measurements we can take, the more accurately we can represent the wave

④ the measurements can then be stored as a list of numbers (digits) in a computer file

0.01,
0.011,
0.0121,
0.01331,
0.014641,
0.0161051,
0.01771561,
0.019487171,
0.0214358881,
0.0235794691,
0.025937424601,
0.0285311670611,
0.03138428376721,
0.0345227121143931,
0.037974983358324,
etc.

Figure 1.3 Analogue to digital

of preserving this electrical current as a groove on vinyl or as magnetised areas on tape with a magnetic covering. In the late twentieth century, digital recording became commonplace. The simplest explanation is that the electric current is now measured and the resulting numbers stored as a computer file.

Digital recording

Since it is the most common current method of recording, let's dwell on the digital recording process for a moment. I will just outline the key concepts.[8]

An audio signal needs to be *sampled* so we can get a list of values, where each one corresponds to one electrical fluctuation (which, as we saw, represents a fluctuation in air pressure). Think for a moment about this. You will see that the success of sampling will depend on two things: the number of measurements we can make per second (*sampling rate*) and how many numbers we can represent (more numbers → more accuracy → greater *sampling resolution*).

Computer technology allows us to do this and then use the data to make useful representations of the captured sound. Special software programs and protocols are needed for encoding and, later, decoding the data into audio formats; these are known as *codecs* and we will describe them later in this chapter. For now, just note that this method of capturing sound by measuring amplitudes at a particular constant speed (*quantisation*) and then representing those magnitudes in binary numbers is called *PCM*, or *Pulse Code Modulation*. This term comes from telephony as the technique was first developed for sending voice signals over the telephone. The word 'pulse' refers to each amplitude measurement at a constant speed which is made on the original sound; each quantised pulse is represented by a number belonging to a set of signals known as a *codeword* hence the use of the word 'code'; and, finally, the resulting transformation into binary numbers is a *modulation*: Pulse Code Modulation (for more precise information, you really need to learn about telecommunications!).

If you study Figure 1.3, you will better understand the key concepts. Notice that the fluctuation in current, represented by a simple waveform, has an unbroken curved shape. When sound occurs, our ears naturally perceive all the subtlety of this fluctuation. But if we want a computer to capture this phenomenon, we need to take as many measurements as possible per unit of time so we can approximate how the ear works. We will also need the computer to keep track of time, by use of a clock (the *sample clock*). This is called the 'analogue to digital conversion', and the electronic device used to achieve this is thus called the *ADC*. The list of measurements is kept as an *audio file*, which can be played back by performing a 'digital to analogue conversion' with the (similarly named) *DAC*. All we would need to do is, while keeping time (with the sample clock), output the number values so they can be

Table 1.1 *Commonly used audio sampling frequencies*

Sampling frequency in kHz	Commonly used for:
22.05	Internet podcasts, online streaming videos
44.1	CD recordings, music
48	Audio for video on DVD and digital video production
96 and 192	High Definition audio for digital audio workstations

converted into electrical current values and made strong enough (*amplified*) so they can be connected to a loudspeaker and drive it. The loudspeaker, roughly speaking, functions in an inverse way to the microphone. It takes an electromagnetically produced oscillation (fluctuation of values) and moves a membrane (speaker cone) in sync with it. The movement of the membrane creates differences in air pressure and the audio signal becomes audible again.

Sampling has evolved as computers have become more powerful, allowing us to capture sound with ever-increasing fidelity. There is a threshold level of sampling rate and resolution (or bit-depth) which today we consider a starting point for audio quality and which is used by commercial recordings on CD: this is the 44.1 kHz sampling rate at 16 bits. It is what people actually mean when they say 'CD quality' (see Table 1.1). Now, this is not the best quality possible, but it has become a standard, although it should be superseded thoroughly in the next few years. So, how did it come about?

First, let's make clear that the term 'sampling', refers not only to digital recording, but also to the artistic process of 'lifting' sound fragments from publicly available music tracks. However, both activities are accomplished with the same technology. The sampling rate that is considered acceptable nowadays is a result of research carried out by Dr Harry Nyquist, early in the twentieth century, whose concern with the optimum way to transmit an audio signal arose out of research into improving telegraphic communications.[9] Nyquist, together with Dr Claude Shannon, developed the theory of sampling at Bell Labs in the United States and their theorem is named after them (the Nyquist–Shannon sampling theorem). They discovered that, to reproduce a sampled signal without loss or distortion, it had to have been sampled at least twice as fast as the highest frequency it contained.[10] Since human hearing can perceive up to 20,000 Hz, then it follows that we need a sampling rate of at least 40,000 Hz to make sure we can later reproduce the signal without distortion or loss.

As somebody working in music technology, you will always be trying to get the best quality of audio that you can store in your chosen media. So, the next important item to consider is *bit-depth*, which is to say, how many values can you represent? I think it is safe to assume that everybody knows, at least informally, that computers

Table 1.2 *The range of values some common bit-depths can represent*

Bit-depth	Number range representable	Number of values	How it is worked out[a]
1	0–1	2	$2^0 = 1$
2	0–3	4	$2^0 + 2^1 = 3$
4	0–15	16	$2^0 + 2^1 + 2^2 + 2^3 = 16$
8	0–255	256	$2^0 + 2^1 + 2^2 + 2^3 + 2^4 + 2^5 + 2^6 + 2^7 = 255$
16	0–65535	65536	$2^0 + 2^1 + 2^2 + 2^3 + 2^4 + 2^5 + 2^6 + 2^7 \ldots 2^{15} = 65536$
24	0–1677721	1677722	$2^0 + 2^1 + 2^2 + 2^3 + 2^4 + 2^5 + 2^6 + 2^7 \ldots 2^{23} = 1677722$

[a] To find the largest number, set all bit positions are to '1', then add up the corresponding powers of 2.

A NOTE FROM A MACEDONIAN CLARINET
IN A TIME-DOMAIN REPRESENTATION OF AMPLITUDE

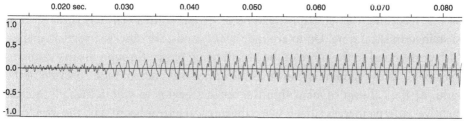

Figure 1.4 Representing amplitude

store information in 0s and 1s. But what does this mean for us? It means that the numbers we can represent are determined (or limited) by how many 0s and 1s we can store in computer memory (see Table 1.2). Thus we will have as many 'degrees' of nuance when measuring sound-pressure levels; the more degrees, the more nuanced and the more accurate the representation.

Sound represented graphically

Representing sound amplitude

Once we have managed to create an audio data file with 44,100 measurements per second and 1,677,722 different amplitude values that can be represented (44.1 kHz and 24 bits), we can create graphics of the audio file. Figure 1.4 is the most typical representation we find in audio sequencers. It is a *time-domain* representation of amplitude as a *continuous function* of time (or in everyday language, as it changes through time when measured constantly).[11] The horizontal axis represents time elapsed and the vertical axis represents the amplitude of the waveform at each instant in time.

The overview is a contour which describes the highs and lows of air pressure around '0' (0 = no change in air pressure). The higher the reading on the vertical axis, the louder the sound at that particular point in time. This is the most familiar representation of sound we tend to come across. Most audio editing software will allow you to select portions of the sound by selecting portions of a graphic such as this and then copying and pasting them or applying sound processes to them. Notice that, for convenience, the amplitude is represented by values between -1 and 1. The software then maps whatever the internal resolution is (given the bit-depth we discussed earlier) to the graphic display. You could, in fact, think of it as a 'percentage of maximum amplitude' representation: 1 = 100%, 0.5 = 50%, and so on. If the sound is 'musical', meaning that you can hear a definite pitch, then the waveform will have repetitive or periodic contours. Notice, in Figure 1.4, how a pattern emerges as the sound develops. We can tell, from this representation, that this recording (which happens to be of a Macedonian clarinet) is the start of a sustained musical note. Up to around 0.03 seconds, we observe irregular shapes, which correspond to the noise of the breath being blown through the instrument's mouthpiece. This segment is known as the *attack transient*, or *onset*, portion of the sound. As the column of air within the clarinet begins to vibrate steadily, a clear repetitive pattern emerges (that is when the musical note is heard) and the waveform enters a *steady state* of oscillation.[12] From about 0.045 seconds, the waveform appears quite stable and we can observe that, after a *zero-crossing*, the behaviour of the waveform in the positive vertical axis (higher pressure) is mirrored in the negative one. This is then repeated each third zero-crossing. As seen earlier, the time elapsed between these is called the *period* of the wave, and the fact that we can detect this repetitive period allows us to call this a periodic waveform. This is what the ear perceives as being 'musical'.[13] The period of a wave is measured as its *phase*. If we take two identical waveforms and layer them, offsetting one from the other, this offset is known as the phase between the two waves. But why do we need to know this?

If we record a sound with two microphones, and one is much further from the source than the other, they will receive the sound at slightly different times. This time difference would be offsetting two identical waves and placing them out of phase with each other. This will create a *phasing effect* in the recording. Unless you are actually looking to create that effect, this will make your recording less faithful to the original. If the microphones are separated such that the delay is equal to half a period of the waveform, this will lead to *phase cancellation*, as the positive amplitude of one is added to the (mirror image) negative of the other, amounting to zero in the end. As you can see, knowing about phase is quite important in the recording process. Another advantage of being able to 'see' amplitude is this: when the sound pressure exceeds the capacity of the microphone diaphragm to vibrate, we get distortion in the recording; this is reflected by 'squared off' (*clipped*) peaks in the waveform and we can see the distortion, even if it is not as perceptible to the ear, as it occurs and then remove it if we want to!

Finally, if we go back to Figure 1.3: in the attack portion of the waveform we see that there is no definite period. This is typical of noise: a series of non-repetitive (*aperiodic*) fluctuations in air pressure. It is lovely to be able to actually see how, from the rich chaos of a breath sound, a clear musical tone emerges (which is not to say that the chaos portion cannot be beautiful too!).

Representing sound frequency

Being able to see the amplitude of a wave only tells us about the strength and periodicity of the audio signal, but not much about its actual content. It is extremely useful to be able to see what frequencies are present in the sound and in what quantity. For this, we use a *frequency-domain* representation.

Vibrating objects in the real world (as opposed to the oscillations of a synthesiser) disturb the air in different degrees of complexity. This means that several different frequencies can be made to coexist.[14] The sum total of these and their proportions within the sound is what we know as timbre.[15] Representations of timbre as it changes in time are known as spectrograms, or Fast Fourier Transform (FFT) analysis. The latter is named after French mathematician Joseph Fourier (1768–1830), whose theory on periodic functions, when applied to audio, is that periodic sounds, even if complicated, can be reduced to a mix of related sinusoids each with its own period and amplitude.[16] If you think about it for a moment, this happens to be the idea behind additive synthesis: to take different sinusoids and mix them together to create new sounds. Inversely, analyse a sound to see what sinusoids it contains (FFT). One advantage is that you can then change the phase, amplitude and frequency of the component sine waves to edit the sound creatively into something else. Applying an FFT to a recording, as seen in Figure 1.5,[17] shows us how the different sinusoid component frequencies change over time.

In this particular example, a short recording of a Bollywood singer, the darker areas show which are the loudest frequencies within the sound. If you study the illustration, you will see, for instance, that at around 0.5 seconds the lowest frequency is near 100k, which is approximately the note 'G' as sung by a baritone. If you made a different graph, where you had all the component frequencies side by side, their amplitude represented as height, it would make it even easier to see how much presence each sinusoid component has inside the sound.

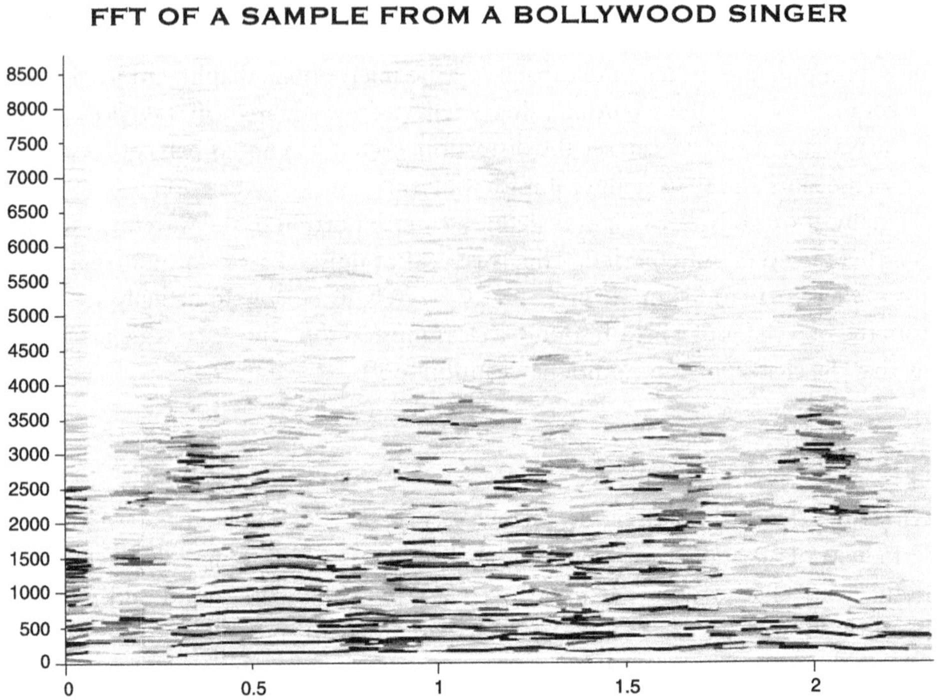

FFT OF A SAMPLE FROM A BOLLYWOOD SINGER

Figure 1.5 FFT representation

Other representations

Although we have highlighted the *amplitude vs. time* and the *frequency vs. time* representations, bear in mind that these are not the only ways to visualise sound, and indeed there have been all kinds of innovative ways developed by artists and scientists (or creative technologists) to allow us to 'see' sound. One of these, for instance, is **cymatics**. In cymatics, you place a shallow container with a fluid (like water or anything else you might want to experiment with) on top of a speaker and when the sound plays back you can observe intricate patterns formed by rippling on its surface. This can also be done with a metal plate covered in sand. The particles will group on the surface of the plate to form patterns as the sound changes.

Representing sound is a challenge to the imagination. Further, you can use sound to represent something else. For instance, if you had a spreadsheet with your student transcript and you assigned each mark range to a different sound and then mixed them, you would come up with a unique sound which identifies your academic achievement! Composers have used **sonification** procedures such as this to give an artistic perspective on otherwise purely scientific data. British composer John Eacott, in his piece *Flood Tide* (2008), created a music score by translating tide measurements from the river Thames in London.[18]

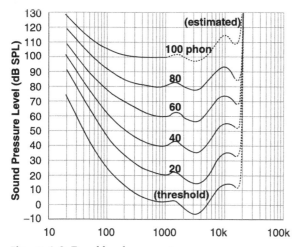

Figure 1.6 Equal loudness contours

Actually perceiving sound

So far, so good. By now you are probably thinking everything is under control. You can capture sounds of any frequency, store them, represent them, play them back. However, there is one very tricky issue in our dealings with sound: perception. This is a huge topic and we cannot even scratch the surface, but for our purposes we will briefly look at how we perceive the loudness of different frequencies.

The human brain does not give the same importance to all sounds, or even to the different frequencies contained in a sound. In general, it appears that the ear favours frequencies between 2 kHz and 5 kHz — which is the range that makes speech intelligible. Lower frequencies are not as important for localisation of the sound source as high frequencies.[19] In fact, the way the ear responds to sound varies at different intensities for different frequencies. Figure 1.6 shows what is called a 'normal equal-loudness-level contour graph'.

Early on, we mentioned that the amplitude magnitude of a waveform is perceived as loudness and that loudness is measured in phons. A phon is defined as 1 dB SPL at 1 kHz. As mentioned before, we do not perceive all frequencies as being equally loud, even when their amplitude is the same. In layman's terms, this means that a double bass will sound softer than a piccolo, even if individually they are actually producing the same amplitude. In other words, low frequencies need to be amplified more than high ones to be perceived as having equal loudness. Several reference graphs containing curves created by mapping loudness against frequency have been used over the years. For instance, the Fletcher-Munson curve was defined in 1933, but was refined by Robinson and Dadson in 1956, and this latter one became the basis for a revised international 'ISO' standard developed by research from several countries (ISO 226:2003).[20]

Understanding the equal-loudness-level graph is useful for seeing how our brain regards frequencies, and it can help us make decisions about mixing and equalisation, as we will see in Chapter 2. Observe, for instance, that it is necessary to boost a bass signal of around 20 Hz by 80 dB SPL to achieve the same loudness as a frequency of 1 kHz at 1 dB SPL (1 phon). The way to read the graph is to see how many dB SPL you will need for any given frequency as you increase the phons. So, for instance, if a clarinet is playing A ♭ just above the treble clef (an octave plus a minor sixth above middle C) and we call that 0 dB, to feel equal loudness from a bass playing G at the bottom of the bass clef (an octave plus a fourth below middle C) we need to play it at +20 dB.

These equal-loudness curves can also be described as giving different 'weight' to different frequencies in terms of perceived loudness. Sound-pressure levels can be then correlated to whatever weighting scheme has been adopted. In the USA the A-weighting is used for instance; this leads to sound engineers talking about 'dB A'. In the UK and Europe, the more common weighting is ITU-R 468 (a standard of the International Telecommunications Union, ITU) because it is considered more accurate for measuring the loudness of noise (which our ear perceives differently from pure tones, and, yes, all of the above needs to be reconsidered when comparing tones with noise!).

Sound as computer data

We have already introduced fundamental aspects of representing and storing sound as numbers, but we also need to cover some conventions and technical terminology. The lifespan of this terminology is not as short as you would think. For instance a file format such as Apple's AIFF has been in use for about twenty years, as has the PC's WAV. New formats come along but we have now accumulated so much sound material in the world that just for the purposes of recovering our archives we need to keep legacy formats. For this reason alone, it would be useful to know about them.

Formats for storing sound files

Sound files can be stored in a variety of data formats, but we can classify them all into two groups: those which aim to store the sound while trying to keep as much data as possible, which we call **lossless** formats; and those which aim to store it while trying to lose (in the interest of storage space) as much data as possible without significantly altering our perception of the sound, these we call **lossy** formats. Much research is done into how we hear sound and, by looking at what an average person perceives, researchers work out what can be safely lost when storing audio in the interests of transmission speed and memory space.[21]

The two most popularly used lossless formats are found in the Waveform Audio File Format (WAV) and the Audio Interchange File Format (AIFF). It should be mentioned that these formats also cater for sound compression and thus lossy storage, but the general usage is for their lossless varieties.[22] WAV was developed jointly by the Microsoft Corporation and IBM for the early Windows operating system. AIFF was developed by the Apple Corporation with the introduction of its first Macintosh computers. There are many other formats and we will mention some of them below, but it would be useful to answer two questions first: why do we need a format? And, what is included in that format?

We need a format so that the computer knows how to handle and playback the audio data: number of channels, sample rate, etc. What we include in the format is a choice that different software developers have made. Let's examine the WAV format first because it is simpler. In a WAV file you will find, in this order, the following components:[23]

- a format tag
- the number of channels
- the sample rate
- the average data transfer rate
- the block alignment in bytes
- the bit-depth
- extra format information

Of these, most are self-explanatory, but it is worth explaining that the format tag carries information also about compression formats created by Microsoft. The average data transfer rate (the speed needed for the computer to play back that format, basically) is expressed in *bytes* (sets of eight bits) per second and, finally, that the block alignment is the minimum size of a data element for this format; i.e. the computer cannot start playing back a file half way through a block, but only at the beginning of the block.

The AIFF format is more interesting because it is ready to carry more musical information as well as raw audio data.[24] Users of Apple software since the late 2000s have found that samples in Apple loop libraries, for instance, may also contain MIDI information.[25] The contents of an AIFF file are divided into 'chunks'. The first chunk is known as the 'Common Chunk' and it tells the computer about format, length and sample rate. This is followed by a Sound Data Chunk, which will contain all the sample data. The other chunks are optional but it is interesting to know what they are:

- Marker Chunk (any markers pointing to a point in the waveform, like loop points for instance; this is useful for samplers, etc.);
- Instrument Chunk (tells us what MIDI instrument could be used to play the sound data; it goes so far as to specify base note, detune, note range, velocity range and gain, as well as loop points);
- MIDI Data Chunk (mainly for MIDI System Exclusive Data, but can be used for other MIDI data as well);
- Audio Recording Chunk (information for audio recording protocols);
- Application Specific Chunk (here, the application which creates the AIFF file can store any parameters that the software author wishes to have available, such as sound-editing parameters, for instance, for editor software);
- Comments Chunk (for comments or annotations);
- Text Chunks for Name, Author, Copyright and further annotations.

Remember, though, that not all AIFF files will bring all this data with them; it is just that they can be made available if the software that encodes them wants to give the user more access and flexibility. Most AIFF will probably only contain the Common and Sound Data chunks, but Apple Loops make extensive use of optional chunks. Other lossless formats you will find include SD2 (Sound Designer 2, which was introduced and used by Digidesign in the '80s, but is mostly in use today as a legacy format), AU from Sun Microsystems (also legacy) and the Free Lossless Audio **Codec**, known as FLAC.

As mentioned before, there are compressed versions of WAV and AIFF, but when it comes to lossy formats, the most used at present is *MP3*. This format was developed by the Motion Pictures Expert Group. It was intended specifically for audio, and its actual name is MPEG-1 Audio Layer 3. MP3s are very popular because when compressed at a good *bit-rate* they appear to be of good quality to most people and they only take up about 10 per cent of the size of an AIFF or a WAV file. Most MP3 encoders available allow the user to set the bit-rate and bandwidth. The higher the bit-rate, the better the sound; yet when using low bit-rates (for encoding speech, for instance), bandwidth needs to be reduced and the audio may even need some processing to eliminate unwanted *artifacts* created by the **compression** process.[26] MP3s also carry some metadata known as an ID3 tag.[27] In this tag we can store the artist's name, song title, year and genre of the MP3. A more advanced form of MP3 is the AAC, or Advanced Audio Coding.[28] It is meant to be a successor to MP3 and a measure of its success is that it is widely used by Nokia, Sony, Apple and Nintendo. AAC is perceived as being of better quality than MP3 at similar bit-rates. Other lossy formats you will find include Ogg-Vorbis and some versions of WMA (Windows Media Audio).

The success of lossy formats in terms of sound quality and ease of exchange has prompted the music industry to seek ways to prevent copying music files from one computer to another (or if copied, not playing back on a different computer). These are called, in general, 'digital rights management technologies' and are proprietary to different manufacturers. It is worth noting that digital rights management (DRM) systems can wrap around any audio file formats (lossless and lossy), although for many reasons this is not popular with consumers and its use is diminishing in the music distribution business.

Standards for carrying digital audio

Connecting audio signals from one digital device to another is known as a *digital interface*. Various standards exist to serve different digital interfaces and some proprietary ones have been created; the most used are described below.

Digital interface standards have been developed by industry professional associations such as the Audio Engineering Society or *AES* (founded in the USA in 1948) and the European Broadcast Union, or *EBU*. The AES formed its Digital Audio Standards Committee as early as 1977. By 1985, it had agreed with the EBU on a standard known as the AES3 digital audio interface. AES/EBU carries the digital clock and two channels of digital audio data at up to 192 kHz sampling rate, at 24-bit-depth, over a balanced cable using three-pin XLR connectors. These cables can extend up to 100 metres without having to use further special cabling, equalisation or termination.[29] The AES[30]/EBU protocol is already twenty-five years old and, although optical connections are now increasingly frequent, AES/EBU is still strongly in use from professional audio applications to consumers. Similar protocols are used at consumer level, the most popular being *SPDIF* or Sony–Phillips Digital Interface. It also carries two channels (as well as multichannel surround sound information) but the difference being that the maximum sampling rate is 96 kHz with 24-bit-depth and that in this standard the connections are unbalanced (thus more liable to noise) and quite limited in cabling length. The type of cable is coaxial and the connectors are RCA type (as used in normal stereo systems); this makes it easy to find anywhere and friendly to semi-professionals and consumers. The size of the phono connectors also lends itself well to computer sound cards. SPDIF can also be carried over optical cable with **Toslink** connectors.

For carrying multichannel audio, the most used standard is the ADAT Lightpipe, or Adat Optical Interface. This standard uses fibre-optic cable and was developed by audio hardware company ALESIS. Even though their multitrack tape recorders are no longer in great demand given the rise of laptop recording, the ADAT standard remains very popular. It can carry up to eight channels of audio at 48 kHz/24-bit. The optical cable used, like SPDIF, has Toslink connectors.

Finally, it is worth mentioning MADI, or the Multichannel Audio Digital Interface. Most consumers may not get to use it, but it is an industry standard and can carry up to sixty-four channels at 96 kHz over fibre-optic or coaxial cable. The advantage over the other interface protocols and standards is the multichannel connection and that the audio signals can travel well over 100 metres and up to 3,000 metres. This makes it ideal for location recording or sound reinforcement in public arenas.

Chapter 2

A studio overview

In this chapter we will look at the sound studio and its elements. We will consider the role of the mixing desk and how it is organised for the management of the audio signal. We will also discuss using microphones and how they fit into the recording workflow. Today, recording is not just a matter of capturing sound on hard disk or (digital) tape, it is also the process of recording data about performance through MIDI sequencing. For this reason we will discuss the MIDI protocol and examine it in some detail. Since audio sequencers capture both MIDI and audio within essentially the same workflow, we will look at how they differ from, yet complement, each other in creative applications.

In Chapter 1, we examined sound; now we need to look at the business of working with sound in the studio. When sound is turned into a signal to be transmitted or recorded for later reproduction, we refer to it as audio.[1] The sound studio has traditionally been the place for working with audio, whether for broadcast or for the recording industry. The computer age has changed all this and anybody with a personal computer (or even a smartphone!) can have access to sound studios implemented through software. Since software studios aim to emulate the traditional hardware studios, we can use them as useful models to illustrate how we deal with audio. In this chapter, I would like to give an overview of the basic elements of the studio, with emphasis on the mixer and possible listening environments. In Chapter 3 we will look at software recording, and this will complement the topic by further examining the recording of both audio and MIDI.

The resources you will need can be safely grouped into categories of audio input, processing, storage and audio output. In the first category, we will find the tools we need for capturing the sound source (mics) or creating it (turntables, synths or electric guitars); in the second we have tools for managing different sources of sound at the same time, setting their levels and changing the character of the sound (pre-amplifiers, mixers, effects units compressors, gates, etc.); in the third we have devices for storing the sound (hard-disk recorders, digital tape, solid-state memory or even analogue tape); and in the fourth we have loudspeakers and listening environments.

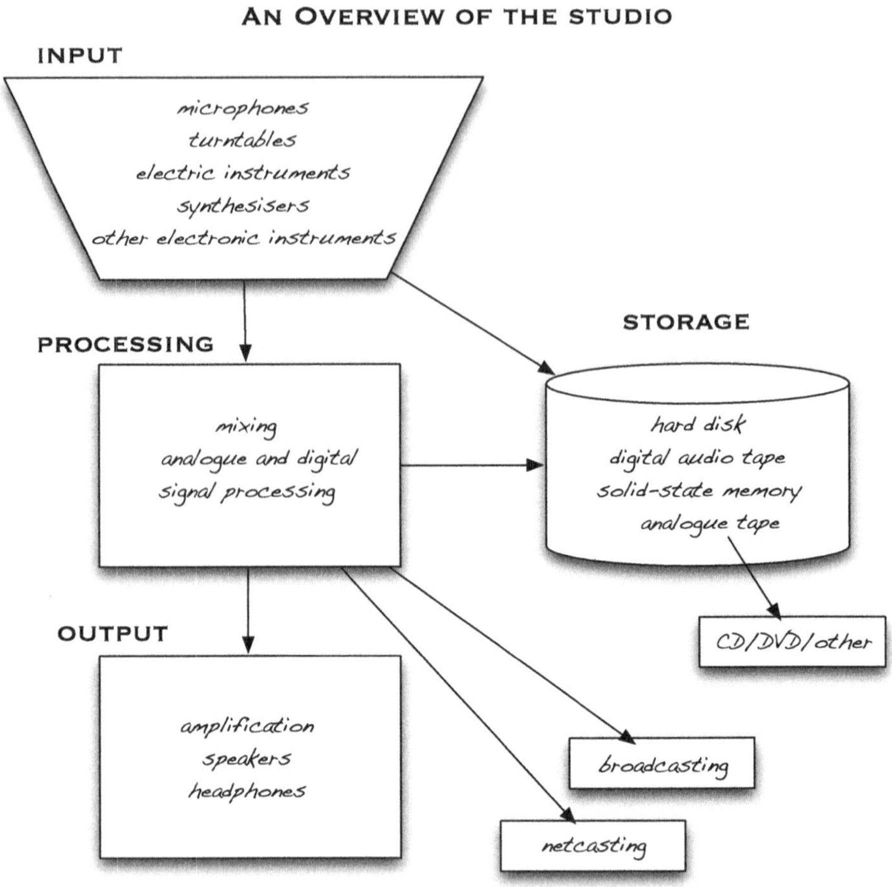

AN OVERVIEW OF THE STUDIO

INPUT

microphones
turntables
electric instruments
synthesisers
other electronic instruments

PROCESSING

mixing
analogue and digital
signal processing

STORAGE

hard disk
digital audio tape
solid-state memory
analogue tape

CD/DVD/other

OUTPUT

amplification
speakers
headphones

broadcasting

netcasting

Figure 2.1 An overview of the studio

So, where should we start discussing the studio? Since there is so much software available for audio, both commercial and freeware,[2] and thus so many mixing interfaces that musicians often come across, I thought we could start with processing/management and in the next chapter focus on input/recording. We will start, then, by examining the device we use as a control centre for managing recorded, live or playback audio: the mixer.

The mixer

The first 'commercial mixer' was apparently offered by the Swiss company Willi Studer in 1958.[3] Since then, although the basic idea of a number of input lines being summed to a common output remains, many sophistications have evolved. To better

Figure 2.2 NEVE 5088 Discrete Analogue Mixer (by kind permission of Rupert Neve Designs)

understand its concepts I would like us to look at the mixer, initially, as an idea, leaving aside electronics for the purpose of this discussion. And, because there are so many implementations of mixing-desk concepts, by thinking about what a mixer needs to be able to do we can form a mental image to help understand any variations we might encounter in professional life.

As mentioned earlier, most users' first experience is probably with a mixer on a computer screen, so we will refer often to software mixers here. Note that mixing desks[4] can be used for live sound reinforcement, sound diffusion,[5] sound recording or DJ performance. We will look at ideas on sound reinforcement in Chapter 5, below. It is worth noting that live-sound mixing desks are essentially similar to studio desks: they simply have features that are more suited to concert presentations. DJ mixing desks are also similar, but will have a selection of the most useful features for DJ performance. Both live-sound and DJ mixers have many software equivalents, yet the use of actual mixing hardware is more common in these applications.

Sections of the mixing desk

Let's carry out a 'thought experiment' and imagine what one would need from an ideal mixer. The list includes:

- Somewhere to be able to control all your sounds at the same time so you can amplify them or send them to a recording device;
- Some way to change their relative levels so we can achieve the right mix;

- Some way to take a sound, add an effect and blend the result into the final mix;
- Some way, when recording/playing, to have different mixes so we can send them through headphones to our players to help them focus on their own playing while the rest of the track can be made slightly quieter;
- Some way to group related tracks so we can treat them as a unit (a drum kit, a brass section or a string section).

From this list we can extract three broad tasks: mixing (technically known as **summing** the audio signal),[6] routing and processing. Everything that is done on a mixer falls within one of these areas. To do their job, mixers have a number of input channels with channel 'strips' to control the signal that is coming through on each input channel. On this strip you will find potentiometers (the technical term for 'knobs') for gain, equalisation and routing, and a fader for level, as well as buttons for attenuation, further routing and other options, depending on the manufacturer.

In the past, when routing a sound for processing we would send the signal to outboard equipment through insert channels and send channels and receive the signal for further routing from return channels. Today, this is only done when the user has specialised equipment they want to treat the signal with. Otherwise, processing can be done through plugin applications within the audio software. Thus, even though we are still 'sending' the signal, it is not going outside the system but is being processed by a separate yet compatible software application. The paths through which audio travels inside a mixer are called busses, so we speak of 'sending the signal through Bus X' and 'returning the signal through Bus Y'. Busses are received by auxiliary channels, called this because they are used for routing purposes as opposed to containing signals coming through a channel input directly. Figure 2.3 shows basic routing options in an ideal recording mixer.

Note also that several channels can be sent through the same bus to be processed in a specific auxiliary channel. For instance, instead of having four different reverbs for four different channels we could have one reverb inserted into an auxiliary to which we send our individual channels, using a bus to get them all there.

In terms of how many channels a mixer can have, the more the better! Hardware mixers tend to be defined by the number of inputs, busses and outputs they allow ($24 \times 8 \times 2$, for instance to signify twenty-four input channels, eight available busses and a final two channel stereo output). With software mixers, we can have as many channels, processing and outputs, as our computer allows. However, hardware is always a limiting factor. Let's now examine the different sections of the mixer as introduced in Figure 2.3.

BASIC MIXER ROUTES

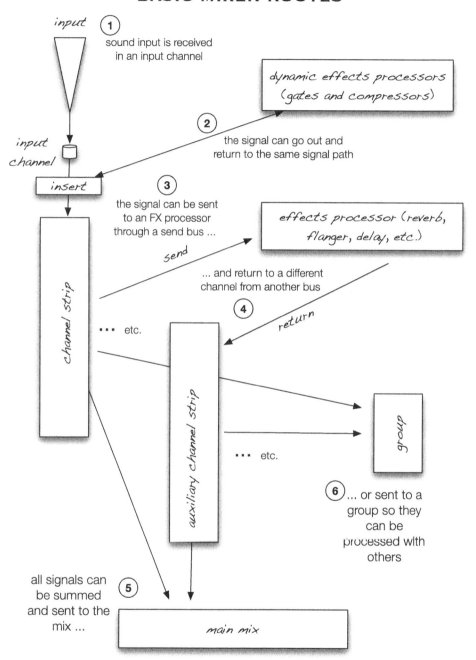

Figure 2.3 Basic mixer routes

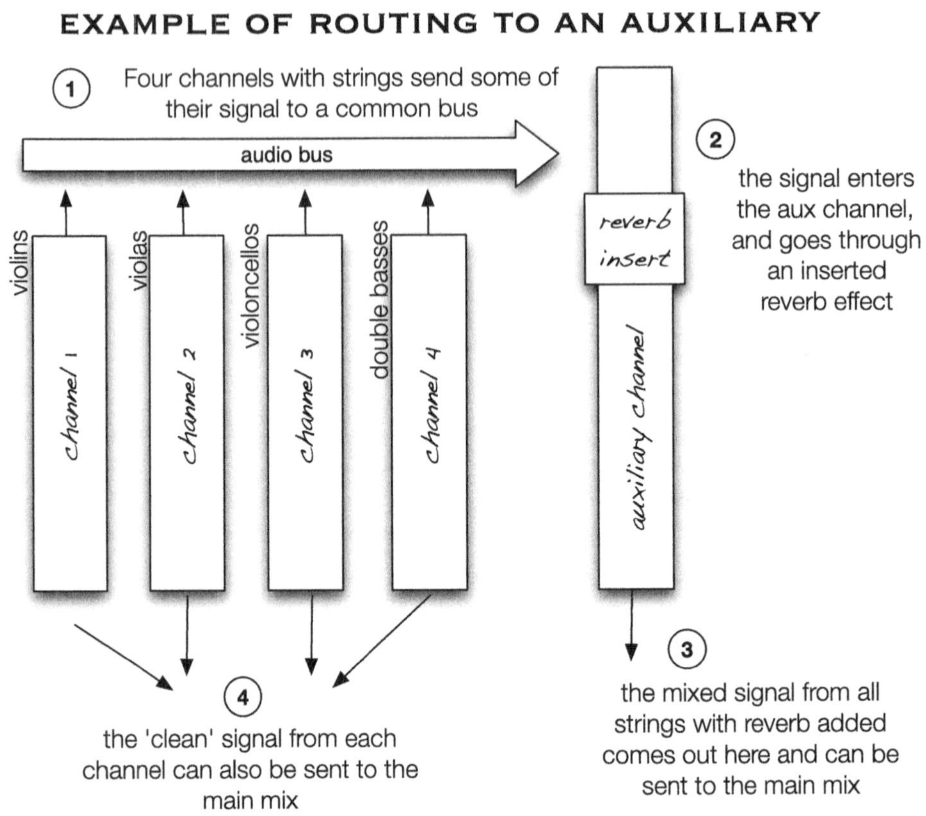

EXAMPLE OF ROUTING TO AN AUXILIARY

(1) Four channels with strings send some of their signal to a common bus

audio bus

(2) the signal enters the aux channel, and goes through an inserted reverb effect

violins — channel 1
violas — channel 2
violoncellos — channel 3
double basses — channel 4

reverb insert

auxiliary channel

(3) the mixed signal from all strings with reverb added comes out here and can be sent to the main mix

(4) the 'clean' signal from each channel can also be sent to the main mix

Figure 2.4 Routing to an auxiliary channel

The mixer input section

The actual soundcard or hardware audio interface will limit your inputs and outputs. On audio sequencer software you will have some control over the hardware and its settings, but this will vary for different soundcards. These will be determined by your soundcard audio driver (software that enables your computer to use the card) or stand-alone software provided by the manufacturer for your audio interface. Here you will be able to select the kind of input level you need (see Chapter 5), either instrument level for electric guitars or bass guitars (which also may need a pre-amplifier), phantom power to boost the signal of a microphone or line level for other audio equipment. In the input section of the soundcard, whether on the actual hardware or through the software, you will be able to power the signal further by adding gain.

The mixer channel strips

The channel strip is the place where the audio signal will appear. In Digital Audio Workstations (**DAWS**) or Audio-MIDI Sequencer software (I will refer to both as audio sequencers) there are different channel strip configurations, depending on what you want to do with the signal (see Fig. 2.5).

A channel that deals with a signal coming into the mixer from an external device (real or virtual) is an input channel. Channels that deal with the signal once inside the mixer, as briefly explained earlier, are either auxiliary channels, busses or groups.

Input channels

These are for bringing the audio signal into the mixer environment. They can represent the physical entry of sound into the soundcard or the virtual entry of an instrument plugin to the mixer. For the software mixer these are both 'external' signals, even though, for us, the first comes from outside the computer and the second (the plugin) resides within the computer and is being plugged-in to the sequencer software or DAW of which the mixer is a part. In software mixers the channel strip also represents the track where sound will be recorded, and for this reason they have a record button to enable you to capture whatever is coming into that channel.[7] The input channel will allow you to select which hardware input to 'listen to' or which plugin to **instantiate** (launch within the sequencer).[8] Let's examine the different stages of the input channel strip.

Input → Gain

Adding gain to the signal is usually a hardware feature and may not be represented in the audio sequencer software; instead it may feature either on the hardware device itself (dedicated consoles or audio interfaces) or on their own proprietary mixer software, which can be confusing because you end up running another mixing 'layer' at the same time as your audio sequencer in a separate stand-alone application. (The economic reality of 'mix and match' studio configurations is that you will often be dealing with this!)

(Input → Gain) → EQ

Input channels can have an equalisation section, or EQ, where different frequency ranges of the sound can be boosted or attenuated. Some software mixers allow you to see the sound input and the effect of your changes upon the signal, by having an amplitude vs. frequency display. Some EQs allow you to receive a signal

INPUT CHANNEL STRIPS

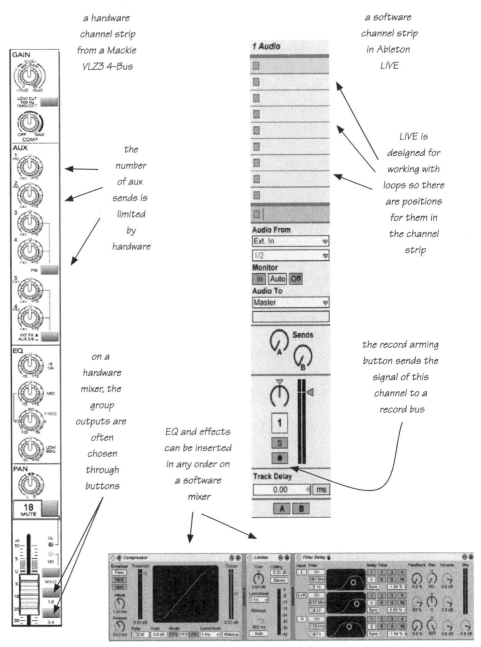

a hardware channel strip from a Mackie VLZ3 4-Bus

a software channel strip in Ableton LIVE

the number of aux sends is limited by hardware

LIVE is designed for working with loops so there are positions for them in the channel strip

on a hardware mixer, the group outputs are often chosen through buttons

EQ and effects can be inserted in any order on a software mixer

the record arming button sends the signal of this channel to a record bus

Figure 2.5 Input channel strips. Courtesy of Mackie and Ableton LIVE

(audio amplitude information) from a different channel altogether to control the attenuation of a selected frequency range; this is known as a sidechain.[9]

(*Input → Gain → EQ*) → *Inserts*

An insert is a point where we can 'hijack' the signal chain and connect a sound processor that will be for the exclusive use of that signal as it will now form part of the channel strip's signal chain. Typically, processors dealing with signal amplitude, known as dynamic processors, will be used here. You will be able to instantiate as many inserts as your computer will allow. Some systems will also allow you to use the insert for patching-in a hardware unit into the signal chain.

(*Input → Gain → EQ → Inserts*) → *Sends*

A send is a link between channels through which part, or all, of the signal may travel. This link between channels is possible thanks to an 'internal' channel called a bus; so, for instance, you can decide to use *Bus 1* to gather everything that will be sent to a delay-effects processor. Any input channel that is connected to *Bus 1* will then be sending some of its signal to the delay processor. This also means that several input channels can send their signal through the same bus to a processor, previously instantiated as an insert in an auxiliary channel. This allows us to maximise our computing power by sharing resources wherever possible. The auxiliary channel will then return the signal to the chosen output bus. In hardware mixers, as the number of sends will be hardwired, you may find dedicated channels which only have a potentiometer: these are called 'returns'. They are essentially a dedicated bus for bringing the signal back into the mixer. Although only the power of your computer limits how many internal sends/returns you can have from plugins, sending a signal out into the physical world is always limited by how many outputs are available on your soundcard.

(*Input → Gain → EQ → Inserts → Sends*) → *Panning*

The panning control, usually represented by a rotary potentiometer, is known as the pan-pot.[10] Panning allows you to choose a position within your audio image. If it is stereo, you will have a choice of anywhere from left to right, but if it is surround, you will also have to deal with speakers behind the listener. In the latter, your mix has the potential to be more 'immersive'. When using the panning control, you are simply deciding how your signal will be shared between your speakers. The listener will then perceive that the audio signal is coming from a particular position in the audio image. Note that pan is not the same as *balance*. We speak of 'panning' mono signals and 'balancing' stereo ones. When an input channel in an audio sequencer contains a stereo signal, the panning control becomes a balance control. Instead of sharing the whole signal between left and right speakers (in a stereo image), it allows you to attenuate either side of the stereo recording, giving you some sense of position. Note that if you place the balance control completely to one side, what you are potentially doing is losing one of the sides of the stereo image. Make sure you understand the difference between pan and balance.

$$(Input \rightarrow Gain \rightarrow EQ \rightarrow Inserts \rightarrow Sends \rightarrow Panning) \rightarrow Faders$$

The fader allows you to control the amplitude of the whole signal after it has gone through all the steps above. Its visual representation (in the case of a software mixer) or its physical placement (in the case of a hardware mixer) helps you see the level of the signal in comparison to other input channels in your mix. Faders will usually be measured in decibels, with $0dB_u$ as the 'unity gain': they represent the point at which the signal is not being reduced or boosted from its original input strength.[11]

$$(Input \rightarrow Gain \rightarrow EQ \rightarrow Inserts \rightarrow Sends \rightarrow Panning \rightarrow Faders) \rightarrow$$
$$Groups/Outputs$$

Finally you will want to decide where your main signal goes. You could send it to a group channel if you are working on a hardware mixer so you can create *stems* of tracks you want to process together (typically you would group all of your drums). On software mixers you will normally use busses to auxiliary channels for that purpose, as well as grouping the tracks into a 'control group', which ensures that when you make changes to levels or panning (and whatever else is available) it affects all tracks in the group. Audio interfaces or soundcards will provide you with a choice of either stereo or multiple outputs. Often when using software audio sequencers, these multiple hardware outputs are what you will use for external sends/returns. In any case, although you can send to any output, remember that the final output of your channel strip may also go into a bus for further processing.

Auxiliary channels

Although we have already mentioned these, note that on a software mixer, an auxiliary channel ('aux') is almost identical to an input channel. The difference being that, in software mixers, they can also be used to bring in signals from other audio softwares with protocols such as *ReWire* for remote control and data transfer (this standard was developed by software companies Propellerhead and Steinberg). On a hardware mixer, an auxiliary channel is more of a pared-down input channel. It is essentially the same module, but may be lacking gain controls or EQ, depending on the console. In hardware, the idea is to provide maximum channelling facility while keeping electronic component costs down. This is not as much of a problem in software.

Output channels

The number of output channels will be determined by your audio hardware. Output channels can have inserts but no sends. This is because they represent the final summed signal, or a sub-mix for other purposes. What I mean by the latter is that your soundcard may have four outputs, of which you may be using 1&2 for your loudspeakers but 'secretly' you can try out other sounds you may want to use in performance by sending them to 3&4 which you patch through to your headphones. That would be normal practice for a DJ or a laptop performer. In recording situations, you may want to send a percussionist her own mix so she can hear more of the bass than you would add into the main mix.

The mixer control section

Software mixers will have several controls that allow you to further route and control your signal:

Record

Available on software mixers, digital consoles and mixing control surfaces. They exist in software mixers because the channel strip in this case also represents the audio recording track and so can be enabled directly on the strip. This is traditionally called 'arming' the track for record. It makes sure that everything that comes into the armed track, once recording has started, will be registered as audio data on to the hard disk or any other storage media.

Solo

Pressing this button will suppress everything else in the main mix and allow you to hear only this channel. You can solo several channels/tracks at once.

Mute

The opposite of solo: it removes the signal chain on this track from the main mix.

Group

Also mentioned earlier; on a hardware mixer these are specific 'master' channels for receiving a number of individual ones to control them together. On a software or digital mixer, grouping is a feature that allows you to control several parameters of your channels at the same time without necessarily sending them to a separate 'master' channel. This is useful if you want to be able to change, say, panning, volume and send levels on several channels at the same time but in proportion to one another. This means that group changes will not override the settings before the channel became grouped but simply change each one relative to the rest. For instance, if two faders are set, one at 0 dBu and the other at −3 dBu, pulling the first one down to −3 will automatically offset the second one to −6.1 dBu, thus keeping the relative loudness within the group. The same will happen to any other controls associated to the group.

Automation
Automation allows you to record and playback the mixing process itself (movement of faders, etc.), typically encoded as MIDI.

Talkback
The talkback is a bus that carries a microphone signal from the mixer into the player's headphones for communication with the sound engineer. The talkback control will temporarily 'duck' the level of any other signal in the console so you can hear the engineer clearly.

The mixer output section

The output section comprises not only control over the mix outputs of our soundcard but also other kinds of outputs that have specific uses. Very specific features may only be accessible through the audio interface's standalone control software.

Main outputs
In hardware consoles you may find a 'monitor' and a 'stereo' output, which are used for monitoring speakers or for diffusion speakers, but in audio interfaces you will find outputs that you can use for any purpose. Inexpensive interfaces will provide between two and four outputs; more sophisticated ones will allow greater numbers.

Digital outputs
Your software mixer will enable output through dedicated digital channels. By using standards such as the ADAT Lightpipe or Adat Optical Interface, multiple outputs can be sent through a single fibre-optic connection. S/PDIF and AES/EBU outputs will allow XLR connectors to carry individual digital outputs.

Sync outputs/inputs
If you are connecting your audio interface to other digital equipment, you will need to send or receive a sync signal known as the **word clock**. In some interfaces and with software control you may also have an analogue signal input/output known as the *SMPTE* signal; this will allow your software mixer to sync with a timing audio signal from multitrack tape or from video.

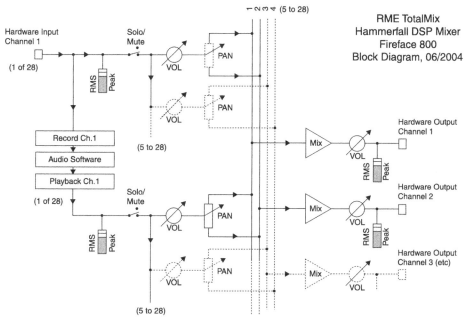

Figure 2.6 Block diagram for the Fireface 800 DSP Mixer (Courtesy of RME Audio)

Data outputs/inputs

Yours software mixer will, in most cases allow you to control MIDI and select what kind of MIDI data are output/input. Normal uses are for sync information through MIDI timecode or for using a hardware controller surface which will provide tactile control over your software mixer's features.

Audio signal paths

The way a signal flows through an audio system is often represented by block diagrams. You will find these in the manuals for audio equipment as a guide to how the electronic components are organised to treat your audio signal.

If you study Figure 2.6, you can observe how it represents the signal flow. The path has arrows showing the direction of the audio signal. Whenever the signal can be tapped, there is a node that represents this (a circle). A signal can be tapped for monitoring its intensity (RMS, or peak) but it can also be tapped to divert it elsewhere. In our block diagram, the signal can go directly to the mix with no processing at the same time as it goes through the audio software. The diagram shows how we can control volume, pan, muting and soloing for each channel, both direct to the hardware outputs (top line path) or through the audio software. Although this diagram looks like an electronic schematic, it is more of a representation for the user than a recipe for building the mixer. In a proper electronic schematic we would find the specific resistances, impedances, amplifications, etc. being applied to the signal flow. We would also have components represented in detail so that anybody could re-create the circuit on a prototyping board.

As sound is converted into an electrical signal and goes through circuits for mixing and processing, the components it goes through affect the current in various ways. This means that when the signal is converted back into sound, it will also have been modified. The simplest illustration of this is when the signal goes through an amplifier it gets louder, but other less obvious things can also happen to the signal. For instance, when the audio signal goes through a **capacitor** in an **alternating current** circuit, lower frequencies will be **filtered** (attenuated). In similar fashion, when it goes through an **inductor**, high frequencies will be filtered. Analogue signal processing for music is, then, about creating circuits to affect audio signals in ways that will make the sound more musically useful. Digital signal processing is an extension of this: the sound is digitised and then, while being processed as numbers inside the computer, its character is changed so that when it is converted back into the analogue domain it will have been modified.

Tracking, mixing and mastering

Tracking is the process of recording individual instruments, or groups of instruments, onto multitrack media (tape, hard disk or solid state). The tracking process was traditionally carried out by a different engineer from the one who would mix and the one who would master the recording, preparing it for distribution via vinyl or CD. What is interesting to us is that if we are to produce a piece of music by layering the different musical elements separately, then there are some things we should take into account. The most obvious is that if we are to record several different instruments we need a common rhythmic reference. This is normally done by use of a click-track, but there are creative alternatives, like using break-beat loops or dispensing with machine-guaranteed regularity and laying down a rhythmic instrument, say the drums or rhythm guitar, which all successive overdubs may use as a reference.

Effects

During tracking, your recordings may be effected by processors such as delays, phasors, flangers or distortion; given that today we use digital audio sequencers where these processors are mostly software plugins, it is usually safe to record your instruments without effects and then to make use of the mixing facilities, auxiliary

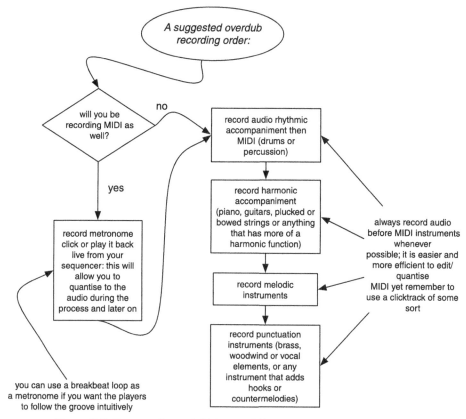

Figure 2.7 Suggested overdubbing workflow

send tracks in particular, to add the effects. This also allows you to fine tune them at the mixing stage. If you are using hardware effects, it may be useful to at least make a separate re-recording of the file (known as a *bounce*) with all effects added in case you are not able to reproduce them at a later stage due to lack of hardware (this is a good idea in software systems in case plugins don't work properly at a later stage; the effected sound is already safe!).

Knowing how to effect your sounds is essential to developing your own production style, so it is useful here to sketch an overview of audio effects processors.

Dynamic effects

Depending on the amplitude of the sound itself, or of a secondary sound which is side-chained to it (this means that the sound is being used as a control of some parameter of the effect applied to the original sound), the original sound may be suppressed, as in a *noise-gate*, or changed in level in a certain proportion, as in a *compressor* or *expander*.

Table 2.1 *Common audio signal processors by type.*

Commonly encountered signal processor	What it does	Similar processors	Type[a]	Example
Parametric EQ	EQ, or equaliser, allows you to emphasise or dampen frequency areas (bands) of your sound	Low- and High-Pass Filters and Shelving EQs (simpler versions); Wah-Wah and Auto-filtering; Spectral processors	d, mod, psy	Pultec EQP-1a Program Equalizer by Pulse Techniques, c.1951
Reverb	It simulates a space different from the one the sound was recorded in, adding degrees of spatiousness	Plate and Spring Reverbs (old-school send–return units using an actual metal spring or plate); **Convolution** reverbs (sampling the impulse response of an actual physical space and using that to synthesise the new spatiousness)	tb, sometimes mod, psy	EMT Model 140 Plate Reverb by Elektromess-technik c.1957
Delay	Buffers the signal and plays it back some time later; in analogue technology delay processors were also known as echo machines and were limited by the distance between the record and playback head of a tape-delay system	Tape delay; Echo machine; Digital delay; Sample delay (delays by sample units)	tb, sometimes with mod capabilities	The Watkins Copy Cat Echo Unit developed c.1958.
Distortion	A clipping circuit generates a distorted version of the input signal; can also be obtained by overdriving analogue circuits that involve valves	Digital distortion (by bit-depth reduction or by clipping); Phase distortion; Fuzzbox and related analogue guitar stomp pedals	mod	Big Muff π, by Electro Harmonix, c.1969

Compressor	The incoming signal is attenuated by a ratio whenever a given level threshold is reached; basically, if the sound is louder than the threshold it gets turned down by a set factor	DeEsser (like a compressor but selects to attenuate by frequency); Expander (boosts sounds below a certain level); Limiter (sound will not be allowed to exceed a set level); Noise Gate (the opposite of a compressor: cuts the sound below the threshold)	d	Universal Audio 1176 Peak Limiter (1967)
Flanger	Mixes the input signal with its own delayed version by a varying delay amount, usually under 20 ms; the varying delay creates phase cancellations and emphasis creating resonating timbral artifacts	Chorus; phasor; Ring modulator and tremolos; Rotor cabinets	tb, mod, psy	Deluxe Electric Mistress Flanger by Electro Harmonix, c.1971
Pitch shift	Changes the pitch of the input signal to conform with a preset tuning template	Harmoniser	mod, psy	H910 Ultra Harmonizer by Eventide, c.1975

[a] d = dynamic; tb = time based; mod = modulation; psy = psychoacoustic

Time-based effects

The original sound is **buffered** in some way and played back with a time delay ranging from a few milliseconds to a few seconds, as effected by a Digital Delay, a Tape Delay or an Echo machine.

Modulation effects

The original sound is modulated or transformed in terms of its harmonic spectrum and amplitude **envelope**, affecting timbre, pitch and loudness over time. Effects that modulate the source sound include equalisers, pitch shifters, flangers, phasers, ring-modulators and tremolos. We could also include distortion effects here as they affect timbral content – the most common are fuzz pedals or analogue overdriven valve amplifiers – but in electronic music digital 'bit crushers' and other effects that force the audio resolution are greatly used as well.

Psychoacoustic effects

The original sound is made to be perceived as more or less spacious or enhanced in terms of its frequency content. This is effected by stereo spreader imaging (to enlarge the perceived stereo image), *exciters, enhancers* and *sub-bass processors.*

Once you have recorded your separate instrumental tracks (assuming you are working on a multitrack production), you can make use of the effects described above to enhance the music. Adding compression to a solo instrument, for instance, can help bring it out in the mix. Similarly, drums can be compressed for a more uniform perception of their level and to help give presence. The latter can be moulded with EQ to help bring out weaker parts of the timbre or attenuate parts that are too prominent. Modulation effects will help you 'blur' your sound for a thicker texture, and delays or echoes can introduce rhythmic elements that complement percussion.

Mixing

Mixing is referred to as an art form as much as it is grounded on science and technology. The problem is that no matter how much you can measure and know about sound, the way you finally present it will depend on personal aesthetics and stylistic considerations. Yet you need to know your console to route the signal in the most efficient and clean way. When you are working with audio sequencers you may find yourself tracking, pre-mixing and editing all at once; this is part of the flow of digital music production, but it is important to check the following points before the final mix:

- Set up your speakers so you can monitor your work at the stereo hotspot (place yourself at the tip of an equilateral triangle of which the base is formed by an imaginary line that goes through the two speakers. If you are looking directly at the centre of the base line, the speakers should be directed at $\pm 30°$ from your direct sight-line).[12]

- Only monitor with headphones if the resulting track is to be heard exclusively through headphones.
- Make sure you know what you have on each track/fader and what it sounds like on its own.
- Check for efficient routing to software plugins; group signals whenever possible.
- Make sure the perceived loudness of each track is similar when monitored on its own (solo) – this makes it more likely that you won't have to over-compensate gain when it comes to combining everything together.
- Have a feel for the spectrum of your tracks independently; in this way if your mix sounds like it's overemphasising a certain frequency area, you may already have a possible suspect.
- Place (through panning) your instruments on a virtual soundstage; no need to limit yourself by reality, though, the aim is to have a more diverse and seemingly wider image.

Mastering

One of the common pit-falls of home and bedroom-studio production is the mastering stage. This stage is essential if the music is going to be distributed even at a semi-professional level. Mastering is the preparation of a recording for reproduction and distribution, so it is important to take into account the various formats in which the music will be presented. One thing to bear in mind is that if you intend to press vinyl copies of your work you should engage a specialist, as it is a very different art form to preparing music for CD duplication. In general, mastering should be done by people who have experience in the field, but if you wish to learn mastering skills, bear in mind the following points:

- Listen to other recordings that have been released and you consider successful: note things like overall level, stereo image, equalisation and compression (dynamic range). This will help you form a critical stance from which you will be able to evaluate your own work.
- Master in an ideal (as possible) listening environment – later on it is impossible to tell what went wrong if the mastering room itself is not a neutral starting point.
- Try out different orders of the pieces that will constitute the CD and try different spacings between tracks.

- Decide on an overall approach to compression of your tracks to help get a unified sound.
- Match your track levels so the loudness is consistent throughout.
- Become informed as to the different dithering algorithms available on your audio sequencer so you can work at the highest possible resolution yet produce high-quality versions with lesser resolutions.

Listening and editing environments

Creating an adequate listening environment is a thorough and complicated task. Different musical styles may require different listening environments and you need to bear this in mind; however, for the purposes of editing and mastering you need a room as neutral as possible. For a person beginning to use music technology, rather than telling them what to do, I have chosen to discuss some issues that will help them decide about their working acoustics.

Noise, absorption and diffusion

In contemporary recording, our concern with noise is mostly centred around the source itself (noise in the recording), as digital media are practically noiseless. For most independent musicians and music technologists, the home listening environment is also an important consideration. Consider that at a distance of 90 cm, an air-conditioning unit may produce up to 55 dB SPL, and a regular desktop computer may produce 37–45 dB SPL. Add to that the noise from your amplifier (if you don't have active loudspeakers, which have typically quiet amplifiers) and you already have a **noise floor** to deal with! Imagine what it was like when, to all of this, you had to add tape hiss (the noise of the media itself). And, of course, you may also have unwanted emphasis on your music given by the room acoustics (potential **standing waves**).

You can dampen a room with various materials. The amount of sound they absorb can be identified by an *absorption coefficient*, which is a number between 0 and 1 (0 being the absorption coefficient of an open window, i.e. none).[13] By looking up these values you can make informed decisions regarding materials like curtains or drapes, carpets, floors and acoustic tiles. The absorption coefficient for any given material will vary according to frequency; arguably the most useful will be materials that help make the room's response flat or even dip in the 2 to 5 kHz region, as your ear will be most sensitive here anyway. As an illustration: consider that a brick wall will absorb 0.04 at 1 kHz while an audience sitting in a hall will absorb 0.95 at 1 kHz (although only 0.5 at 125 Hz; it is good to bear these figures in mind when sound-checking before a concert), cotton drapes will absorb 0.8 at 1 kHz and carpeting about 0.3 at the same frequency.

Sometimes you will not want dampening but instead wish to simply scatter possible standing waves. For this you will use reflecting panels. These are typically made of wood and can be mounted on the wall between speakers, for instance, or on the back wall behind the engineer. They will create a complex reflecting surface (on an otherwise directly reflective one) that will ensure that sound waves do not reinforce each other to create unwanted resonances and filtering effects.

Speaker choice, position and seating

Although specific applications will call for specific speaker combinations, the most common found in use with digital workstations are *near field monitors*. These are not substantially different from normal monitors – they are simply smaller because they will be closer to the listener/music editor/sound engineer, and you can get a satisfactory sound level with modest power. In the end, the idea is that all the frequency drivers of the speaker can reach your ears with a negligible delay. Consider, for instance, that a large speaker (for example, a studio monitor like the Genelec 1036A) can measure 118 cm wide and 96 cm tall.[14] These dimensions already ensure that if you are too close to the speaker, the sound image will be skewed by the frequency driver that is closer to your right or left ear. You need to stay far enough from it (maybe up to four metres), and at the same distance from both speakers, so that you can get a unified impression of the sound. In terms of listening, what you are doing is actually aiming to reduce what is called the *interaural time difference* and the *interaural level difference* between the ears, so that sound will arrive at both at the same time. Even moving your head will create a shadowing effect, lowering the intensity of the sound reaching one of the ears and giving you a different impression of the sound.[15] Finally, the height of your speakers relative to your ears will influence how your outer ear-folds (*pinnae*) filter the sound and give you localisation cues.[16]

For the reasons discussed above, seating will depend on the size and height of your monitoring speakers. Manufacturer speaker specifications will tell you where they can produce the greatest SPL and this can also help you decide. For instance, the 1036A's mentioned above, when playing back music, will exceed 136 dBA at two metres. You clearly don't want to sit there when playing back loudly if you want to preserve your hearing (the pain threshold is 120 dBA)!

One more thing to bear in mind is that *sub-woofers* (speakers with drivers for frequencies below 100 Hz) will not really be perceived as coming from any particular direction, so their position is less critical than low-, middle- and high-frequency drivers.

In conclusion, evaluate the technical specifications of your speakers and find the spot where you get the most unified audio image, taking all discussed facts into consideration. Make sure you are never exposed to high SPL for long. The most common affliction for working musicians is *tinnitus*, a result of hearing loss through frequent exposure to high SPLs. Tinnitus consists of hearing high pitches and noise components in your ear when there is no actual noise in the environment. Once it sets in, it is irreversible and can lead to sleep problems and even inability to perform daily chores that involve listening or concentrating.[17]

Headphone editing and mixing

Headphones are very useful for editing: they are like magnifying glasses for audio. Imperfections in recordings, rough edits, timing issues, etc. are things we can easily detect when using headphones. Headphones isolate the stereo tracks, assigning each to a different ear, cutting off any crosstalk between them as well as reflected sound from walls and other objects in the listening room. This allows for close inspection of the sound, separated from other pyschoacoustic cues. Yet what makes them excellent for editing, may not recommend them for mixing.

Live music depends on many aural cues for its enjoyment by the listener. Two broad approaches are at work where mixing is concerned. The first aims to represent the source realistically through the speaker array (stereo or surround). In this case individual elements will be levelled and panned during mixdown to represent their actual position when the sound was captured (for instance, in drums from a kit, the snare will be placed so it can be heard to the right of the kick). The second approach is a continuum that stretches from liberally enhancing the source to creating an unrealistic blend of sounds that disregards notions of acoustic reality. This approach has been employed by sound crews in film and radio to paint colourful audio canvases for narrative fiction.[18] It was then taken up by electroacoustic composers from the birth of *Musique concrète* onwards to create compositions for loudspeaker playback. In the '60s, probably with the release of the Beatle's *Sgt Pepper's Lonely Hearts Club Band* (1967), the 'studio album' was born. It brought to popular music the possibility of sound exploration and studio manipulation of sound as a creative complement to live performance. The common thing about these two approaches is that, up until the end of the twentieth century, the preferred mode of consumption of recorded material was through speaker playback. This meant that the activity of mixing was optimised taking into account the different psychoacoustic cues produced by speaker placement. An ideal listening scenario involves sitting at the same distance and height from both speakers. This means that most of the left channel is heard in the left ear and the same for the right. Yet a lot of crosstalk between channels occurs as a result of head shape and mass, which help filter the sound, resulting in what is described as the Head-Related Transfer Function, or HRTF. Also, the shape of the exterior ear, which helps us localise sound source by filtering it relative to the angle of incidence,[19] plays an important role when listening to loudspeakers. Combine this with the acoustic characteristics of the listening environment and you may have a veritable carnival of reverberation, phase cancellation and standing waves (which, by the way, can actually enhance the listening experience!). But all this happens external to the ear . . . in other words, if you are wearing headphones you lose most of these cues that are due to the transmission of sound through the air. This can have a dramatic effect on our perception of the music, especially if the mix was intended for speaker playback. Conversely, if the mix was created on headphones then possibly none of these things will have been important at the time of making decisions regarding levels and equalisation. Speaker playback then becomes a liability for music mixed on headphones.

A great many people, since the advent in the late 1990s of relatively inexpensive audio computing resources and laptop computers, tend to mix on headphones. What has been called the 'iPod revolution' by journalists has meant that listeners, in the order of hundreds of millions (and counting), are now consuming music through headphones. Although one finds many online articles on the topic, not many books deal with this issue. Mixing and editing on headphones is a subject that needs to be addressed, so we will discuss it here.

Given the spread of personal music players, there is a strong case for creating special headphone mixes when releasing a track. As of the early 2010s, the trend is to mix for loudspeakers, always making sure a pleasing headphone mix will also result. So if we mix on headphones for loudspeaker playback, what do we need to take into account? Here are some pointers.

On choosing the right headphones

Open-back headphones will allow some channel crosstalk that is slightly more realistic but at the expense of isolation. They will also generally provide a flatter frequency response. Bear in mind that the frequency response of different high-quality headphones will have been weighted (equalised) already to mimic a given listening situation considered ideal by the manufacturer. In the '70s, a standard for headphone EQ was the 'free-field equalisation', which sought to reproduce a flat frequency response, generally assuming frontal incidence on the ears (HRTF at frontal incidence, which means basically that you are placed in front of your sound source), but more common today is the 'diffuse field equalisation', which aims to reproduce a flat frequency response with respect to the diffuse field average of HRTFs from all incidences,[20] meaning that it also takes into account how your head mass and position would affect the sound if it is coming to you from many different angles, as in a reverberant room. High-quality headphones will tend to have this kind of EQ already (or a similar secret manufacturer proprietary one based on their own research!).

The headphone stereo image

As we mentioned above, the left and right tracks will be pumped directly at the corresponding ears; this means you will perceive no room colouring, frequency masking or reverberation from the usual speaker playback. Channel crosstalk will also be negligible. Reverb at source will become more apparent and your end mix may sound quite dry on speakers. On headphones, your mix will sound very 'wide' even if the panning at source is subtle; remember that you have an aural magnifying glass on each ear. Because of this, you need to pan wider than it sounds on headphones to get a broad image from speakers. Finally, you will hear everything 'inside' your head (you will have no speaker localisation cues) as opposed to in front of or around you, and sounds which may have been masked when playing from speakers will be unmasked on headphones. Although there are 'virtualisers' and sound processor plugins on the market that will compensate for all these things, there is no substitute for trial and error and becoming very familiar with how your headphone work translates to speakers.

Headphone frequency response

Headphones don't allow us physically to feel the bass frequencies in the way we can from a subwoofer speaker, so we are likely to over-emphasise low frequencies when mixing. A good rule of thumb is to set up a **high-pass** (HP) filter starting at about 100 Hz with a steep roll-off (perhaps 24 dB per octave) and then begin lowering the cut-off frequency until we cannot tell the difference in EQ. At that point you will have reached the limit of what your headphones can actually reproduce and you can be sure that you are hearing all the bass content there is. If you don't do this, you may find that your mixes 'boom' or distort badly on speaker systems that have subwoofers. On average, you may find that you can set the HP filter between 30 and 50 Hz and still have a nice full mix image.

In terms of mid-frequency-range sounds, i.e. between 2 and 5 kHz (which your ear is most sensitive to), you will need to emphasise this area slightly to translate your mix well to average speakers (meaning: not very expensive ones!). This will feel counterintuitive because your ear canal is already boosting those frequencies, but if you don't pay attention to this, you risk mixing this area too low for loudspeakers to reproduce well.

Regarding levels, the standard recommended safe hearing level that tends to be used in studios (and recommended as a tolerable workplace noise level) is around 85 dBA SPL, but this is in dispute when it comes to personal music players.[21] The idea is that around that level, our ears exhibit the flattest frequency response that is still considered safe (look back at Fig. 1.6: the louder the sound, the flatter the contour, but how loud before you get hearing loss from trying to achieve a flat response?). A little bit of research will immediately show you how the 85 dBA level is almost a health-and-safety standard, but it would seem that for working on headphones and, indeed, for reproducing music it is best to keep below this level in the interest of avoiding noise-induced hearing loss.

In conclusion, I would propose that producers label their headphone mixes as such. This would allow them great creative freedom to work with the nuances of headphone listening, and by keeping the above-mentioned points in mind they could make sure their headphone mixes are 'speaker safe'.

Sound recording

One key thing to consider when discussing recording in the context of music, and thus of creativity with sound, is that the sound quality of a recording does not equate to the musical quality of the recording. I don't mean the musical quality contained in the recording, lent to it by the performers, but the musicality of the recording itself. This sounds more complicated than it is. Consider this: the song 'Da Do Ron Ron', by the Crystals and produced by Phil Spector in 1963, when heard alongside contemporary 24-bit 48-kHz recordings could be described as limited in **frequency bandwidth** and noisy, thus lacking in quality by today's standards. Yet nobody would deny that this recording, as an artifact, is a beautiful (albeit minor!) musical object. It is evocative of the era in which it was made: it brings to mind beehive hairdos and the beginnings of a revolution in music and lifestyle, perhaps even echoes of the Cold War and, for some people, the year J. F. Kennedy was assassinated; a recording can be evocative, musical and beautiful regardless of its sound quality. This also extends to recording techniques or microphone techniques. At the Glastonbury Music Festival in 2010, the band Gorillaz could be seen performing with one of its members (rapper Pharcyde) singing into what seemed like a Shure 520DX microphone, used commonly for harmonicas, to get that **band-pass filter** sound on his voice.[22] Would that be the optimal way to amplify or record the voice? Well, maybe not from a technical point of view, but from a musical point of view not only is it valid and effective but it is beautiful and essential to the songs in which it features. With all this in mind, let's discuss microphones.

As an introduction to music technology this book does not have the technical scope to delve deeply into microphone technology, but rather will concentrate on the musician's point of view when using microphones. For in-depth information on microphones I would refer you to excellent sound technology books like Rumsey and McCormick's *Sound and Recording,* or Huber and Runstein's *Modern Recording Techniques.* There you will find detailed schematics on the different microphone types. Here we will provide an overview and look at some of the practicalities.

Musicians need to remember that a microphone is a transducer, something that converts one form of energy into another: in this case it converts sound waves impacting on its diaphragm into electrical energy. In a sense, it is a musical instrument 'played' directly by sound and yielding a version of that sound coloured by the microphone's quality (as well as the other elements in the recording chain).

Two things are fundamental when deciding how to record a given sound source. The first is where to position the microphone to best capture the sound we are looking to reproduce; the second is: what inherent sound does our microphone have by reason of its design and build (size of the diaphragm, sensitivity of the microphone, directionality, etc.), in other words, as mentioned earlier, how will it colour the sound?

Microphones are classified according to the technology by which sound is sensed.[23] The most common are dynamic mics, which need no electric powering, and condenser mics, which need what is called *phantom power* – a direct current sent to the mic from the console or a preamplifier. Apart from these you will find ribbon mics, which are delicate and should be used mostly with acoustic sources, and more specialised mics, like electrets, contact mics, rifle mics and others.

As musicians, we should try to picture how a microphone 'listens' and therefore how it can provide a sonic perspective on the instrument or sound source recorded. This will then suggest where it can be positioned to capture the sound we want.

One thing is for certain: recording a sound so that we can play it back and mistake it for the original is a very difficult task. This is because of the way we listen. We perceive the vibrations of the air through our body at different times, and what our brain construes as sound will depend both on the timing of these vibrations being felt at different points and their strength. Acousticians and sound psychologists describe how sound arrives at our ears both at a slightly different time from each other, and filtered by our head.[24] Depending on the intensity and wavelength of the sound, we may feel our bodies vibrate, as with very low frequencies, or even resonate in our head, as when standing next to a fire alarm that has just gone off! To add to all this, we also receive reflected vibrations from the different surfaces the sound impacts on. As you can see, it is a very complicated process. A microphone on its

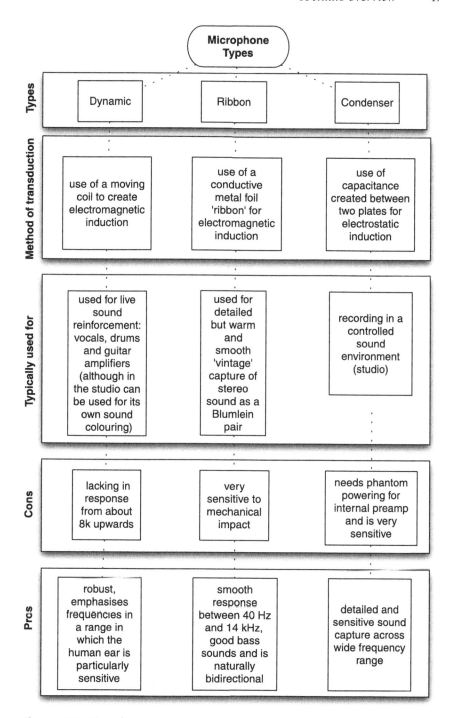

Figure 2.8 Microphone types

own is rather like one ear on its own with no head, yet by combining microphones we can build an 'image' of the sound we are trying to capture and this is, of course, where all subjectivity comes in and why recording is an art form.

Polar diagrams: representing how a microphone 'listens'

Microphones respond differently to the direction from which audio sources arrive depending on their internal construction (how the diaphragm is presented to the soundfield). This response can be shown with a type of graphic known as the microphone's *polar diagram*. A polar diagram is a flat (two-dimensional) representation of the position of something regarding a given point, or *pole*. This is done by measuring two things: how far from the point and what angle to a given axis (straight line) drawn through that point. This is the *polar axis*. A distance measured along this axis is called the *radius* and the angle from this axis is called the *azimuth*. Have a look at Figure 2.9: the pole is the centre of the diagram; this is where the microphone's diaphragm is theoretically placed, flat and facing upwards.

The polar axis is the line drawn up from the pole at 0°. The dotted lines allow us to map any measurements (radius) made against the polar axis; in this way, say, the second dotted line out from the pole will measure the same radius at any given angle. This is useful because sound approaches the microphone from all directions and, although it is only in two dimensions, we can make a fair representation of how sensitive the microphone is and from what angle. The sensitivity is represented by a dark pattern drawn around the pole and it portrays how, given a frequency to which the microphone responds at a given amplitude from a given angle (azimuth),[25] it will then respond at other frequencies. Figure 2.9 tells us that if we try and capture, say, a 1 kHz frequency directed straight (0° azimuth) at the diaphragm, the microphone will be perfectly sensitive to it as long as it comes from 0°; but if it came from 90° (an azimuth of 90°), the frequency would have to be played 10 dB louder than at 0° for the microphone to sense it. Bear in mind that polar diagrams, or polar patterns as they are also called, are measured in a free-field, meaning no sound reflected from any surface.

There are three basic directionalities for microphones: *omnidirectional, bidirectional* (or 'figure of eight') and *unidirectional* (or cardioid and its variations). Mixes between these are also achieved depending on how the microphone is built, and each make of microphone and specific model will have an individual response which colours the sound to a greater or lesser extent.

Microphones also respond to different frequencies in different ways; so, for instance, in the case of an omnidirectional microphone, it will respond omnidirectionally up to about 16 kHz (as depicted in Fig. 2.10), from which point it will respond bidirectionally (as in Fig. 2.11).

reading a polar diagram

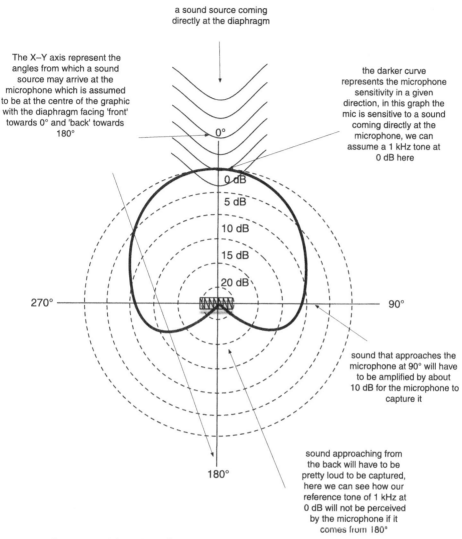

a sound source coming
directly at the diaphragm

The X–Y axis represent the
angles from which a sound
source may arrive at the
microphone which is assumed
to be at the centre of the graphic
with the diaphragm facing 'front'
towards 0° and 'back' towards
180°

the darker curve
represents the microphone
sensitivity in a given
direction, in this graph the
mic is sensitive to a sound
coming directly at the
microphone, we can
assume a 1 kHz tone at
0 dB here

0°

0 dB
5 dB
10 dB
15 dB
20 dB

270°   90°

sound that approaches the
microphone at 90° will have
to be amplified by about
10 dB for the microphone to
capture it

180°

sound approaching from
the back will have to be
pretty loud to be captured,
here we can see how our
reference tone of 1 kHz at
0 dB will not be perceived
by the microphone if it
comes from 180°

Figure 2.9 The microphone polar diagram

Bidirectional, or 'figure of 8', microphones respond in a fairly uniform bidirectional pattern throughout their range with little variation.

Unidirectional, or cardioid, microphones will respond to sounds directed towards the microphone and tend to be used for situations in which we want less response from other directions (vocals or solo instruments). The amount of directionality varies by design; extreme directionality can be achieved through hypercardioid and

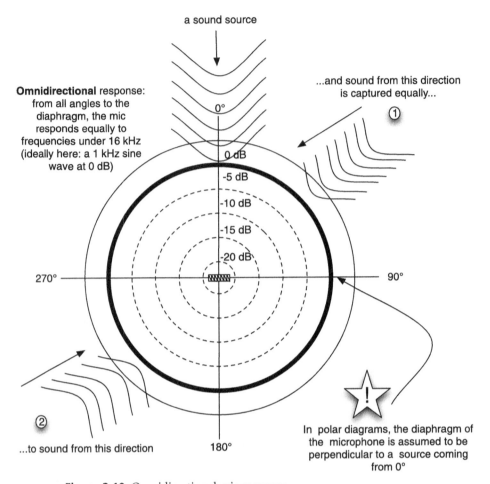

Figure 2.10 Omnidirectional mic response

'shot-gun' microphones, but the general response is a cardioid, or heart-shaped, pattern (Fig. 2.12).

In all these graphs I have illustrated the response at one frequency, but you will find graphs in other books where key frequency responses are overlaid and represented with different dotted lines to show an all-in-one response. However, bear in mind that no reading of the diagrams will substitute for what the microphone sounds like to *you*. For this reason, you should experiment and try them out rather than rely solely on diagrams: by listening proactively you put the music in music technology!

Perhaps now you are wondering if there is any simple way to capture sound 'holistically', as heard by an individual. People are rarely placed in perfect free-fields in the way microphone polar patterns are measured. They will be situated somewhere

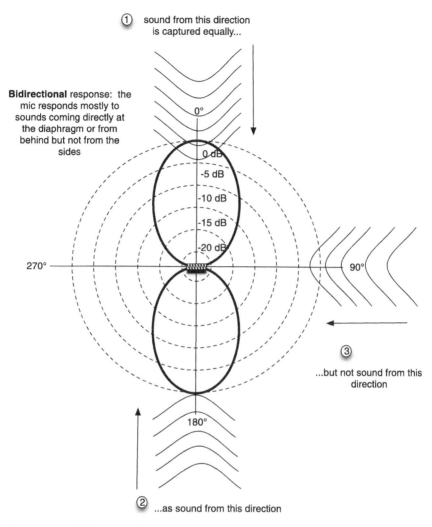

① sound from this direction
is captured equally...

Bidirectional response: the
mic responds mostly to
sounds coming directly at
the diaphragm or from
behind but not from the
sides

0°

0 dB
-5 dB
-10 dB
-15 dB
-20 dB

270°

90°

③

...but not sound from this
direction

180°

② ...as sound from this direction

Figure 2.11 Bidirectional mic response

that sound will be a sum of both the direct source and the way it is reflected from any object present (Fig. 2.13).

A way to capture the sound as a whole from the listener's perspective, and control stereophony precisely, can be achieved by using headphones and by recording in a way similar to how we will reproduce the sound. This is *binaural* or *headphone stereo*. We can make a binaural recording by using a dummy head with special microphones stuck inside it and peeking through what would be the ears (see Fig. 2.14), surrounded by a rubber mould to help simulate the human *pinnae* (the part of the ear outside the head, or *auricula*) as well as the ear positioning. The

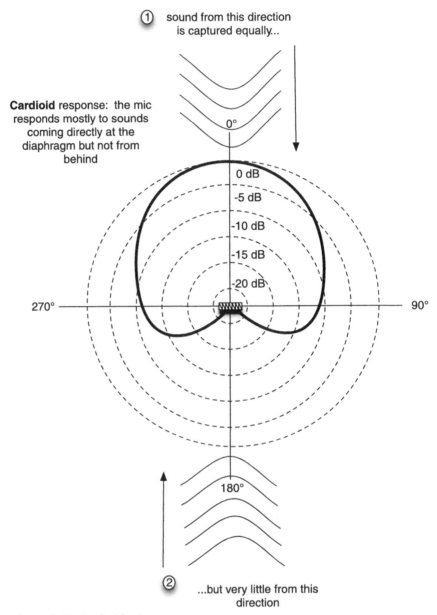

Figure 2.12 Cardioid mic response

dummy head itself will act as a filter so that sound arriving at either microphone is a combination of direct, reflected and filtered sound waves. When sound is recorded in this way and reproduced through headphones (thus avoiding any extra reflections at playback) we get a very convincing surround-like field.

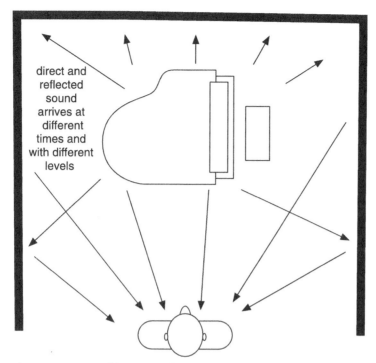

Figure 2.13 Sound bounces off every available surface and arrives at each ear with a slight time difference and timbre

Binaural recording and reproduction is interesting in that the setup is relatively straightforward and the results quite pleasing and immersive. However, at this point it is far from widespread practice, perhaps because headphones are needed to perceive the immersive effect correctly.

Next to the idea of binaural recording, you may think that recording sound in stereo would be a simple affair. Nothing is further from the truth. A whole host of microphone techniques are applied to recording in two channels for stereo reproduction. Even mono recording has its nuance as we decide the angle and closeness of the selected microphone.

Microphone placement

Since we have examined how microphones listen, we should now discuss the main approaches to miking so we can work out some guidelines. Your choice of microphones and their position will vary according to how you want to capture the sound. If your representation is to be realistic, you will want to think of where you want your listener to be placed and how much detail they should be able to hear. This will depend largely on the music you record. Generally, in classical, jazz, folk and

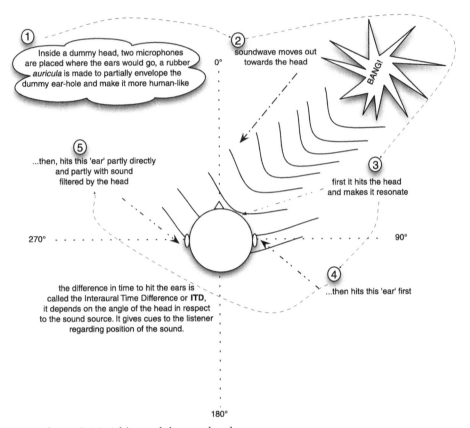

Figure 2.14 A binaural dummy head

any kind of unamplified music, you may want to try and reproduce the 'best seat in the house' experience. For this you may need a combination of distant miking for ambience and close miking for detail and accentuation. It also depends on how large your soundfield is. In a large orchestral concert the image will be very wide, so you may want to emphasise that for playback. At the other end of the scale, a classical guitar recital may need a very narrow image, with presence and some ambience for warmth. You may also choose to pick up the ambience of the concert hall itself with microphones that mainly pick up reflected sounds. For this you need to make sure that your microphones do not pick up information that will conflict in phase, as this will lead to cancellations and unwanted colouring of the sound. A rule of thumb used in miking is that the distance between two microphones recording the same source should be at least three times that between one of the microphones and the source (so, if there is a distance 'd' between mic1 and source, then mic1 should be at least three times 'd' (3 × d) removed from mic2).[26]

Remember, though, that there may be no reason why your miking has to be realistic. You could chose to close mike an acoustic guitar so you can hear the picking noises in great detail and at the same time complement that with a broader, more ambient miking; in a sense this would reproduce a giant guitar!

Musical instruments tell you the way they need to be miked. The first thing to determine is where the sound is emanating from, and how much you would like it to be coloured by reflections from the surfaces of the recording space. If you intend to use the recording as an overdub, you should aim to get a close-miked image so as to exclude ambience that will eventually result in noise when superimposed on ambiences from other overdubs.

Instruments with an obvious sound-source point like, say, the trumpet will be miked realistically by a cardioid mic facing the trumpet's bell. The same is true of trombones, smaller brass and woodwind. The larger the instrument, the more you may want to consider picking up some sort of stereo image. Thus, the techniques you need to master concern both picking up a stereo image, on one hand, and, on the other, picking up a well-defined area of the soundfield. For instance, you may want to mix a contact mic on the body of a sitar with a stereo pair directly in front of the instrument plus a spot mic on the gourd by the top tuning pegs. Or, when dealing with an ensemble like a jazz orchestra, for instance, you may want to have a spot on a solo saxophone. This can be achieved by a mono mic placed so as to blend with the total stereo image.

To record stereo images using two microphones we use the following techniques: *coincident pairs* (also referred to as an X/Y pair), *near-coincident pairs* and *spaced pairs* (also referred to as an A/B pair). In coincident placement, the mics are next to each other, set at different angles; the aim is to capture level differences between the two diaphragms but not arrival-time differences. In near-coincident pairs, the mics are quite close, but with a distance of between 5 cm and 40 cm between them, thus introducing small arrival-time differences. Spaced pairs are any pair separated far enough to create big arrival-time differences, the aim being to create a sense of spaciousness in the recording. Time and amplitude differences will create the stereo image, but we need to be aware of possible phase problems. Another potential problem is a weak imaging of anything in the centre position, so a spaced pair may be enhanced by adding a third microphone placed slightly forward in the centre. This advanced mic position, aided by what is known as a precedence effect, will help counter phasing problems and better anchor the centre of the stereo image while retaining the sense of space provided by the spaced pair. This three-mic arrangement is also known as the Decca Tree, after the Decca record company engineers who began using it in the mid 1950s.

Finally, a surround-sound image may be captured by tree arrangements similar to the Decca Tree; in fact, a surround Decca Tree may be set up by simply arranging five cardioid mics in a circle configuration similar to the speaker placement in a 5.1 playback system. Figure 2.15 shows some of the key techniques for recording in stereo.

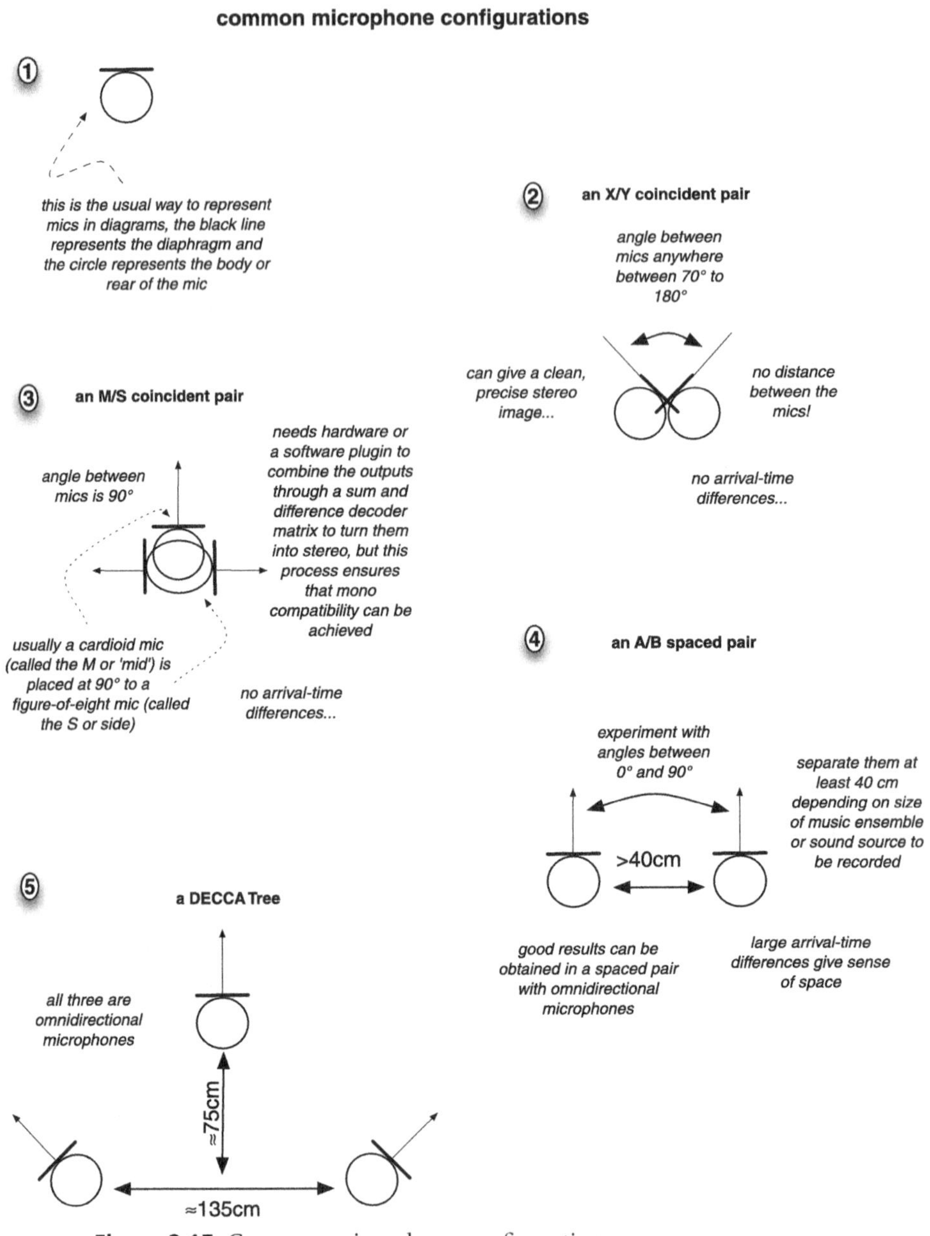

Figure 2.15 Common microphone configurations

Enveloping the listener

So far, we have discussed how microphones 'listen', how their sensitivity varies throughout the frequency range and how they are used to capture sound for a more or less realistic representation. So, thinking of the listener's experience, at this point it may be useful to discuss sound 'envelopment'. This term is used to describe the sense of being immersed and involved in a soundfield.[27] Envelopment is pleasing to the listener partly because it transmits a sense of what it must be like to actually be in the live presence of that sound source as opposed to just a recording, and partly because it places the listener somehow inside the soundfield (even if it is not an accurate reproduction of the soundfield in terms of the placement of sound sources). Music producers try to re-create this feeling through two main approaches. In popular music, the soundfield is synthesised or artificially created by recording musical elements on their own and later positioning them on a virtual stereo field through panning, or the relative amplitude of the sound coming from the left and right loudspeakers. Further, sounds are often overdubbed and thus the placement is an artistic decision (not to say an arbitrary one!). Sometimes this approach may be mixed with the capture of a live performance, and efforts will be made to correlate all music tracks to create a unified stereo soundfield. In classical and jazz music recorded during live performance, the prevailing method is to reproduce the musical soundfield through microphone placement that will allow for stereophonic reproduction. Stereo itself is an attempt to re-create the live sound by using two speakers to reproduce the recorded soundfield through differences of level of a signal coming from these two speakers (early research carried out at Bell Laboratories in the 1930s used three speakers, but this was less viable commercially). Thus, to put it crudely, by positioning two microphones in such a way that they capture two separate versions (and so, amplitudes) of the same sound, we are able to capture a stereophonic recording.

Stereophonic reproduction is pleasing, but not as immersive as being surrounded by speakers containing discrete programme information, whether it is different musical instruments or, as in audiovisual applications, different elements of the soundtrack (see Fig. 2.16). As musicians, we have not really caught up with the potential of surround in commercial applications; so, for instance, although there may be some experimental instances, it is not usual to find a recording of, say, a jazz quartet where a loudspeaker or sets of speakers reproduce just one instrument of the band. In this way we could have the drums on two speakers, the saxophone and the double bass on their own speakers and perhaps the piano on a stereo pair. This experiment itself raises many issues, but it is not so dissimilar to the separation of music, sound effects, dialogue and atmospheres we find in cinema-surround audio reproduction.

Reproducing aural envelopment in the cinema is mainly achieved today through the use of different forms of multispeaker surround sound. This approach consists in using loudspeakers to re-create as many angles as possible for the playback sound to envelope the listener in an attempt to re-create the original soundfield. Surround formats are well established in audiovisual applications, but the obvious problem

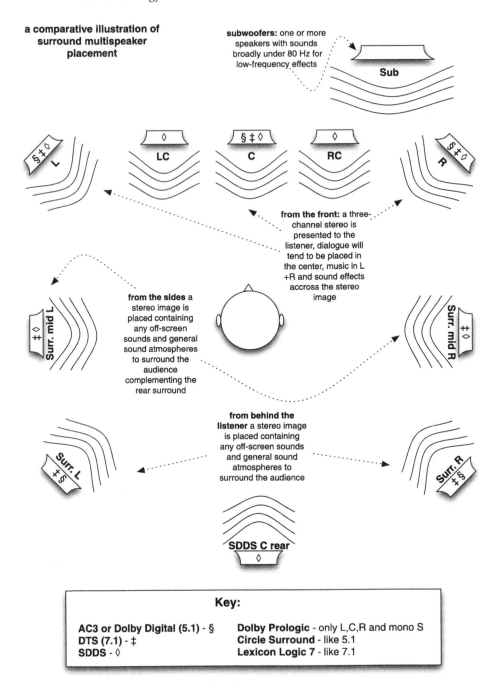

a comparative illustration of surround multispeaker placement

subwoofers: one or more speakers with sounds broadly under 80 Hz for low-frequency effects

Sub

L   LC   C   RC   R

from the front: a three-channel stereo is presented to the listener, dialogue will tend to be placed in the center, music in L +R and sound effects accross the stereo image

Surr. mid L

from the sides a stereo image is placed containing any off-screen sounds and general sound atmospheres to surround the audience complementing the rear surround

Surr. mid R

from behind the listener a stereo image is placed containing any off-screen sounds and general sound atmospheres to surround the audience

Surr. L   Surr. R

SDDS C rear

Key:

AC3 or Dolby Digital (5.1) - §	**Dolby Prologic** - only L,C,R and mono S
DTS (7.1) - ‡	**Circle Surround** - like 5.1
SDDS - ◊	**Lexicon Logic 7** - like 7.1

Figure 2.16 Surround speaker placements

is: how many speakers will eventually be enough? At present we could possibly be asked to create audio masters for up to ten speakers and two subwoofers (in the 10.2 system devised by Tomlinson Holman, inventor of the THX system for film audio), although the 5.1 system (left, centre, right, left surround and right surround plus a subwoofer) is still the most popular, especially for home theatres. An interesting development, which is still in an experimental stage, is Wave Field Synthesis (WFS, created at the Delft University of Technology in The Netherlands), which aims at creating a holophonic reproduction of the sound independent of listener placement. It relies on arrays of speakers, but the most obvious hurdle is the commercialisation of a system that needs so much hardware. In the pursuit of envelopment it is worth considering the compromise between realism and representation and how it may apply to different situations. In film, we are aware of being in the presence of represented sound and are tacitly accepting its imperfection, whereas perhaps in a sound art installation the creator may want to confuse one's perception of the sonic reality.

The variety of surround formats and methods is large, and keeps growing. It can be difficult to keep up with every new format that appears in the audio industry, yet there is no escaping that music production has to be tailored to the format of delivery, be it stereo or a variety of surround. The format will depend on the content to some extent. If the media contain audiovisual material you will need to deliver some form of surround. If it is music, with the exception of academic electronic (known as electroacoustic) music, the format will tend to be simply stereo. The reasons for this are closely related to the way music is consumed, with stereo being largely preferred by people. The present trend is to have high-capacity optical media such as the *Blu-Ray* disc, which seems positioned to supersede the DVD by allowing high-definition video and audio as well as games; what this may mean is that surround may be delivered more often as discrete channels.

Surround is today delivered in two main ways. One is by matrixing, the other is by digital surround in discrete channels. In matrixing, the different channels are encoded using an algorithm that will later allow the signal to be decoded into separate channels. In digital surround, the channels are provided separately but, due to storage space restrictions, the discrete channels are compressed with proprietary methods that allow for a minimum loss of quality. It is not difficult to envisage a near future where no compression will be needed to have truly discrete full-resolution audio encoded with video or film. Finally, apart from the systems displayed in Figure 2.17, surround can also be encoded into internet distribution formats such as Windows Media Audio (WMA) and others.

The kinds of surround used for film and video are what we could call 'representational surround', meaning that they do not really aim to give a true 360° image placement of any given sound, but rather to give the listener an

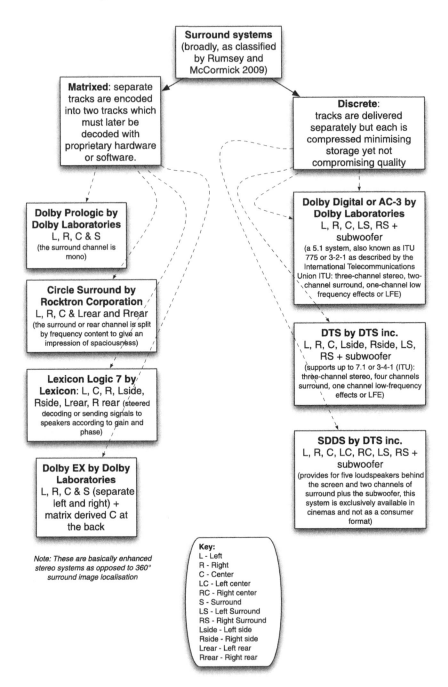

Figure 2.17 Surround systems overview

impression of being immersed in the sound world that is shown on screen. This is why there is such a set style of mixing in surround: placing the music left/right, and effects and 'atmospheres' in the surround channels as appropriate. It would be interesting to have bolder mixes where the music can navigate the whole theatrical surround space, for instance, or instruments placed off the three-channel stereo, as it were.

We have described attempts to create true sound placement earlier through binaural recording. There is a further method to provide envelopment known as *ambisonics*. This method is probably the best way to encode surround and play it back, but unfortunately it has no commercial support and thus no marketing promotion in the way AC-3, SDDS or DTS have.

Ambisonics was invented in the early 1970s by Michael Gerzon from the Mathematical Institute, Oxford.[28] Its theoretical and practical aspects were developed by Gerzon together with Peter Fellgett, David Brown, John Wright and John Hayes. Without going into technical facts, ambisonics attempts to capture a soundfield through directional pickup by means of a set of coincident microphones capturing in all directions and then to encode it for further reproduction by any number of speakers. Whether one soundfield mic with several diaphragms is used, or three figure-of-eight mics are setup, the aim is to receive sound from the front, back, above and below. Ambisonics may include height information, which then can be reproduced with a speaker setup that decodes height to a loudspeaker, or set of speakers, above the listener's head. The basic tenet is that the ambisonic recording is 'whole' and independent of how it will be reproduced, so you can choose to listen through four speakers and not to decode the height; however, this information will still be in the master and not affect the quality of what you hear. This also means that a four-speaker system will suffice to render an ambisonic soundfield recording, but a six- or eight-speaker one may be better; the recording does not need to take into account the playback requirements, these are decided at the decoding stage. Ambisonics is a fascinating area for further research and, since many free ambisonic software plugins are available, as well as language classes or externals for SuperCollider and MaxMSP among other computer music programming languages, we will probably see more future development in this area.

MIDI and recording

In my experience of teaching students about music technology I find that almost everyone will respond in the affirmative when you ask them if they know MIDI, but then if you pursue the subject beyond what the acronym stands for, Musical Instruments Digital Interface, most students will have a weak grasp of MIDI. In a sense they cannot be blamed for this as the rise of virtual synthesisers through software plugins integrated in DAWS tends to make a lot of the MIDI workings invisible. The generation that saw MIDI appear had to deal with cables connecting MIDI-In and MIDI-Out and MIDI-Through, so we could see and touch the cables through which MIDI travelled and there was no confusing them with audio cables! – mistaking MIDI for audio is a common rookie mistake. The apparent success of the DAW interface that makes MIDI connections invisible to the user (you just select a new software instrument in a pop-up menu and there are no physical connections to be made) promotes a superficial grasp of MIDI. There are far better tools that could do the same job today as MIDI (like Open Sound Control coupled with computer languages for one, enhanced by the message resolution of USB controllers, which is much better), yet MIDI is very convenient and simple, and is used throughout the world in commercial music technology applications to a point where it is safe to say that anything that comes next will have to deal with MIDI as a legacy standard. So, here is a basic overview of MIDI for the benefit of more than would care to admit they need it.

Why and how did MIDI come about?

Synthesisers of the '70s worked mainly with control voltages that triggered the playing of notes. If you wanted to have two layered sounds from different synths, you had to share that control voltage from one synth into the next (and if you already are a musician who uses synthesisers you know that sounds can never be 'fat' enough, so given the chance you will always want to layer sounds, at least to try it out). This was a very limited system and only allowed real-time interaction between the synths, and then mostly for the triggering of notes, so you could play your *Minimoog* synth keyboard and get your *ARP Odyssey* synth to 'beef up' the sound. This was common practice in the late '70s at the same time as microprocessors were becoming cheaper and more readily available. It was simply a matter of time before microprocessors were used for synthesisers. Max Mathews at the Bell Laboratories wrote his first program for sound generation, MUSIC, in 1957. So computer sound generation for the masses was on its way. But before synths would actually have a digital sound-producing engine, they had digital technology to control them.

The first inclusion of a microprocessor in a commercially available synthesiser was Dave Smith's Prophet 5 (1977–84), built by his company Sequential Circuits. This instrument had an on-board memory chip for storing the configuration of the different sounds (called *patches*) as well as sound synthesis chips. Smith's innovation did not stop there. In particular, we could say that the general idea of storing the instructions to make a sound must have seeded the idea of looking for a computing standard to understand and transmit the sound-making actions as well: playing a key, releasing a key, rolling the modulation wheel, using the pitch-bend wheel, and so on. In 1981, Dave Smith and Chet Wood presented a paper at the 70th Audio Engineering Society meeting,[29] proposing a Universal Synthesizer Interface:[30] 'The Universal Synthesizer Interface [USI] is a specification designed to enable interconnecting synthesizers, sequencers and home computers with an industry-wide standard interface.'[31] This idea was based on meetings with Tom Oberheim of Oberheim Electronics and Ikutaro Kakehashi from the Roland Corporation. Both Oberheim and Roland synthesisers were in much demand at the time and this cooperation proved strategic. By the end of 1983, at the winter gathering of the American National Association of Music Merchants, or NAMM (now internationalised and known as the International Music Products Association, yet still using the acronym NAMM), USI had been morphed into a better standard to be known as the Musical Instruments Digital Interface, MIDI, and a demonstration was presented. David Smith's Prophet 600 was hooked up to a Roland JP-6 and music technology history was made.

The next milestone would be the appearance of an entirely digital keyboard using frequency modulation synthesis (FM): the DX7, produced by Japanese company Yamaha. This keyboard made extensive use of the MIDI standard, and the digital synthesis and communication floodgates were open. At the same time, computers became personal, affordable and more powerful. MIDI became a staple in studios, along with growing racks of synths, drum machines, sequencers and samplers, with studio control rooms expanded to house all of this gear (thus blurring even more the traditional distinction between the recording or live room and the control room). From the 1980s, the original MIDI spec was further enhanced with features such as MIDI Sample Dump, MIDI Time Code, MIDI Show Control, MIDI Machine Control and General MIDI, as well as incorporating MIDI sequencing into the DAW environment.

MIDI is not sound

Nor does it travel through audio cables, as mentioned earlier. Although most sequencers tend to present the user with a total recording interface that resembles audio recording, MIDI recording is actually a hybrid activity involving live playing, programming (step recording) and editing in a continuous work-flow. Facilities of audio recording like punch-in/out, overdubbing and even effects (in this case MIDI-effects) are common with MIDI recording, but anybody who is experienced in using MIDI will be very familiar with editing and tweaking MIDI events through **quantisation** and other batch processing of MIDI events (creating crescendos, customising pitch-bend data or velocity, etc.). MIDI events are simply data that can be shared among synths.

MIDI is indifferent to timbre

In MIDI terms we can specify that a stream of notes will be played by a synth with a detuned square-wave lead sound, but this same stream of notes can be sent to a sampler loaded with a banjo sound and MIDI is none the wiser. You can send a message to change the soft-synth or hardware synth sound preset if you like, but it is simply a binary computer message, not the sound itself. By the same token, sending a middle-C note is just the act of sending a binary message with the number that the synth will associate with the pitch for middle C, followed by how loud it should be played, further followed by any other performance nuances transmitted through other MIDI messages.

and . . . MIDI has low resolution!

Because of the way the standard is designed, MIDI messages use values that range between 1 to 127, except when transmitting pitch-bend when it actually uses 16,129 values (-8064 to $+8064$). So, yes, an actual MIDI-note can simply be G5 or the note G in the fifth octave (more about octaves, below), but you can bend it in about 8,000 increments or decrements.

What does the MIDI protocol actually specify?

The MIDI protocol specifies all the messages needed to play a synthesiser remotely, usually, but not exclusively, by means of a keyboard controller (other controllers are used, of which probably the most successful have been the wind controllers, but MIDI was made with keyboards in mind; this is one of its drawbacks). MIDI messages are expressed in series of binary numbers, sent in bytes (binary numbers made from groups of eight bits). These messages consist of a *status byte* and one or more *data bytes*:

<status byte>

or

<status byte> $++^{32}$ <data byte 1> ++ <data byte 2>, etc.

Status bytes define whether the message is something like a *note-on*, a *program change*, a *pitch-bend* value, or a setup message exclusive to the manufacturer known as *system exclusive* (among up to sixteen types of *system status bytes*). Data bytes set the value for the status where necessary. This sounds obscure, but it isn't that bad! Let's see how.

A note is sent to a synthesiser on a MIDI channel – each synth voice can respond on a different channel; the message should at least tell it what note it is and how loud to play it, right? So in this case we would have three bytes, one for the fact it is a note to be played, one for what note it actually is (a number identifying the note) and one for how intensely to play it; so, in pseudo-computer language, it would look something like this:

<Status byte = Channel in use + Note-On> ++ <data byte 1 = Pitch> ++ <data byte 2 = Velocity>

or simply:

<Channel & Note-On> ++ <Pitch> ++ <Velocity>

Musical dynamics such as *forte, piano* or *pianissimo* are known as velocity in MIDI – this measurement is taken by how fast a keyboard key is depressed. In guitar controllers the actual amplitude of a plucked string is measured, and in wind controllers the strength of the breath is measured. Note (pitch) values can range from 0–127; this is enough to cover all the (eighty-eight) notes of a piano and more, but that is just adequate to cover loudness and intensity. Here is where MIDI falls short and you have to make do with the capabilities of individual synths to nuance volume and expression. If you want to go more deeply into message formats you should consult the MIDI specification published online by the MIDI Manufacturers Association.[33]

Channel voice messages

Even if you don't know the low-level details of data bytes (how they are differentiated in binary, their hexadecimal representation, and so on), as an introduction to MIDI you should be familiar at least with *Channel Voice Messages*, even though not all hardware synths respond to all existing MIDI messages (the fullness of the implementation depends on individual manufacturers). These are messages sent on a MIDI channel to affect the receiving voice on that channel, hence the name 'channel voice messages'. For instance, if the synth has a Moog bass sound on channel 3, voice messages are sent to channel 3 to tell the synth what and how to play the Moog bass. They are:

- *program change*: selects preset sound or patch;
- *note on*: plays a note;
- *note off*: releases a note;
- *polyphonic key pressure*: how much pressure is applied on each key;

- *control change*: what additional nuances to add (panning, modulation, volume, etc.);
- *channel pressure*: if the synth does not respond to polyphonic key pressure, a general channel pressure message is determined by how hard you press the keys;
- *pitch wheel change*: the amount of pitch-bend sent with the pitch wheel; this is an exception among MIDI values since it combines two data bytes to produce a range that covers −8064 and +8064.

Working with MIDI control messages

Of particular interest for expressive and creative use of MIDI are the control change messages mentioned above. These are mostly unspecified, with the exception of a few common ones. Basically a control message is one that a specific manufacturer defines for their instrument and which we can change by sending MIDI messages with that controller's ID or number. If you are using programming languages to control hardware or software synths you will definitely be using these so it is worth becoming familiar with them (*coffee alert, maybe boring but essential to know!*).

MIDI devices have a synth engine. This engine specifies how the sound is produced and what aspects of the sound can be altered as you play the synth. These aspects of the sound can be controlled by MIDI messages. The messages will enhance the expressivity of the synth sound; so, for instance, while you sustain a screaming lead synth high G, two octaves above middle C, you can change the timbre of the note to it to make it sound something like 'aaaaaawooooowaaaaah'. The necessary changes to the filter to achieve this (that's the synthesis parameter that would cause that timbre change normally) will be values sent on a controller number that corresponds to the cut-off point of that filter on that synth.

There are 128 possible types of controllers, represented by MIDI controller numbers (0–127). These are also known as *continuous controllers* or 'cc' numbers. Their structure consists of a status byte & channel plus a data byte:[34]

<cc # & ch# > ++ <data for the cc>

so for instance:

<channel number & modulation-wheel status byte> ++ <a value between 1–127>

For the most common agreed controllers the following are preset:

- cc # 1 = modulation wheel or 'mod wheel' (anything that has been assigned to receive information from the mod wheel will get it when this cc is selected and the mod wheel turned);

- cc # 7 = channel volume (a volume value for the MIDI patch being played on that channel);
- cc # 10 = panning (a panning value for the MIDI patch being played on that channel; the centre value is 64);
- cc # 64 = sustain pedal (any value ≤ 63 will release the pedal; any value ≥ 64 will apply the pedal).

You will find a few other preset cc's, but their implementation depends on the nature of the instrument and manufacturer. However, bear in mind that you can reassign any cc within a MIDI channel if you are using it for control. For instance, with the rise of USB control surfaces many different hardware controls can be directed to change synthesis parameters or control MIDI machines like hardware sequencers (see Fig. 2.18). It is very likely that as a music technologist you will be using one or more of these control surfaces or even building your own (see Chapters 9 and 10).

   The MIDI specification is still evolving and there are many other MIDI messages for you to explore, although they are for more advanced use. Here is a guide for further exploration:

- MIDI modes for hardware synths (how they receive messages and whether they receive them in a polyphonic or monophonic manner).
- Channel Mode Messages to control the internal connection of hardware synths (local control, 'all notes off' messages, etc.)
- System Common Messages (mostly for hardware sequencers to locate song position, frame subdivisions and the like).
- System Real Time Messages (timing clock information and controls for sequencers like start, stop, continue, and active sensing to determine if a MIDI instrument is connected and receiving/sending MIDI.
- System Exclusive Messages (messages that are exclusive to a particular manufacturer and allow MIDI to send all the configuration information for particular synth engines; these can also be sent in real time to modify configurations 'on the fly').

   Finally, the MIDI spec extends to defining a compatibility standard so device manufacturers and content providers can take for granted things like some universal system exclusive messages (previously determined individually by manufacturers, yielding very little or no compatibility) or what programme number is assigned to what kind of instrument sound and further enhancements to the controller specification. This is known at present as *General Midi 2*, or GM2. There are plans by the MIDI manufacturers association for a faster and more complete implementation known provisionally as the MIDI HD Protocol, yet at the time of writing this is not available.

**USB controller surfaces send MIDI cc messages to any assigned channel
as well as midi notes and midi machine control messages**

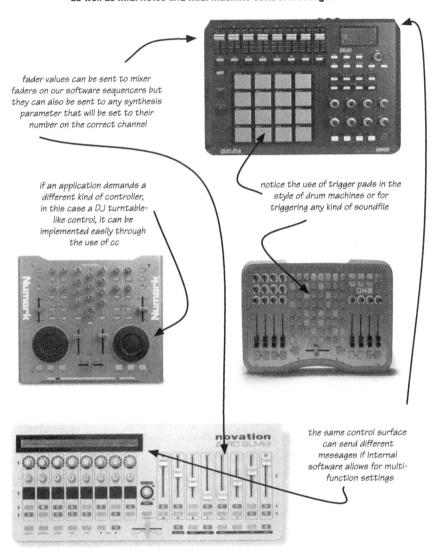

*fader values can be sent to mixer
faders on our software sequencers but
they can also be sent to any synthesis
parameter that will be set to their
number on the correct channel*

*if an application demands a
different kind of controller,
in this case a DJ turntable-
like control, it can be
implemented easily through
the use of cc*

*notice the use of trigger pads in the
style of drum machines or for
triggering any kind of soundfile*

*the same control surface
can send different
messages if internal
software allows for multi-
function settings*

Figure 2.18. Various Controllers surfaces. Images of Numark Stealth Control,
courtesy of Numark, Akai MPD32 courtesy of Akai Professional, OHM64 courtesy
of Livid and ZeRO SL MkII courtesy of Novation

There are no initiatives similar to MIDI that are backed by music instrument
manufacturers, but in music technology research there is a useful and potentially
fast protocol called *Open Sound Control* (OSC), invented by Adrian Freed and
Matt Wright at The Center for New Music and Audio Technologies (CNMAT)
at the University of California, Berkeley. OSC is a 'digital media content format

for streams of real-time audio control messages. By audio control we mean any time-based information related to an audio stream other than the audio component itself.'[35] OSC is so genuinely open that it is widely used in robotics and show control, as well as music and audio. OSC is implemented in MaxMSP, PD, SuperCollider, Isadora, Csound and others, and used commonly for communicating between applications as much as with custom-built hardware (for more, see Chapter 10).

Combining audio and MIDI

In terms of recording, there are possibilities for using MIDI together with audio which at first may not be apparent. One of the most interesting is how MIDI can be used to trigger audio files that have been split by transient. Let's look at this briefly, as an example.

In the mid '90s, with the widespread use of hardware samplers for customising breakbeats, the need to be able to change both the original feel and tempo of a groove appeared. Since commercial time-stretching algorithms were relatively new and computationally expensive, beat slicing became a cheaper and accessible alternative. The idea was to take a recording of, say, two bars of a drum pattern and split the audio into individual slices, one per main audio transient. This would approximately give a separate time-slice for the kick, snare, hi-hats and any percussive event. The drawback was that you were separating by time-slice, which meant getting sometimes more than one instrument at a time (see Fig. 2.19).

In practice, though, some quite interesting results could be obtained perfectly in line with the remix aesthetics that were becoming increasingly popular. The first commercial software application for this process was developed by Steinberg and called, fittingly, ReCycle. With this software, your audio file could be sliced, loaded into a sampler and each slice assigned in ascending order to a note from the chromatic scale (C, C♯, D, D♯, E, F, etc.). This meant that if you played a chromatic scale on your sampler, steadily, you would obtain the original groove at whatever tempo you played in. It also meant that you could play back the slices in any order and create unusual patterns. This is a good example of how MIDI can be used to harness audio creatively and not just to play discrete musical notes of, say, an electric piano sound or a string patch.

More recent and related techniques have consisted of extracting a groove pattern from audio that can be used as a template for MIDI recordings, or simply as a pattern to be varied so the audio can be regrooved, as it were. Most major audio sequencers, like Ableton, Cubase and Logic, allow you some form of this technique. It works, again, by looking at the main transients, which means identifying loud

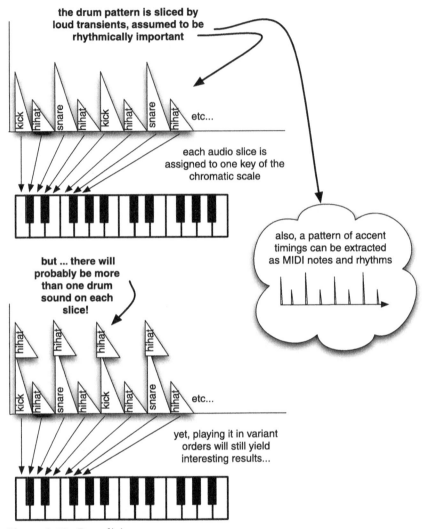

the drum pattern is sliced by
loud transients, assumed to be
rhythmically important

kick hihat snare hihat kick hihat snare hihat etc...

each audio slice is
assigned to one key of the
chromatic scale

also, a pattern of accent
timings can be extracted
as MIDI notes and rhythms

but ... there will
probably be more
than one drum
sound on each
slice!

hihat hihat hihat hihat

kick hihat snare hihat kick hihat snare hihat etc...

yet, playing it in variant
orders will still yield
interesting results...

Figure 2.19. Beat slicing

events and creating a template of MIDI accent-timings, as it were, which can be used
for quantising audio as well as slicing the file for sampler performance.

Beat slicing and the whole subject of identifying transients to determine which
ones are the most important, as well as analysing their spectrum, has been a growing
area since the early 2000s in computer music. The growth of the 'intelligent dance
music' style, or IDM, and related electronica style has placed much emphasis on
stuttering slices of sound files and creating new beats from a sliced pattern. An
excellent toolkit for slicing, BBCut2 by Nick Collins,[36] can be found in SuperCollider.
The BBCut2 toolkit has been extremely successful and has been ported as a VST

plugin called Livecut by Mdsp@Smartelectronix.[37] Also, MaxMSP brings an example
of slicing in its ModSquad example patch by Atanau Tanaka.

MIDI can be further used beyond audio. We briefly mentioned that MIDI was also
used for hardware controllers. The MIDI Machine Control subset of MIDI messages
(MMC) appeared as a result of needing to control multitrack recorders, while
MIDI Show Control (MSC) is a subset of real-time system exclusive messages for
communicating show devices (lighting, video, music, pyrotechnics and animatronics
can be sequenced on show-control software to coordinate them in complex cues). In
particular, MIDI can be translated into a lighting control standard called DMX512-
A, which is of interest to musicians in that you could create precisely synchronised
lightshows for your music by using the right software and hardware MIDI to DMX
converters. And in the context of electronic music performance with video, it can
be used to help to link music to changing images and video control. There are many
VJ software applications available that deal with video control, and, of course, you
can create your own mappings of MIDI to picture parameters with the computer
languages mentioned earlier.

Although relatively slow (compared to signals running at 44.1 kHz or more), and
with low resolution, MIDI is a very useful control standard for music technologists, and with new related standards like General MIDI Lite for mobile devices its
development is ongoing.

Chapter 3

Synthesisers, samplers and drum machines

In this chapter we look at basic synthesis concepts and discuss their practicalities for musicians. We will review the different synthesis methods and the most common elements of modules that are found in synthesisers, and look at some practicalities of sampling and drum machines.

Sound synthesis

Since the appearance of programmable synthesiser keyboards in popular music, performers, composers and producers have gradually developed a new musical skill: sound programming. Today, anybody interested in electronic music needs to have a grasp of synthesis. In a sense we could say that learning about oscillators, filters and envelopes is to an electronic musician what learning scales is to a traditional musician. For this reason, in the following sections I would like to introduce you to some basic concepts of sound synthesis.

Synthesis methods

Methods for synthesising sound by using analogue and/or digital techniques can be classified usefully into four broad types first proposed by Julius O. Smith III in 1991 at the International Computer Music Conference that year:[1]

- *Processed recording*: which consists of creating new sounds by the use of pre-recorded sounds (as is done in *granular synthesis* and *sampling*).
- *Spectral models*: based on highlighting or selecting certain characteristics of the frequency spectrum or timbre of a sound to sculpt them into new sounds (for example, *subtractive synthesis*).
- *Physical models*: these methods aim to synthesise the physical elements of natural sound production. For example the Karplus–Strong algorithm, which simulates the plucking of a string.

- **Abstract algorithms**: these are properly digital or computer music techniques. Although they may be inspired in acoustic behaviours, they are based on using mathematical functions that can be quite counterintuitive to the user (for example, *Frequency Modulation synthesis*, or *FM*).

These are not exclusive types. Many hybrids have appeared that make the best of different methods, but they help us categorise the basic approaches. Synthesis methods have appeared in history gradually, as they have been technologically feasible. Sampling (which is a forerunner of processed sound synthesis) was practised by Pierre Schaeffer and Pierre Henri in *Musique concrète* in the late 1940s and early 1950s. Some rudimentary sample manipulators were invented then (like the **Phonogène** of 1953), yet this technique did not really come of age until digital means were available thanks to microprocessors.

Subtractive synthesis was available relatively early as it is based on the judicious use of impedance within an electrical circuit. Radio broadcast studios had filters as part of their signal processing equipment and indeed were available to Pierre Schaeffer in the late 1940s as well as the German composers of the Cologne School in the early 1950s and indeed to all the pioneering electronic music studios across the world, in the USA and Europe but also in Latin America, Scandinavia and Asia. The bare-bones explanation of subtractive synthesis (which may be the best-known form of synthesis) would be that if you have a very rich sound being produced by an electrical circuit and you channel it through a resistor that works on certain frequency ranges, you are attenuating the sound in those ranges. Controlling these frequency-dependent resistors allows you to sculpt the sound.

Physical model synthesis depends extensively on computers, and the earliest practical example is the Karplus–Strong method, which models the acoustic wave dispersion of plucked sounds, mentioned earlier and available to computer synthesists in the late 1970s and 1980s. Finally, as an example of abstract algorithms being available for synthesis, Frequency Modulation was only practical in the early 1970s for computer musicians and about a decade later for keyboard players. In 1983, the Yamaha DX7 brought this method, arguably one of the least intuitive, to the masses in what turned out to be a key period in synthesiser and music technology history.

Synthesisers, analogue or digital, hardware or software, appear to be quite complicated things. And mostly they are. You need to know and understand the synthesis method to effectively shape the sound. The effect of changes in synthesis parameters may not seem apparent at first sight. For instance, in a subtractive synthesiser you would need to have a high *cut-off* point, to generally get a bright sound, but to know this, you need to know what a 'cut-off' point is and understand something about filters. Unfortunately there have been precious few attempts to make

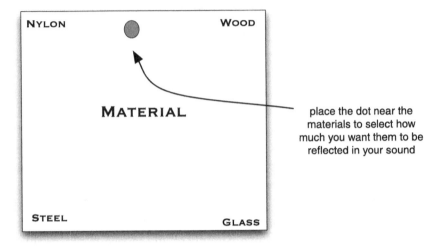

The waveshaper section of the sculpture modelling synthesiser allows the user to make their sound reminiscent of the use of physical materials in making it

NYLON   WOOD

MATERIAL

place the dot near the materials to select how much you want them to be reflected in your sound

STEEL   GLASS

Figure 3.1 An example of a user-friendly interface idea in physical modelling

synthesis usable by non-geeks. We could mention here the *Sculpture* virtual modelling synthesiser plugin included in Logic Studio (Apple), which tries to ease the user into manipulating the sound by providing categories like nylon, wood, steel and glass, proportions of which you can determine by positioning a control dot within a rectangle where each of these properties is represented by a corner. The closer to any particular corner, the greater the similarity to that sound type you obtain as a result. So if the dot is half way between the nylon and the wood corners you can obtain a sound that has properties of nylon strings and wooden objects.

So, given the field is so varied and complex, how can I help you navigate and explore the intricacies of different synthesis methods? I have thought that perhaps by looking at the most common building blocks of synthesis, found across methods, we could get a good start.

Synth signal flow and modules

You may be slightly confused with so many synthesiser facts in just a few paragraphs, but there are many commonalities to all synthesisers and perhaps by looking at what these are, we can prime ourselves for exploring any synth. When we first come across a new synthesiser, we need to understand the signal flow. This is how the audio is made and delivered to the listener. Once we understand that, for a given synthesis method, identifying its elements on a graphic user interface is easier (assuming there is one, which will more often than not be the case). Presumably you will then be able to make some changes to the sound by manipulating the key sound creation elements in the signal flow.

The way the different sound creation and control elements are laid out in a synth is sometimes called the *synth architecture*. This is particular to every synth and method and, as mentioned earlier, we find many common elements throughout. Let us try to identify and describe them as synthesis modules. Figure 3.2 is an attempt to show how the modules I am about to introduce could be related to each other.

All synths need to work from a basic audio signal. We can call this the sound generator module. Once we have a basic sound from our synthesis method, we need to change two broad aspects: how it will be amplified and how its timbre will change (*modulate*) in time. Then we need to decide how these elements will interact with each other (which is called *routing*). See Table 3.1 for a 'cheat sheet' of well-known synthesis methods.

Sound generator modules

All synths must have a sound generation module. This is the core of the synthesis method; it is how the sound is created. Depending on which approach is used, this module is designed to produce a raw signal from an electrical circuit (if it is a hardware synth) or a digital signal from a mathematical function appropriate to the synthesis method. These modules are known by different names, all broadly meaning the same: *tone generators* and *operators* as in the Yamaha synths of the '80s and '90s; *oscillators* as in Moog, ARP and Oberheim synthesisers; *partials* as defined by Roland on the legendary *D50 synthesiser* and *Unit Generators* as referred to by the MUSIC-N series of languages devised by Max Mathews.

You will be able to identify sound generation modules in some graphic interfaces for spectral models because they offer a selection of waveforms, including noise. Figure 3.3 shows the kind of graphic representation you can expect to encounter in synthesiser interfaces when the method is subtractive synthesis or similar.

If the synthesis method is obtained by waveforms that are made to modulate each other (like FM), then you may encounter oscillators without a choice of waveforms. This is because the range of sound you can produce with sine waves as a basic waveform set to modulate each other with different intensities and frequencies is already very broad. However, many FM synths do offer the possibility of modulating waveforms other than sines, and even sampled acoustic waveforms (this latter modulation is known as *convolution*).

In processed recording synthesis like granular synthesis and sampling you will find that the sound generator is a playback module, allowing you to play, loop, cut-up and mix pre-recorded sounds.

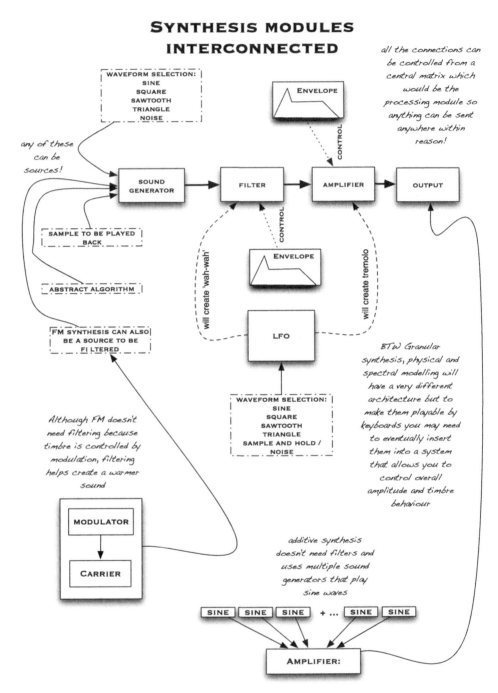

Figure 3.2 A general interconnection diagram for synth modules

Table 3.1 *A cheat sheet of well-known synthesis methods noting what you need to know about them*

Synthesis method	How it works, in a nutshell	Things to try...
Subtractive synthesis	A rich sound source, often from a combination of oscillators, is fed into a filter which controls which range of frequencies are enhanced and how. With envelopes you can control the behaviour of the filter over time.	• How to change filter cut-off point • What happens when you change filter types • How to connect envelopes and low frequency oscillators into filters
Additive synthesis	Any number of sine waves at different amplitudes, frequencies and phases are mixed together. In theory any musical sound can be broken down into sine wave components. This method is easiest to implement in computer music languages as it is very expensive to do so in hardware.	• How varied the sound results can be from a mix of sine waves • Filters are not necessary here • Interesting sounds are obtained by getting oscillators very close (a few Hz) in frequency
Frequency Modulation (FM)	The output of one oscillator called the modulator is fed into another oscillator called the carrier. The modulation effect is heard through the carrier. The greater the amplitude of the modulator, the deeper the effect. FM is usually implemented with a set of carriers and modulators connected in varied ways.	• How different frequencies are brought out when the ratio between the frequencies of both oscillators is changed • make inharmonic sounds by obtaining irrational ratios between the modulated frequencies • You can have more than one modulator to a carrier and you can mix several carrier-modulator systems
Processed recording or sampling	A recording/sample is played back with the possibility of looping and changing its pitch and tempo (if it is rhythmic). It is often coupled with filters in the style of subtractive synthesis as samples are a rich sound source.	• Given its lack of synthesis complexity, it seems less interesting than it actually is, but clusters of played-back sounds can yield impressive results • Looping rhythmic samples • Modulating the start point of the sample

(cont.)

Table 3.1 (*cont.*)

Synthesis method	How it works, in a nutshell	Things to try . . .
Granular synthesis	A sound (synthetic or sampled) is cut up into short segments between 20 and 100 ms, each segment is called a grain. Each grain has the same kind of envelope. Grains are played back repeatedly, often like a stutter; they can be crossfaded with one another. They can be played in random order and changed in pitch.	• Experiment with different grain lengths • Experiment with how fast the 'playhead' reads through the sound thus jumping from grain to grain • Experiment with different grain envelopes, also known as windows
Physical modelling	A theoretical model of how a sound is produced is implemented in synthesis. The process is broken down into component elements and different sounds are achieved by changing the parameters of the components. In a physical model for a marimba, for instance, there would be a model of the mallet (how hard it is) and a model of the wooden slab (to give pitch and a wood-like sound).	• After you get over being impressed by how the best ones work, try subverting the model: imagine a marimba played with water drops or a violin bowed with rubber.
Abstract algorithms	The result of an interesting mathematical function is mapped onto values that can be interpreted as audio frequency. There are many of these synthesis methods, particularly implemented in computer music languages.	• Understand what the relevant values are in each individual method • These are usually based on non-linear functions so tend to be good for rich sound sources that can be filtered or used as modulation sources • Great for creating complex clicky noise sounds!
Spectral modelling	A sound is analysed to create a model of how its spectrum behaves; this model is then used to re-create the sound.	• As in physical modelling, for a musician, look to subvert the model. Nobody really wants an 'almost violin' when you can have a real violin played by a human! • Synthesis is usually aesthetically more fruitful when not used to imitate instrumental sound

Many software instruments will represent their sound generator modules in a way reminiscent of the Minimoog: oscillators that can be detuned from each other, in different range and with possible different waveforms

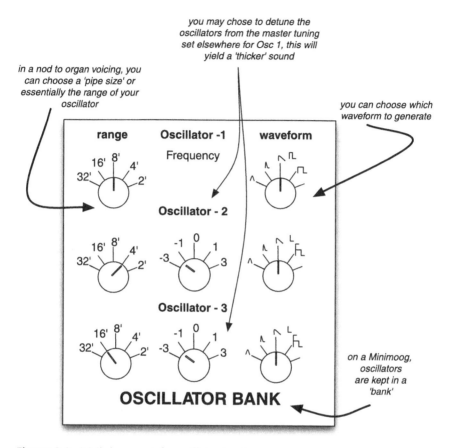

you may chose to detune the oscillators from the master tuning set elsewhere for Osc 1, this will yield a 'thicker' sound

in a nod to organ voicing, you can choose a 'pipe size' or essentially the range of your oscillator

you can choose which waveform to generate

on a Minimoog, oscillators are kept in a 'bank'

Figure 3.3 A Minimoog-style oscillator bank

More complex synthesis systems like those based on non-linear mathematical functions are common in computer music languages where their sound generator modules will be text-based for the user, until (and if!) some graphical user interface element is decided by the programmer that accounts for the different elements in the function's formula which you will be able to change.

Filter modules

A filter, as mentioned earlier, allows you to emphasise or dampen selected frequency ranges; in fact, usually many ranges or *bands* at once. There are three key elements in a filter: the **cut-off point** or centre frequency of the filter, the *resonance* and the *roll-off*. The cut-off point is the frequency around which the filter operates, for instance, a **low-pass** filter's cut-off frequency tells you that all frequencies below it will be heard perfectly while above it they will be dampened. The resonance controls how much gain you apply on the cut-off frequency. The roll-off is a measure of how gradually a filter is applied from the cut-off frequency upwards or downwards and is expressed in decibels per octave.

Control modules (envelopes)

Regardless of synthesis method and architecture, all sounds need to be controlled as they are produced. They can be controlled in real time, like when you switch on a sound system and you crank up the volume gradually by turning a knob, and they can be preset to behave in a certain way as they are being generated. This is what we call enveloping. An *envelope* – curious word for this – is simply an instruction to change a synthesis parameter by a certain amount and in a certain time. Now, one may think of this as just processing, and for synthesis to be exclusively the stage where the signal is born. While that is a valid view, as a musician, anything that changes the resulting sound once the synthesis method has been implemented in hardware or software should be considered part of the synthesis. This is because timbre alone doesn't identify a sound, it is the envelopes of its characteristics (or the way the aspects of the sound behave) that tells us what a sound is. This was described by Pierre Schaeffer in his *Solfège de l'objet sonore* (sol-fa of the sound object) in 1967, and perhaps formally researched earlier by Jean Claude Risset around 1964.[2] Essentially, if you hear a series of notes played by the piano, but where the beginning of the sound for each note is faded in so we never hear the percussive hammering typical of the piano, you may well mistake the sound for a flute!

In particular, it is important to understand envelopes. An envelope can be made of any number of changes at any number of times (by the way, each pair of values and times is called a stage), but there are certain stage presets or 'envelope forms' that are often used. Probably the best-known envelope form is the traditional hardware synth *ADSR* envelope used for amplitude, pitch and filtering. For our purposes, it is easiest to first look at it as applied to volume level or amplitude. ADSR stands for 'attack–decay–sustain–release', or how fast/slow to bring the sound in or *attack* (also known as onset), once the sound has reached its highest level how it *decays* until it reaches a steady state or continuation known as *sustain*, and when the sound is ordered by the synth to stop (by releasing the key on the keyboard or by pre-setting it) how it disappears, fast or slow, in what is known as the release (see Figure 3.4).

In computer music programming languages as well as some hardware synths, instead of an ADSR you can change a number of stages of the sound and assign

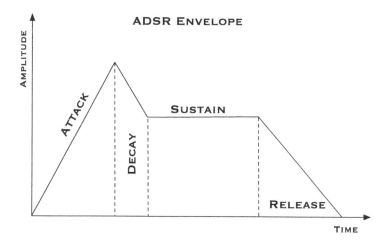

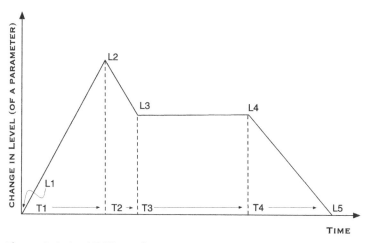

Figure 3.4 An ADSR envelope

durations for each stage. If we abstract an envelope to be just levels of change and times in which those levels are reached, then an envelope looks (less friendly than an ADSR but more flexible!) like a list:

[[L1, T1], [L2, T2], [L3, T3], [L4, T4], [L5, T5], etc.]

meaning, to start at a certain level (L1) and in a certain time (T1) to reach another level (L2) and in a certain time (T2) to reach another level (L3), and so on until you reach the last level for which you will have no time value as that is where your envelope will end (see Figure 4.2: Generic stages envelope). By the way, the rate of change between levels doesn't have to be linear, and different envelope implementations will allow different rates of change or curves between the points (levels).

Envelopes as explained above can be found on any implementation of any synthesis method. One can have envelopes controlling any parameter, not just amplitude and filtering. Yet as we move away from spectral models with the more intuitive amplitude, filter and pitch envelopes, we may find envelopes described as 'windows', as when dealing with individual grain envelopes in granular synthesis. In physical modelling we may find envelopes for controlling the friction and dampening within the model of a ball, for instance; and in abstract-algorithms based synthesis, for instance, envelopes to control probabilistic distributions of amplitude values.[3]

Amplifier modules

As the name suggests, the amplifier module is simply the stage where the signal is amplified so we can hear it. The exception to this is FM, where the sound generators or oscillators can themselves be 'amplified' since the depth of their modulation when interconnected depends on level. In most synths there are usually dedicated envelopes for control of amplitude of individual oscillators, thus they are known as amplitude envelopes.

Low Frequency Oscillators (LFOs) module

In essence, a low frequency oscillator, or LFO, is a looped envelope generator. Sounds wordy, but consider this: an oscillator that produces a low frequency is one that works at anything below 20 Hz, which as you know is the lowest threshold of hearing for humans. These oscillators are used for modulation tasks where the modulation needs to happen over and over again. The typical real-world example is the vibrato of a string player. As the violin player rubs the bow against the string, they obtain a note, but with their left hand they modulate that note in pitch by moving the finger rapidly up and down. The speed of the finger will be less than twenty times per second (or 20 Hz) and thus not perceived as a pitch but as a slow repetitive effect on the main pitch made by the bow. Envelopes, as we mentioned earlier, have a set life. Once the stages are progressed through, the envelope is finished. An oscillator simply produces a wave form, for instance a sine wave, the shape of which is not much different to an envelope. It is a series of values that can be applied to any parameter of synthesis but in this case repetitively, because that is how oscillators work.

Low frequency oscillators can be used to modulate parameters of all synthesis methods if the module is available to the user for interconnection (routing). In computer programming languages you can include them as a tool when you design the implementation of your synth. In hardware synths they tend to always be available as a modulation source. The most common shapes of LFOs are sine waves, square waves, sawtooth waves and a random wave shape produced by a function known as a *sample and hold.*

Routing modules (modulation)

By routing one module into another, various changes can be effected on the sound. Synthesisers will provide users with ways in which parameters can be effected by envelopes or by external control. To illustrate the idea of routing, think of this very simple concept: the harder you play a synthesiser keyboard, the louder it should sound. On a physical instrument this is a given: hammer a piano and you will get a loud sound. In synthesis, this only happens by design! So, playing intensity must be *routed* to amplitude. In this way a relationship is established: more intensity in playing → louder volume. In terms of MIDI, velocity is normally routed to amplitude. If you want a sound brighter, the harder you play, then *route* velocity to the filter so it opens more, the greater the velocity. So far so good, and this may be intuitive in spectral models and in using envelopes to control timbre, amplitude or pitch, but what happens with more complex synthesis forms like physical models or abstract algorithms? Well you have to think outside the box, use your imagination. For instance, in a physical model that emulates the behaviour of a spring, you could have an envelope that changes the input force to the spring over time. In one that emulates a bouncing ball, you could change the force of 'gravity' with an envelope so the ball falls very fast to begin with and then slows down until it hits the 'surface'. In abstract algorithms, envelopes can be set to change the parameters in pre-set ways so the sound is not static. Bear in mind that by routing LFOs you can also give life to the sound, and to make things more interesting, you can envelope LFOs to define how they will begin to effect, and in time fade out, the modulation.

   In all implementations of synthesis we can also use real-time external controls like synth modulation wheels, or sliders or knobs, all assigned to different parameters that they will change in time. These external controls allow the performer to interact with the synthesis process and shape the sound as it is being produced, making it more expressive. In Chapter 9 we will look at how we can control synths with custom-built controllers.

   Finally, to illustrate how powerful *routing* can be, consider that Frequency Modulation is in fact a form of synthesis in which one oscillator is routed into another to produce a complex waveform which bears no resemblance to either of them!

Samplers

We have just explained how processed sounds are synthesis methods, and playing back and processing sounds is what samplers do; so why give them their own heading? Well, in theory we may have covered them above, but in practice samplers and looping software have become such a vital part of music technology that they deserve some separate discussion. Samplers make recordings playable. Or to put it another way, since the early days of *Musique concrète* (late 1940s) through later avant-garde turntablism and hip-hop scratching (late 1970s), recordings have become more than sound to 'play back', but sound to 'play with', and samplers are the best way to do this. Consider also how looping softwares, as pioneered by Sonic Foundry's ACID pH1 – now Sony – and Ableton LIVE, are in essence the natural development of samplers. In academic and experimental electronica circles we have also seen a growth in the popularity of looping software (it seems like any music programmer worth their salt has designed their own looping system!).

Samplers were initially developed to re-create acoustic instruments by a method called multi-sampling (recording as many notes and playing styles of the instrument as allowed by sampler memory capacity) so they could be played from a keyboard and a realistic sound obtained. In music this amounted to something like a mini industrial revolution, as it allowed composers and producers to create credible arrangements with fewer live musicians. Although it has impacted on the economy of commercial recording, it soon levelled off and samplers as a substitute for live players tend now to be a feature of low-budget projects or demo productions. When used by high-end professionals, orchestral tracks made with samplers will tend to be replaced or heavily complemented by live players. The truth is, though, that the days of needing a studio orchestra to test your orchestration skills are over. Today samplers are also much used for playing back rhythmic loops as well as recordings of musical phrases or special effects that can be performed in a track or synced up via MIDI. In the following lines I would like to explain the key features you should look at to understand about sampling when programming them yourself.

Original pitch and root key

When loading a sound into a sampler, a root key needs to be designated to play the sample back at its original pitch. You will normally choose this root key depending on how far you want to transpose the original recording in playback. Depending on available memory you can record the source instrument every three semitones (every minor third), which would allow you to playback an octave's worth of notes with only four samples. However, if you can record every single note of the instrument you will obtain the best results. Remember, as well, that for the best realistic playback, you need the same note played at different intensities; so for instance you could record each note *pianissimo, piano, mezzo-forte, forte* and *sforzando* and program the sampler to crossfade between them according to received MIDI note velocity. Of course, this also gives you the option of recording notes from different instruments for each velocity level, which can be quite an interesting experiment. (Remember that thinking outside the box is the best approach to using technology in the arts!)

Start, loop and end points

Once you have recorded a sample, you need to get on with the delicate task of trimming your recordings. The decision on where a note should start has a subjective component. Often a perfect trim realised by computer analysis of the waveform may result in a sample triggering too quickly or sounding abrupt. Sometimes a little 'air' is needed to get the right feel of the sample's attack portion. The ending may be less crucial when samplers are designed to be controlled by MIDI (as opposed to custom built through programming) as in this case the release portion of the amplitude envelope can hide any imperfections. Looping is crucial for a realistic sound if we want to simulate long notes. Samplers will allow you to choose a stable part of the waveform that can be looped and tuned so that when the sample is triggered and reaches the sustain portion, a convincing held note can be heard. Looping rhythmic samples is also an art form in itself. Further, while modulating the start point of a sample at playback, you can play different portions of it and crossfade between them for creating soundscape textures.

Zones or key-groups

If, as discussed earlier, you record your instrument every three semitones, you are effectively designating a sample to be played back at different transpositions by a group of adjacent notes. This is usually known as a *zone*, or a *key-group*. The closer the notes, the less noticeable the transposition is. If you sample one note per semitone, your zone will be one note wide.

Groups

Samplers have surprisingly complex internal mixing capabilities. By grouping zones, you can treat several samples with the same or offset versions of the basic filter, envelope and amplitude settings. To cater for extended playing techniques, samplers will also allow you to select a group for playing back a specific sound. In this way, although the regular sound you may obtain from a string sample is played with the bow, or *arco*, you will be able to create a group of the same notes playing *pizzicato* (or plucked) which you can select in performance through the modulation wheel or any other assigned controller. Groups can also be output through different channels for further processing or separate mixing (as in the case of sampled drum kits where you may want the snare to be effected differently to the kick drum or the cymbals).

Filters, envelopes, amplifiers and modulation matrixes

Samplers generally follow the architecture of subtractive synthesisers and thus will have all the same resources for shaping the sound. They will also have comprehensive modulation routing to allow for maximum expression in performance.

Warping and tempo syncing

Finally, it is worth mentioning that samplers are not usually set up to preserve sample duration when played back at different pitches (and thus the rhythm changes in speed as we play higher or lower notes triggering the same sound). This is because it is less computationally intensive to just playback a sound at a different rate than to analyse and granulate it before being able to play it. However, there are many programming language resources that will allow you to do just that if you wish. Also, it is quite normal for commercial looping sequencers to cater for repitching rhythmic loops while keeping tempo.

Drum machines

Drum machines have been around for longer than most people realise. The earliest is probably the Rhythmicon built by Léon Theremin in 1931. However this remained something of an isolated experiment, only really to be followed by the **Chamberlin Rhythmate** in the late 1940s, a loop playback machine where the loops were recorded drum tracks. The Chamberlin keyboard and later the **mellotron** also functioned in this way and were precursors to the modern-day sampler. Drum machines were then more of a novelty item, a gadget, but by 1955 the idea had already been put to a practical use. It was around this time that the legendary synth builder Robert Moog recalls his first visit to the studios of commercial electronic music pioneer Raymond Scott in North Hills, New York:

> he had rack upon rack of these stepping relays that were used by the telephone company. You'd dial it and the relay would step through all the positions. He had these things hooked up to turn sounds on and off. This was a huge electro-mechanical sequencer! And he had programmed it to produce all sorts of rhythmic patterns. The whole room would go 'clack-clack-clack-clack-clack-clack-clack-clack' and the sounds would come out all over the place.[4]

Although used in popular music in the '60s and '70s, in specific productions and niche electronic music bands of which perhaps Kraftwerk became the best known in the '70s, drum machines and their distinctive sound and feel would not really

TR-808 - STYLE INTERFACE

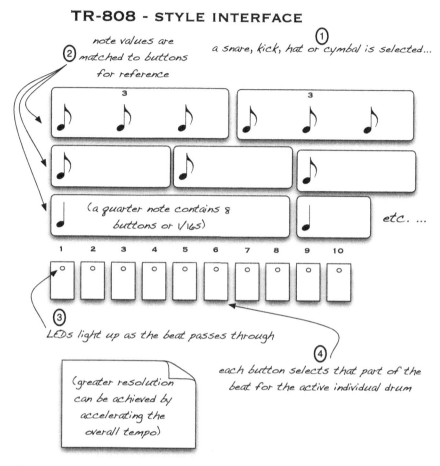

Figure 3.5 A vintage drum machine grid

produce a substantial impact in the pop music world until the late '70s when 'Synth Pop' arrived and then continued to evolve well into the '80s.

At this point there were clearly two trends in drum machine sound production: sample playback and some form of electronic synthesis, mostly subtractive (using noise as a source for snare drum sounds and so on). Yet one common feature, regardless of sound generation, was the increasing integration of a sequencer element as part of the drum machine itself that the user could programme and follow graphically on the hardware itself by means of LEDs and some sort of grid-like arrangement that represented the beat graphically.[5] A good early example of this was the *Roland TR-808*. This machine has a very distinctive sound that has spawned countless imitations and emulations. From a GUI point of view, though, it added an intuitive feel to rhythm programming/creation by graphically showing the progress of the beat (Fig. 3.5). One drawback, though, is that the machine was not performable in the sense that others like the *Linn Drum* were (on the Linn DM-1 you could play the pads in time to a metronome and layer the instruments). On the TR-808 you could select the rhythmic position of a hit but not actually play it. These two approaches to rhythm programming would later come together in drum machines like the *Roland R8 Human Rhythm Composer* (1988). Drum machines seem to have helped usher in the age of sequencing in music production; although the synth pop movement passed, the legacy of drum machines is alive and well. The use of grid-like interfaces with their equal-spacing representation of rhythm encouraged musicians with no traditional training to experiment with beats.[6] These grids would also be influential in the development of the piano-roll representation in MIDI software sequencers and in later grid GUI for looping software and, indeed, virtual drum machines.

Finally I want to briefly highlight some key points for would-be drum machine programmers to be aware of when using a drum machine or sequencing drums.

Realistic or not?

It may just be impossible to make drum machines sound actually real, but combining them with elements of live recorded percussion can counteract the machine-like precision that characterises them. If you are using a virtual drum machine within a sequencer you should become familiar with quantisation, groove and humanise features; these provide virtual alignment grids for beats, regularly spaced, customised to a pattern and randomised respectively. Try also to become familiar with both the placement of the drums on your virtual stage as well as the kinds of things that a drummer would do.

If you are looking for that machine-like precision and sound, you are 100 per cent there already, but remember that drum machines have become associated with styles and you send a very different message if you use the sounds of a TR-808 than if you use the sounds of an AKAI MPC-60 (the first one says 'synth-pop', the second one says 'rap'!). Become familiar with the different drum machine sounds but don't be afraid to customise. Software drum machines will usually allow you to substitute drum sounds for any percussive sound you wish. This is a good opportunity to experiment with sounds you would not usually associate with a drum kit, yet can sound very effective. Finally, many high-end sequencer software programs will allow you to extract the groove 'template' from live recorded drum patterns. Try to apply these to programmed patterns for an effective feel that maintains an 'electro' sound.

Chapter 4

Live music technology (the FAQs)

Presenting music that depends on sound technology beyond microphones and amplification is not something trivial. Where acoustic musicians can perform on stage with relatively little technology beyond microphony and amplification, computer musicians and digital DJs cannot; they are highly dependent on often complex electronic setups. In this chapter I would like to present a number of frequently asked questions regarding that scary step: actually getting people to listen to your music while you tweak, perform, capture and transform or do any other musical interaction with your electronic and digital instruments. This list is compiled from the point of view of the performer as opposed to the sound engineer.

What is sound reinforcement?

Sound reinforcement is the use of amplifiers, mixers and speakers to reinforce the sound of acoustic instruments, or to diffuse the sound of electric instruments like synthesisers, samplers and turntables. In the case of electric guitars, basses and pianos, the system will usually reamplify the individual amplifiers that are normally used for those instruments.

What is a PA?

PA stands for 'public address' system and refers to amplification systems used for piping recorded background music and spoken announcements (public addresses), for example, at airports or convention centres. PA is sometimes used to mean the same as sound reinforcement. Depending upon context, the difference between the use of these two terms is often blurred.

What is sound diffusion or sound projection?

'Sound diffusion' or 'sound projection' are terms from avant-garde and academic electroacoustic music practice referring to the art of placing audio feeds from a

Figure 4.1 Word cloud of Chapter 4

pre-recorded composition in a multi-speaker sound setup. This also includes the use of pre-recorded elements combined with live performance. The result of this can be magical, and unfortunately this practice has not made it into popular music practice, where stereo is the norm.

Sound diffusion grew out of the *Musique concrète* performance practice of the '50s. Pierre Schaeffer and Pierre Henri would prepare several sources on shellac (this is, before vinyl and tape!) that could be mixed in performance. For this they used a device they called *pupitre d'espace*, essentially a mixing desk that allowed them to pan the sound of what we could term a 'soloist track' around an array of speakers. The idea being that this rendering of the sound in live performance was essential to the music.

In the late 1960s this practice was continued by the Acousmonium, an orchestra of loudspeakers from the Groupe de Recherches Musicales founded by Schaeffer at *Radiodiffusion-Télévision Française* (RTF). Their approach was to present all the loudspeakers on stage so that by distributing the sound among the speakers throughout the performance, the sound image would be enhanced and punctuated in a quasi-orchestral fashion by sub-groups of speakers running in different directions across the stage. To this day, the Acousmonium performs in this manner. Yet there are other ways of effectively rendering the sound image in performance. The Birmingham Electro-Acoustic Sound Theatre, or BEAST, is a large sound diffusion speaker system designed and directed by Professor Jonty Harrison at the University of Birmingham.[1] The work of BEAST has been seminal in electroacoustic performance. While BEAST can playback any multitrack tape configuration, it is interesting to note Harrison's approach to rendering a stereo image through multiple speakers. The basic idea is that there is only one sweet spot for a stereo playback in a two-speaker system, so by having several stereo pairs at different distances from each other and covering back, sides, front, ceiling and far front, the sound projectionist at the mixing desk can provide a performance of the sound that allows all listeners to enjoy a different and valid experience of the music. BEAST operates with large numbers of speakers, but the core is made of eight main speakers. Harrison calls them the 'main eight'.[2] These are divided into four stereo pairs, carefully designed to enhance the stereo image in performance. A narrow frontal stereo pair, termed as *Main*, allows for a stable stereo image front and centre of the audience. To enhance lateral movements of sounds recorded with panning, a *Wide* pair is added. The sound diffuser can then bring them into play as the music requires it. To enhance perspective, a *Distant* pair is added to the front of the hall, further from the Main pair and suspended at about eight feet to aid a sense of immersion for the listener. The *Rear* pair is the back version of the *Distant*, also raised above the listeners to promote envelopment. These can also be brought into play dramatically to give the impression of specific directionality of the sound elements. BEAST complements the main eight with subwoofers and tweeters and auxiliary smaller speakers that will take advantage of the concert hall in which the performance takes place.

As you can imagine from the above description, a sound-diffused performance can be very exciting. Here is a lesson that popular musicians would do well to assimilate as it adds to the enjoyment of the music enormously.

Is there a standard setup for a PA or for sound reinforcement?

Not really, but you could say that both consist of an input section, a processing section, an amplification section and an output section. Input and output sections use *transducers* which, as we know, change one form of energy into another. In this case, acoustic energy is turned into electrical energy by the use of input transducers like microphones or instrument pickups and later turned back into acoustic energy by output transducers like speakers. The processing section is the set of audio devices that we need for treating the sound to make it more intelligible or to prevent listener fatigue (for example, for filtering unwanted frequencies or clarifying the sound, etc.). The amplification section consists of amplifiers to send the right amount of power to drive the speakers, which are the output section, for optimal sound projection.

How much sound reinforcement do I need?

This depends on many factors like amount and efficiency of amplification, number of speakers, size of the venue, shape (architectural features), absorption of the surfaces and so on. Bear in mind also that a venue will sound different if it is full of people than if it is only filled to a quarter of its capacity. It has been the practice for sound engineers to estimate the amount of amplification needed by working out a wattage per person in the audience. This varies wildly as you can verify with a few simple internet searches in audio engineering forums. You will find estimates as low as 0.5 watts per person for vocal applications, and as high as 20 watts per person for a heavy metal band in a concert hall. The problem is that even if you work out what wattage can drive a given speaker efficiently to reproduce a typical range of frequencies at an acceptable level for the kind of music you will be playing, you still have to factor in all the other acoustic factors present in the venue. The only sensible answer is that you need to know the venue to have an idea of what to expect.

Where should I setup my laptop on stage?

This is the first question when you arrive to perform. So here are some things to bear in mind: if you are playing as part of a band you will negotiate your position on stage, but if you are a solo artist, you will probably be centre-stage. You need to remember that in that position you will not necessarily have a very good idea of what the audience is hearing. Make sure you have somebody at the main console. Unless it is a very small gig where you are providing all the amplification yourself and controlling it from stage, it is worth having somebody else within the diffusion field of your speakers who ideally can control the general level of your sound. They should receive from you a stereo submix or separate lines if you have several sources (guitar, laptop, voice, etc.). Do this even if all they have in the end is a small console with your stereo output. The FOH engineer (Front of House) will then be able to equalise and level as appropriate when the room is full and the absorption coefficient of the room has risen thanks to the presence of a (hopefully) packed audience. In electroacoustic music, in particular in acousmatic (playback only) or multispeaker sound-diffusion setups, you will be at the centre of the audience or 'best seat in the house' position so you will be in a better location to control and mix your sound live.

Which cables should I use?

Sounds trivial, but many fine sounds from the studio are ruined, when taken on stage, by noise and *ground loops*. The rule of thumb is: if you are going to exceed five meters (to be on the safe side!) between your source (synth, soundcard) and the mixer, you need to use balanced lines. The actual connector – whether a quarter-inch plug or

CONNECTORS

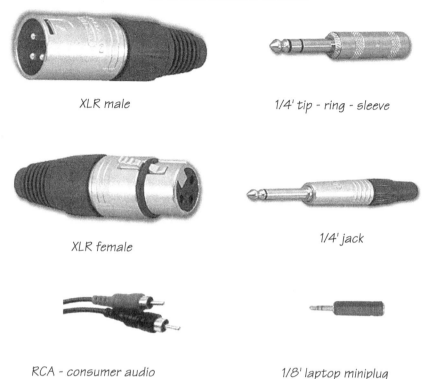

XLR male

1/4' tip - ring - sleeve

XLR female

1/4' jack

RCA - consumer audio

1/8' laptop miniplug

Figure 4.2 Various types of connectors and plugs

an XLR or cannon – is not so important as to whether the line is balanced. Electric instruments like synths, electric guitars or electric pianos are usually connected by an unbalanced cable, with quarter-inch connectors, to their amplifiers. Unbalanced means that the cable consists of two conducting elements, one is the actual voltage varying signal and the other is a grounding element usually in the form of a sheath around the signal wire. The problem with this type of cable is that any noise added to the audio signal cannot be removed. Balanced cables are designed precisely to solve this. In a balanced cable there are three conducting elements or wires. One contains the signal, another contains the inverted signal and the third is the ground. The logic of this is that if the signal picks up noise, all you need to do is subtract the inverted one from the original and divide by 2 and you eliminate the noise. Here is why: the original signal with noise can be represented as (Signal + Noise), the inverted signal also picks up the noise (which itself is not inverted) and can be represented as (−Signal + Noise). If you do the subtraction, you have this:

$$(\text{Signal} + \text{Noise}) - (-\text{Signal} + \text{Noise})$$

and so you obtain, after simplifying the signs:

$$\text{Signal} + \text{Noise} + \text{Signal} - \text{Noise} = 2\,\text{Signal}$$

but since the signal has been now duplicated, it needs to be halved to obtain the final signal, and so:

$$[(\text{Signal} + \text{Noise}) - (-\text{Signal} + \text{Noise})]/2 = \text{clean signal}$$

In any case, you can still use unbalanced lines if you are close to an extension box of a multicore connection on stage, because the multicore itself will be balanced.

How will my instruments be connected to the venue's PA?

This depends on how far you are from the mixer; normally a special cable called a *multicore* is used on stage. It carries many different signals in their individual cables, or *cores*, which are grouped into one larger cable. On stage you will find the inputs to this composite cable individually accessible through an input box and then, at the other end, the multicore breaks out into individual cables and connectors that can be patched into the mixer.

How many mixers/consoles do sound systems use?

There will be at least one if the venue is small enough that no separate monitoring is needed for the players. The main mixer is called the Front of House mixer (FOH). If the venue is large and the players need monitoring, then there may be a second (or more) mixer(s) to create a separate mix for the players on stage.

How many monitors will I need to be able to hear myself on stage?

You will need to at least be close to one monitor speaker, but the ideal is to have at least one per player with a separate mix for each player. The best way to achieve this is through the use of *in-ear monitoring*. Together with a wireless system, this can ensure that players have a very good idea of what their sound is and how it may be perceived by the audience. In-ear monitoring can also reduce feedback problems as microphones can pick up the signal from monitor speakers. A crucial point to bear in mind is that with in-ear monitoring the performer can be quite isolated from other sounds that are not being fed into their personal monitor mix, so it is good to have microphones set specifically for the audience and other elements on stage that may not be going directly to the monitor mix. This will ensure better communication with other players but also a greater rapport with the audience.

Can I connect my consumer sound card with phono connectors (RCA) or a 1/8″ mini-jack from my computer to the mixer?

No, but maybe yes! Here is what you need to know to decide. Not all audio signals have the same voltage and thus electric potential. There are average voltage conventions you should know about.[3]

Microphones, guitar pickups, turntable pickup cartridges and tape heads (taking into account that so much retro technology is fashionable!) work at very low level, as low as −60 dBu and sometimes up to −20 dBu. Your mileage may vary, but be sure to know the operating level which is optimal for each device you work with.

For consumer electronics, the average level is −10 dBu. This means that consumer-level signals will operate or reach a maximum of −10 dBu below the reference of 0.775 volts, known as 1 dBu (the 'u' means that when considering voltage in an audio circuit, decibels will be referenced to 0.775volts as 0 dBu). Home Hi-Fi, consumer playback devices like mini-disks or personal solid-state playback/recorders and MP3 players operate at −10 dBu. If the mixer has specific inputs that state −10 dBu, then you can connect into those. Sometimes you will be able to select the voltage on your hardware as well for a set of inputs. Mini-jacks and phono inputs are most likely an indication of a 'consumer-grade' connection. One thing to bear in mind for computer musicians using the 1/8″ mini-jack of a laptop to output audio is that these outputs have an amplified signal ready for headphones (unless the laptop manufacturer offers a hardware or software switch). This means that the signal will be louder than −10 dBu and you may need to attenuate it when connecting into other consumer electronic devices.

For pro-audio in most of the world, the nominal line level (level at which the device is designed to operate) is +4 dBu. This is evidently a 'hotter' signal than consumer electronics and usually transmitted through XLR cables or Tip-Ring-Sleeve (TRS) 1/4″ balanced jacks.

What is the ideal way to output audio from my laptop?

A soundcard with balanced outputs at +4 dBu, connected directly to the console. Of course, if you can connect digitally from the soundcard or audio interface to a digital mixer, that is even better.

What audio processing devices can I expect to find in a PA?

You can expect to find multi-effects processors to provide reverb and delay processing to aid the impression of space in the venue. You should also find equalisers to help present the best sound possible and dial out unwanted frequency areas or simply attenuate a problematic frequency range. Finally, compressors and noise-gates are used to help unify the overall level of the music items being presented (preventing the amplification from going to dynamic level extremes).

How do I setup for live mixing, capture and looping?

In a live setup you will typically want to play back some sounds you have selected as well as transform and remix them. You may also want to record live sounds either from an instrumentalist or from noise-making devices that can yield interesting sounds (toy instruments are great for this). This is a way to keep your performance interesting and for the audience to witness the creative process from capture to output. Of course, you may also simply wish to perform a DJ set. All these scenarios have a basic setup which is illustrated in Figure 4.3. Study it for a moment.

Regardless of performance scenario, one of the key elements is to decide where the headphone mix comes from. If it is to come from the mixer, then you will have to coordinate the sampling setup (audio capture) with the front-of-house engineer; this may be necessary in larger venues. If at all possible, you should control the capture yourself by connecting the microphone directly to the audio interface. If performing the sound to be recorded is part of the performance, you may also need to amplify it, but this is better achieved with a separate microphone (and again, either directly to the mixer or through your interface first depending on the venue; the former may be preferable in a larger venue as the sound can be balanced by somebody with a perspective closer to that of the audience).

What sort of microphone is best for live performance?

Although this will also depend on the venue and the sounds/instruments being amplified and sampled, the safe bet is on dynamic microphones. Condenser mics will give a better sound but in live performance they tend to be too sensitive and thus more susceptible to feedback. However, supercardioid condensers, like, for instance, the DPA4099G clip microphones, will allow you to focus very precisely on close miking plucked instruments like the guitar, thus permitting greater gain

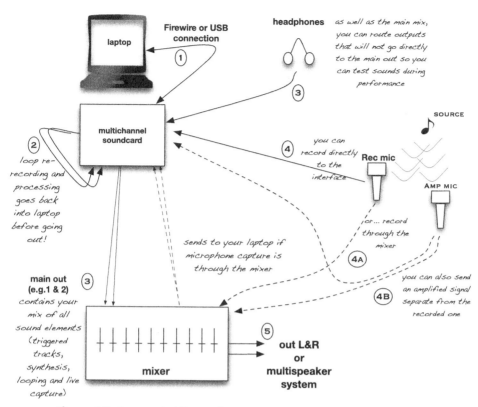

laptop

Firewire or USB connection ①

headphones

as well as the main mix, you can route outputs that will not go directly to the main out so you can test sounds during performance

③

SOURCE

multichannel soundcard

②

loop re-recording and processing goes back into laptop before going out!

④ *you can record directly to the interface*

Rec mic

AMP MIC

sends to your laptop if microphone capture is through the mixer

or... record through the mixer

④A

main out (e.g.1 & 2) ③

contains your mix of all sound elements (triggered tracks, synthesis, looping and live capture)

④B *you can also send an amplified signal separate from the recorded one*

⑤

out L&R or multispeaker system

mixer

Figure 4.3 A suggested live performance set-up

before feedback becomes an issue. Microphones like, for instance, the Shure SM58 for vocals and the SM57 for instruments have been around for decades now, and are used widely in rock, pop and jazz performances. They are unidirectional or cardioid mics that will minimise the chance of feedback and represent a relatively inexpensive solution to sound reinforcement. They are also more forgiving of poor microphone technique. For instance, speaking too close to the microphone will accentuate implosive vocal sounds (like the sound of syllables that include the letter 'p'). Also, closeness to the microphone will accentuate lower frequencies. An important part of live performance is knowing how to handle microphones to minimise extraneous noises and get the best response from them. In general, you will want to avoid omnidirectional microphones as you cannot control well what will get picked up. Finally, good wireless microphone systems are an excellent solution to reduce cable clutter and allow mobility for the instrumentalist in performance, yet the less expensive wireless systems will not have very good frequency response so you may decide to bear with the clutter!

IMPEDANCE

Electrical impedance is the total opposition presented by a circuit to alternating current by resistors, capacitors and inductors. An audio signal can be affected by the combination of these components to emphasise or attenuate certain frequencies

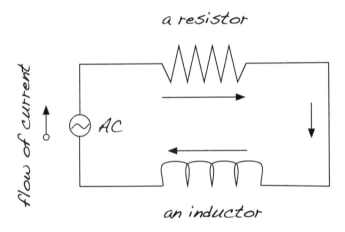

a resistor

flow of current

AC

an inductor

the resistor plus the inductor together impede the flow of current

Figure 4.4. Impedance

What do I need to know about impedance and nominal levels and how do they affect my sound in live performance?

While it is true that current electronic equipment makes it easy for users not to know much, if anything, about impedance, it is useful to have an idea of what it is in case you are tempted to plug a cable somewhere just because it fits, or you use vintage equipment now and again (like valve amplifiers). By the same token, if you are setting up your connections you need to know that you are feeding the correct levels into the right inputs (nominal levels were described earlier in the FAQ about connecting your laptop's 1/8″ plug).

Impedance is an electrical term referring to the total resistance to the flow of electricity in an alternating current circuit. (Fig. 4.4.) To fully understand that last sentence, you may actually need some knowledge of electricity, but you can still understand how it affects your sound without detailed technical knowledge.

Whenever you are drawing electricity from the mains – and this probably means always in live performance – you are working with alternating current, or AC. This is perfect for audio because as air-pressure changes produce sound and microphone diaphragms move back and forth in response, compression and rarefaction can both be represented positively and negatively by a current that alternates going forwards and backwards, as it were (think back to Chapter 1 and the nature of sound). This is different from battery-operated circuits where *direct current*, or DC, is used. In these circuits, the total resistance is simply called resistance, and measured in Ohms, just like impedance is. What is interesting to music technologists is that impedance varies with frequency. This is important, because it means that the audio circuit behaves differently according to the sound content. Forgive me if this doesn't look too technical, but for musicians it means that the sound becomes coloured according to what sorts of impedances are presented in a circuit. It makes electrical circuits more like musical instruments. Some will sound warm as they present impedance due to inductors that favour low frequencies and some may sound bright as they present impedance from capacitors which favour high frequencies. In fact, if you know your circuits, you can carefully balance the colour of your sound. And, if you are following this thought process, perhaps you have even begun to see that this is the foundation of filtering.

In live performance, know that your beautiful studio sound will be coloured by every circuit that you need to use, from the venue's mains to your stomp pedals. In vintage analogue equipment, impedances were carefully matched so that as the current flowed from one device into another, the other properties of the circuit, like power and intensity, did not vary. In modern equipment connected via analogue inputs and outputs, impedance at the outputs of your machines will be very low and impedance at the inputs will be actually as high as possible. This is so you can interconnect various devices together without loss of signal: an output from your audio track can be compressed, limited, equalised, etc., while the final signal remains strong. Imagine an irrigation system connected to a dam: the dam itself has all the water ready to flow unimpeded, but as you tap into the dam with pipes that will carry the water to your various crops, each pipe carries only a small volume of it, making sure no single pipe drains the dam and you have an equal supply for the different areas of your farm.

You probably have understood the metaphor by now. Modern-day equipment is impedance fool-proofed thanks to this low to high impedance convention (not so vintage gear, so don't even try connecting an old, classic, valve amp to speakers if you don't know what you are doing, and never load it with an input if it is not connected to speakers because you will blow it up!), so redirect your attention during setup to matching nominal input/output levels. Consumer equipment only plugs into consumer inputs, and professional equipment will do similarly. No matter how easy it is to use a connection adaptor bought at the local electrical shop, you will get unwanted noise if you try to connect your MP3 player to a balanced, +4 dBu input! This is why many popular consoles will have phono inputs just for what is known traditionally as 'tape returns'; this is where you would plug your MP3 player, without need for an adaptor.

Can I connect my electric guitar into a microphone input if it accepts a ¼″ plug?

No and yes! No: although the connection may be a ¼″ plug and so it looks like an ideal place to put your guitar lead, this type of input is called a TRS which stands for Tip-Ring-Sleeve, and it refers to the fact that it carries a balanced signal (see above) using the tip and ring for the positive and negative versions of the signal and the sleeve for grounding. Yes: you may in fact connect your electric guitar or electric bass or any instrument with a pickup if you use a device known as a 'direct box', also known as a *Direct Injection* box, or a *DI* box. This device is a transformer which will present a high-input impedance to your unbalanced line and present a balanced low impedance source signal to your console input. DI boxes also have the facility to separate the grounding of your instrument from that of the console and so prevent 'hums' or ground loops.[4]

What can I do when there are hums, buzzes, hiss or static crackle sounds that I do not actually intend as part of my music?

This may seem a rather facetious way of posing this question, but bear in mind that many electronic musicians will actually be trying to make hums, buzzes and crackle!

Hum is the result of *ground loops*. These are unintended connections between the groundings of separate but interconnected equipment. A circuit needs to have a ground point for safety reasons and there will normally not be any current flowing through this ground connection. It is there so that electricity can find an escape route in case of a short-circuit and for fuses and breakers to trip, breaking the circuit and thus saving the user from electric shock. In audio equipment, as balanced audio cables are grounded, if the gear connected by these audio cables is itself connected to the same mains earth ground, then you can actually complete a circuit via the grounds! This will result in noise being introduced in the audio signal path. Also, if you place power transformers inadvertently close to low impedance components, you will also induce noise into those components: a phenomenon called *inductive coupling*. This basically means that an electromagnetic field is being created that can be picked up by any audio component that is sensitive enough (i.e. has a low impedance). Because this electromagnetic field is induced by AC, the rate of change will be that of the current: if you are in the USA or the UK this will be 50 or 60 Hz. The resulting advice for you is to keep your power amplifiers in their own separate racks. Inductive coupling can also result from microphone lines running too close to power cables. Keep your audio cables separate from your electricity or power cables. If you cannot keep them separate, then make sure they tend to cross at right angles.[5] Not that you can do much about this unless you are performing in your own studio, but your main sources should all be grounded to the same ground point. A good device to have for audio installations is a *balanced isolation transformer*. Through the use of specially designed transformers and filters, this transformer effectively gets rid of the inductance problem and thus the hum.

Buzzes are sounds that contain repetitive high frequencies, hence the description 'buzz' to signify a very fast and high-pitched rattle. The fact that the sound is repetitive may give us a clue that it has to do with some sort of inductive coupling as described above, yet of a higher frequency. You would hear buzzes through high-frequency speakers in your audio system. If you also hear a hum in the low-frequency speakers or woofers, then it will be due to a grounding problem. If there is no low hum to accompany the buzz, then check for the cables that feed the high frequency speakers. They may have grounding problems. Another common source of buzzing is from microphone cables running too close to light dimmer circuits. As mentioned above, you can try different angles of the cable run against the dimmer circuit.

Hiss is most often due to amplifying a signal that is being fed at a lower than optimal operating level. You need to check that all connections are carrying the right nominal level and the integrity of the cables themselves, and that they are used for the right inputs/outputs. If you plug the unbalanced electric guitar cable into the microphone input and then try to amplify to compensate for the poor gain of the signal, you will also be amplifying noise. In general 'don't try to get out more than you have put in'.

Crackle and static are usually due to connections coming on and off very rapidly, perhaps because the signal itself is intermittent due to faulty cables or, again, faulty grounding. Last but not least, your system may be subjected to radio frequency interference (RFI), which is a more sophisticated form of hum, simply because it is caused by electromagnetic induction over a great range of frequencies and once in the signal path is difficult to isolate. Mobile phones are a well-known culprit, but even emissions from the sun can cause RFI!

Distortion is the opposite of hiss. If, instead of trying to amplify a weak signal, you send a very strong one into an input which expects a weaker signal, then the sound will be distorted. Distortion of itself tends to colour the sound in different ways. In valve electric guitar amps this is an effective way of getting that 'tube' sound: overdrive the input stage of your amplifier. Modern amplifiers that do not use valves will distort quite differently and present a harsher more metallic sound when overdriven. The history of guitar amplifier design seems to shadow the evolution of guitar tone production. Remember that what may seem undesirable today, can sound very fashionable tomorrow.

Finally, if you are creatively looking for hum, hiss, crackle or distortion sources, not only do you have an idea of possible causes but now you know how to make them happen!

Chapter 5

Select, remix, mashup

DJs have come a long way from being selectors of music to creating new music from those selections. In this chapter we look at the rise of DJ practice and some of its practical implications. We also consider some technical points before briefly discussing the sticky issue of copyright and an alternative represented by the Creative Commons permissions scheme.

The question of the Deejay

'You take something hip, and you hop on it'

Nile Rodgers[1]

Although people who select and play records (or CDs!) have been around since radio began, the DJ as musician is a relatively recent phenomenon. In the '70s, the radio DJ was like a guru. You followed their programming avidly because they introduced you to new music that was cool, stylish and interesting. It had nothing to do, as one would tend to associate today with the term 'DJ', with dance music. Famous American DJs, like Alan Freed in the '50s (who popularised rock & roll and helped introduce black R&B to white audiences) or Wolfman Jack in the '60s and '70s, were arbiters of musical taste. It was not until perhaps the '80s, really, that radio DJs became more like simple voice-over artists tying together the song rotation imposed by radio executives.[2]

Regardless of all the terms coined for the role of a DJ in different musical styles, it would not be controversial to say that DJs are part of a continuum of recorded-music creativity that ranges from mere selection to composition and performance. The original radio DJs were selectors of music and they developed audiences of like-minded listeners. Yet at this point their creative input was arguably non-existent.[3] Meanwhile, the Jamaican *sound system* operators of the late '60s developing the first versions of mixes from dubplates[4] were adding an element of creativity as well as opening a performance possibility to be fulfilled by DJs *toasting* over the instrumental rhythms extended through looping.

By the early '70s, in a not-so-separate development, DJ Kool Herc was extending rhythmic breaks on vinyl at New York block parties by creatively cueing two turntables with identical copies of a record and, in so doing, helping give birth to the Hip-Hop genre. By the late '70s Christian Marclay was using skipping records as part of his performance art.[5] Remixes and mashups would almost immediately start following, ranging from disco medleys to purposefully built copyright-breaking compositions like John Oswald's 'Power' (made up from Led Zeppelin and a Southern preacher's impassioned sermon), to self-remixed compositions like Frank Zappa's 'Rubber Shirt' from *Sheik Yerbouti* (1979) built from different recordings of his own music (a technique he termed *Xenochrony*).

Let's not forget that earlier than all of this, in 1948, Pierre Schaeffer had been experimenting with creating compositions that used edited and remixed sounds from sound-effects disk libraries and music records while working at Radio France in Paris. As tape became available, he would later co-invent a working sampler instrument called the *phonogène* as well as numerous devices for manipulating and remixing loops (roughly at the same time, the *Chamberlin* would compete against the now better-known *Mellotron*), but these advances dealt with tape manipulation not vinyl.

The important distinction for the purpose of our discussion here is that Schaeffer did not use records for live performance, but as studio composition tools, and in so doing is missing some of the improvisational elements and real-time skills of the later Hip-Hop DJs. Schaeffer's contribution effectively bypassed the stages from composition to performance, creating fixed music. To paraphrase Evan Eisenberg's discussion of the history of recording in his book *The Recording Angel* (2005): composition began to become a 'thing'. No interpretation was involved: once made, the composition could only be heard/diffused through loud speakers. And the latter spawned a craft in itself with the invention of panning (spatialising) contraptions such as Schaeffer's *pupitre d'espace* and later developments like the loudspeaker orchestra, known as the *Acousmonium*, at the Groupe de Recherches Musicales in 1974.[6]

For the purpose of this chapter, we are interested in performing DJs with turntable skills to needle-drop, match beats and scratch, because they signal a moment in music history when the reproduction (in the sense of playback) of music becomes a musical act in itself and gives rise to an instrumental practice. The skilled control of a music-playing machine – the turntable – allowed us literally to make music out of music by developing very specific skills in handling turntables. These skills are just like any musical instrument skills requiring intonation (matching of record speed), rhythm (keeping the breakbeat flowing in time) and manual dexterity (needle dropping of fragments and scratching).

We could say that the variety of DJing we are looking at, later to be coined turntablism by the virtuoso DJ Babu, is a case of pre-digital musical technology performance practice. The early DJs like DJ Kool Herc had a grasp of basic audio systems and it would not be far-fetched to say that others like Grandmaster Flash, Grand Theodore Wizard and Afrika Bambaataa also had to become familiar with the electric (routing) side of their set-ups as well as the performative side. It is difficult to imagine anybody, in fact, interested in the live manipulation of audio who does not have some familiarity with, if not an active interest in, the technology behind it.

By the mid 90s, DJing in the sense of turntablism had become a virtuoso act. Listen to pieces like DJ Babu's 'Suckas (Sucka DJ Dis)' or Mix Master Mike's 'Terrowrist (Beneath The Under)' on the 1995 *Return of the DJ, Vol. 1* of Bomb Hip-Hop Records for examples of great manual dexterity and improvisational imagination. Yet beyond the instrumental promise of turntablism, DJing brought the notion of music appropriation and recombination through sampling and audio editing to the mainstream and in so doing contributed an enormous incentive to the development of digital music technology.

Digital DJing

With the development of digital audio workstations (DAWs) in the '90s, DJ-specific techniques became much easier to replicate and a host of possibilities became available based on the innovations of Hip-Hop artists and remixers in general. In the late '80s, the first usable audio sequencers appeared, Opcode's Studio Vision and Digidesign ProTools leading the way. Yet these were studio tools with no provision for live performance. The Dub/Hip-Hop trend was essentially bringing pre-recorded audio manipulation onto the stage, but the tools for this were not yet available to a mass market. Notice that we are not referring here to tools available at universities or institutions as part of exclusive research projects, but to the access of ordinary people to these tools. There actually was at the time, however, a convergence of academic interests in **algorithmic music** with the consumer market.

This convergence could be seen in software applications like David Zicarelli's *M*, *JamFactory* or *UpBeat*, available commercially at the time through *Intelligent Music in the late '80s*. These applications gave algorithmic control of rhythm and pitch based on a pattern construction model, not dissimilar to drum machine programming; in fact Upbeat was a sort of algorithmic drum machine. In the early '90s, sequencer software began to incorporate tools that could be used for live performance like the much-neglected *touch tracks* facility of Emagic Logic Audio, which allowed the user to assign midi sequences to MIDI notes that could then be triggered live. It could also be seen in the rise of accessible sampling instruments like the AKAI S900 and the EMU Emulator (in contrast to the expensive Fairlight and Synclavier sampling instruments owned either by institutions or wealthy rock stars). Among the S900 and Emulator's standard production tasks, these would eventually be used for triggering samples of breakbeats, brass/orchestral hits and instrumental phrases on stage. But the traditional keyboard used for synthesisers was no longer suited for this kind of performance and a new creation, control and production model was introduced with the AKAI MPC60 MIDI Production Center. This instrument housed what we can now describe as a performance or playable sequencer. The creation, editing and stringing together of patterns was then made possible with the use of soft pads inherited from drum machines and enhanced by sampling and sequencing capabilities.[7] This machine quickly became a Hip-Hop favourite and could be seen today as a precursor of both software and hardware DJ composition and performance systems.

Controls like those found on the AKAI MPC60 are now common in stand-alone music controller devices (with no sampling or sequencing capabilities). Pads and related controllers allow musicians to interact with digital audio files in a similar way to how DJs have interacted with audio recordings on vinyl. Furthermore, the development of virtual instruments in the 1990s and 2000s has been enhanced by this trend for software-independent controller surfaces. Where the old-school DJ has the turntable, the digital DJ and the DJ-inspired producer and remixer has MIDI controllers.

In the same way that virtuosity and skill can be shown on a turntable practically to the same degree as on a traditional instrument, they can be shown on controller setups. Scratching becomes digital scrubbing, needle dropping becomes transient detection, and beat matching is accomplished by time-stretching algorithms. Not to labour the point too much, but as the control of digital sound becomes more sophisticated, keyboards are clearly insufficient to harness it, so sliders, drum pads, knobs and pressure sensors come into their own for triggering, scrubbing and modifying on the fly.

This gave rise to the use of controllers as a true instrumental practice. Also, custom controllers have become easier to make thanks to the availability of cheap sensors and digital interfaces such as the ones made by Arduino.[8] Live performance setups are often now constituted by a mix of off-the-shelf hardware (sometimes modified) as well as custom built.

Finally, we can see two trends evident in controller development: that of creating digital emulations of analogue DJ equipment known as *vinyl emulation setups* (or systems), and the creation of entirely new interfaces often based on mixing-desk models known as controllers. These trends can be mixed and matched by musicians

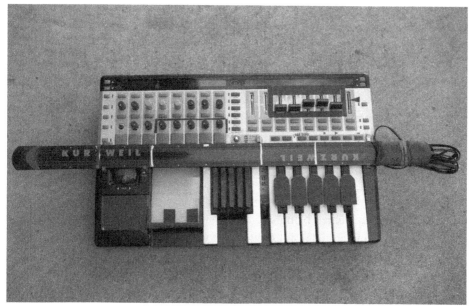

Figure 5.1 A MIDI controller instrument: the 'Frankentroller' created by Moldover. Photo by Sarah Peet

and often are, but they represent diverging design approaches, so we should have a look at them for a moment.

Vinyl emulation setups

Vinyl emulation setups offer a DJ the tactile interface of a standard turntable (usually the *Technics 1200* is the one of choice, first produced in 1978 – not much of a passing fashion!). The idea behind these systems is that you can control the reading of a computer audio file by using a turntable or a turntable-like device (in the case of CDs) to cue the audio. The turntable will simply send an audio signal indicating the absolute position of the needle; this signal is known as *time-code*. The time-code then tells the computer the timing (position) from which to playback the audio file. The computer needs software that will understand the time-code audio signal for this playback. For the turntable to send time-code, it needs to be playing a special disk that has time-code recorded onto it. These are available both in vinyl, if the DJ wishes to use an analogue turntable, or as a CD, if they wish to use a CD/MP3/WAV player with a virtual turntable control. The time-code is sent to the computer via an analogue-to-digital audio converter (traditionally known as a soundcard, although they look nothing like a card nowadays). The computer software that receives the time-code will not only use it for cueing and thus back-spinning or scratching the digital audio, but it will usually provide visual feedback of the audio waveforms involved in the mix as well as a management system for browsing through the DJ's audio collection.

There are many commercial brands dealing with system components for digital DJing, but there are also open-source projects like *xwax* and *MIXXX* that can be used to drive digital audio from time-code. These also happen to be hardware independent, so the user can mix and match resources as they please.

Controller setups

Laptop-based systems can indeed be controlled by time-coded vinyl, but the development of DJing has helped bring about new approaches to music-making which are similar from a conceptual point of view but very different in practice. Electronic musicians working in dance music of various kinds, as well as experimental electronic musicians, have gone far beyond the turntable model of sound manipulation.

Looking at it coolly, the turntable is quite limited as a 'sound-reader', which is what it technically is. The DJ can alter the playback (reading) of the vinyl-pressed sound (encoded soundwave) by slowing it down or accelerating it, reversing it and starting it from any point, but newer sound synthesis methods based on recorded soundwave manipulation benefit from greater control.

Take the use of granulation, for instance (see Chapter 3). The granulation process creates a stuttering effect and if grains are tapered and overlapped the resulting sound will be more like a swarm of bees. Now, think about this for a moment. Granulation is in fact a form of looping, only that the loop is extremely short. Granulation is the sort of looping available to someone who can control such fine reading of a soundwave. This is in essence not different to scratching, where a sound is 'read' back and forth rhythmically. It's just that scratching is what is possible with a turntable, while granulation is what is now possible with digital playback methods, for which different non-analogue controls are devised. Sliders or X–Y touch surfaces are ideal for this kind of sound generation, although with some reprogramming any controller, like for instance a digital turntable, can control granulation. The point is that new sound playback possibilities call for new instrumental interactions. Controller systems allow the digital DJ to work like the traditional DJ but extend the sound possibilities into the digital domain, so their conceptual approaches remain quite similar.

Sequencing environments

The DJ era has promoted the development of sequence tools that address the need for triggering samples and working on pre-recorded audio by looping in real time.

Comparatively, it has taken a long time for these pattern-based sequencers to emerge as distinct from the usual linear, tape-recording model. The key developments are the facility to instantly synchronise rhythmic samples and to be able to make them into performance tools. There is a strong trend towards playable sequencers and an interesting symbiosis has developed between software and hardware developers where controllers for live performance are being made more software specific and the software looks also to support the controllers.

Pattern-based sequencers are very much the product of a popular song-form approach to music-making, and perhaps this is both their advantage and their downfall. The former because of its simplicity and popular appeal, and the latter because they very much straitjacket the musician into a particular workflow and compositional output. It is possible that, given the way in which musical education is integrating music technology, we will see more computer-literate musicians who are more willing to experiment with software programming. This would in turn bring about greater customisation of software tools. We are beginning to see this trend take flight as more sequencers incorporate truly programmable elements within them. The earliest was probably *Cakewalk* with its scripting language in the '80s and '90s, followed by some graphic programming in the Logic Studio *environment* since the '90s. The latest is the integration of the *MAX/MSP* graphic programming environment into *Ableton LIVE*. This allows the user to create custom digital signal processors as well as MIDI processors and thus extend the sequencer's features.

Loop resources, creation and management

There is a little terminology you should be familiar with if you are going to be working with loops. The days when harvesting a good loop was almost certainly illegal have passed. There are now many companies offering ready-made copyright free loops in a variety of formats. Audio file formats, as we discussed in Chapter 1, can contain much more than just the actual audio data. The early loops were distributed as standard audio files that you could edit on your sequencer, but if you needed to match them to a specific tempo you had to do all the processing yourself. Thanks to a trend started by the makers of Acid Pro in the late '90s, a new kind of audio format containing timing information has evolved. The idea was to have loops that could simply be dragged and dropped onto a project and for them to adjust to the tempo automatically and with a minimum of quality loss. For this to happen, the audio file needs to have its loudest transients marked to show where possible rhythmic material is placed.

Transient means 'something that is changing'. In acoustics this refers to changes in amplitude within the waveform. It is a term that can be used quite loosely as if there were no changes in amplitude, then there would be no waveform! But in terms of looping material, the word 'transient' is used to indicate the loud or dramatic changes which suggest that a rhythmic event is happening there. If the software analysing the audio file

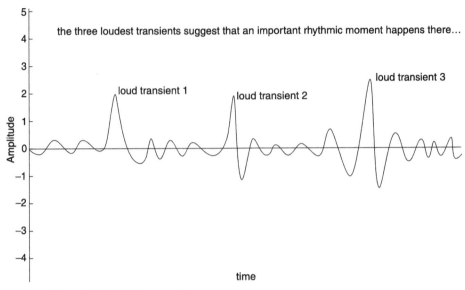

Figure 5.2 Finding transients

finds these transients to be spread evenly across time, it can safely assume some kind of beat. This is what looping software looks for. In packages like Ableton LIVE or Logic Pro, the loops need to be mapped out in terms of their transients. This information is then kept with the file so that the software knows how to modify them meaningfully. These are also called 'analysis' files.

Some loops can even bring MIDI information to re-create the recorded audio contained in the file. This is the case with *Green Apple Loops*; these are AIFF files that contain the MIDI and the instrument settings for the sequencer in the case of Apple's *Logic Pro*.

Knowing where the transients are is also useful as you can automatically slice the audio file into meaningful segments given the right software. This is what the ReCycle software by Propellerhead Software introduced in the mid '90s. In this way, the different segments could be triggered in succession at different tempi. The resulting file format is known as REX2. Many commercial sampler instruments and sequencers will understand this format and it allows you to change the speed of the loop without changing the pitch, within reason!

Loops may be grouped and sold in *construction kits*; these are packages that contain all the elements of a mix broken into its constituent loops. Of course, the last thing you should do is reconstruct the main mix where these elements come from. The most productive thing to do is to combine elements from different construction kit sets to create new and sometimes surprising combinations of grooving material. In this way, R&B horn riffs can be layered onto Latin percussion with a dub bass line, for instance.

DJ-style workflow

The workflow of DJing is useful to examine because it is pervasive in contemporary popular music-making. It consists of selecting music (other artist's tracks or copyright-free loops),[9] sampling (recording useful musical segments for breakbeats or punches/hits), developing a groove, adding vocals (sung or rapped) and finally structuring the material around the words or lyrics.

Selecting music

In the DJ-style workflow, finding loops with memorable stylistic features is highly desirable. Originality comes through recombination of elements in unexpected ways. The key to success is to find music that can be rhythmically related in some way, from actual tempo matching to layering one piece on the other because it contributes to the groove. In the song 'Extreme Ways', American DJ and composer Moby's 2002 single from the album *18*, we hear a looped string glissando that introduces the track. The way it is looped seems to imply a rhythm but it isn't until it is layered upon a drum-sample loop taken from Melvin Bliss's 1973 single 'Synthetic Substitution' (Sunburst Records) that the groove becomes apparent (and in an unexpected way). In fact, the groove comes about precisely because of this layering of rhythmic elements. When the Sugar Hill Gang recorded 'Rapper's Delight' in 1979, they did so by juxtaposing an ostensibly Latin rhythm segment with a loop, almost exactly replayed by the Sugar Hill Records house band, from the disco band Chic's 'Good Times', effectively recontextualising the (at the time) famous bass line and handclaps over piano riff to a four-on-the-floor kick drum. One could argue that the key to the success of 'Rapper's Delight' was due in part to this wholesale lifting of musical material and its presentation in an unexpected way as an accompaniment for rap. Selection is crucial.

Nile Rodgers, guitarist and producer for Chic, has this to say on the use of Chic's 'Good Times' by the Sugar Hill Gang, on reflection, during an interview in 2006:

> 'Rapper's Delight' is one of my favorite songs of all time. At first, I admit, I was p***** off. You work your whole life to write a song like 'Good Times'. It takes all of your experience, all of your music lessons, all the places I got fired, all the times I was robbed – all of that living. But the truth is, I was especially p***** because as innovative and important as 'Good Times' was, 'Rapper's Delight' was just as much, if not more so. . . . Anyway, that's why they call it hip-hop – it's collage art. You take something hip, and you hop on it. And you know, 'Good Times' is definitely hip.[10]

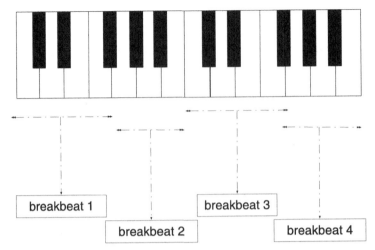

breakbeat 1

breakbeat 2

breakbeat 3

breakbeat 4

Figure 5.3 Key-groups

Sampling

In the DJ-style workflow, once an interesting riff or rhythmic break is identified, it needs to be prepared for use in the production of the track. 'Old-school' DJs will mark their vinyls with stickers showing them where to drop the needle for a particular breakbeat. The digital method is to record the musical segment and edit it into a standard number of beats so it is easy to drop-in wherever appropriate; it can then be loaded onto a sampler and looped or used directly in a sequencer as described above when discussing loop creation.

It can be interesting to assign different samples to the different key-groups (groups of adjacent MIDI notes) of a sampler because quite unexpected results can be obtained by triggering them to a common beat. This process allows you to mix and match in a very expressive way.

If you allow a wide key-group, you may find that the differences in tempo and the sound of playback (due to changing the pitch) will add variety to your performance of the breakbeats. When you use a key-group that spans an octave and you place your original breakbeat in one of the extreme notes, you can obtain twice (or half) the tempo and many relationships in between. For instance if you assign your breakbeat sample to be played back by all notes in the region C3–C4, when you play C3 you obtain the original playback speed. When you play C4 you will get twice the speed and when you play G3 you will get 3/2 the speed. Try jamming on these and you will be surprised at how much variety you can get from simply doubling and tripling the tempo ratio of a rhythmic sample.

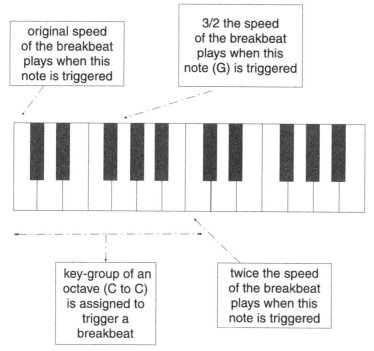

Figure 5.4 Wide key-group assignments

Developing a groove

A rhythmic phrase, a riff, a pattern, does not necessarily give us a *groove*. The word 'groove' itself is a non-technical term which you as a musician will understand beyond any attempt by dictionaries to define it. What we do know for certain is that even if there is rhythm, there may not be 'groove'. For groove to exist, the rhythmic construction has to have 'swing', another difficult to define word! I will not even try to lock these into definitions, but just point out that in modifying your rhythmic samples you will find the groove. It is an ineffable quality that we look for when building rhythmic elements. Often it will arise from performing your samples in the way described above, or scratching and cueing your vinyls, or from controlling your samples with an interface. Any resource that allows you to inject a physical gesture into the playback of the sample should be used to find the groove.

Voice and structure

We could say that electronic dance music differentiates itself from Hip-Hop mainly in that the latter uses the voice, rapping or singing and the former tends to be more instrumental. It is probably at the point of inserting vocals of some sort that structure begins to emerge in DJ-style composition. The breaks and instrumental additions will relate to the structure of the text. This is how music with words has tended to be made. Words provide clear ideas to structure music upon. In traditional music education, punctuating the words by the use of instrumental techniques is referred to as 'word painting'. In music of the early nineteenth century, both words and music worked to predictable patterns offering plenty of symmetry in the building of songs. The interesting aspect about Hip-Hop is that the vocal line may be so free as to only occasionally repeat itself. In 'Rappers Delight', mentioned above, Big Bank Hank, Master Gee and Wonder Mike rap in a linear way, like telling a story. There are repeats of rhythmic or almost melodic motives, but we listen through to something that is mostly two layers: a vocal delivery and the Chic rhythm sample. A hybrid approach is taken by Afrika Bambaataa in *Who's in the House* (1999; 12-inch EP). Here he makes use of many repeating phrases that add to the groove and act as departure points for short vocal excursions with punctuations from the choir. Another interesting example blending rap and song is the 'Zulu Nation Throwdown' from *Bambataa: Looking for the Perfect Beat* (1981–5).[11]

The voice can also be used to create structure, as seen in the work of Moby, who we mentioned earlier. In 'Honey' from *Play* (1999) he uses a sample from singer Bessie Jones's song 'Sometime', where she riffs on the refrain 'get my honey come back' and the choir answers 'sometime'. The song is recorded with unaccompanied voices or 'acappella' – solo voice recordings are very sought after by remixers. The sample is then repeated, harmonised and orchestrated in different ways. Even though the song doesn't follow the lyrics in any way, the groove generated by this sample serves as an excuse to build the piece, giving an impression of song form. This technique has been used very successfully by artists like Fatboy Slim, Art of Noise and French electronic ethno-dance music duo Deep Forest. Although seemingly far removed from the origins of Dub and Hip-Hop DJing, the principle of lifting segments of music that are later recontextualised is elevated here to an art form where whole works are built around short fragments which unify the piece that they give origin to.

In general, DJ-style composing yields 'layered forms' of music. These tend to be built by adding elements to an otherwise static underlying beat and/or musically recontextualising samples. Young producers and composers starting out with music technology tools are often tempted to create pieces where there is little more than the looped sample and some percussion elements. The full sound of the samples themselves may trick them into thinking they achieve something merely by the act of selecting the right groove, but it is precisely those who nuance the beat, add breaks and play with the harmony in unexpected ways to seek variation that contribute the freshest music. In the end, the challenge of structure is the same across all music

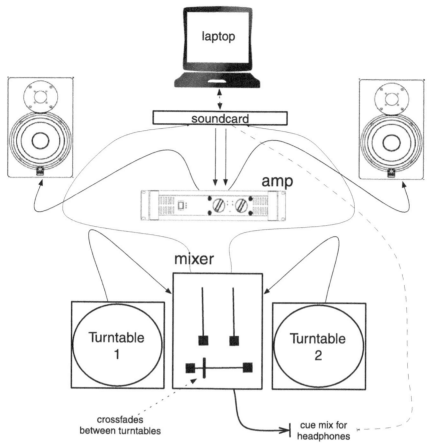

Figure 5.5 In a digital DJ setup, turntables running timecode records can control sound files on a laptop

forms and music technology, although sometimes accelerating certain production tasks, offers no shortcuts to originality.

Performance considerations

In what must surely be a unique case in music performance, DJs audition musical material on stage while other elements are playing back, essentially editing and choosing like a producer, but in a performance situation. In this way turntables can be cued precisely and correct matches of tempo and instrumentation can be estimated. DJ-specific mixing consoles will have both this headphone cueing facility and a crossfader to blend or suppress a selected turntable. Sequencers based on the sample/trigger paradigm also allow you to do some extensive editing while the rest of your material is playing and to audition it through an output dedicated exclusively to this cueing task.

Remix, mashup...

Let us start this section by debunking an urban myth that says (in one of its tellings) you can legally copy two or three notes of a melody or sample a portion as long as it's very short. With the prevailing laws on copyright in most (or perhaps all) of the Western world, a musician cannot use any recorded material that has been credited already to another composer: not a phrase, not five notes, not one second, not one millisecond. Popular wisdom has for years promoted the mistaken view that a short segment is legal to use by virtue of its duration. In reality sampling has been, and is, illegal when not authorised explicitly; yet this whole chapter has been about the creative joy of sampling!

The problem is that artistic creativity is not moral in and of itself. Borrowing and bettering things, or at least varying them, is fundamental to creative activity. If we consider the idea put forward by John Oswald, the creator of *Plunderphonics*, in *Bettered by the Borrower: The Ethics of Musical Debt*,[12] that 'All popular music is (as is folk music by definition) essentially, if not legally, existing in a public domain. [Because...] Listening to pop music isn't a matter of choice. Asked for, or not, we're bombarded by it', then we must conclude that we have actually earned the right to borrow!

Now, consider remixes: they can be traded with according to an established economic model. Remixes can be valuable marketing tools; for this reason alone they are mostly encouraged and sometimes commissioned by large record labels. For the music industry it is a question of packaging. A dance remix will mean that a song that may not have been intended for the dance market makes an appearance there. In the mid '80s, musicians like British duo Coldcut (Matt Black and Jonathan More) benefitted from this. Not only did they become known for their own work but they were asked to remix others, like Lisa Stansfield, Blondie and Queen Latifah among others.[13] As long as the labels could control the royalties due to sample borrowing everything was fine. In fact, it still is.

But the problem becomes more pronounced when the creative result is so mixed that all samples enjoy the same importance. This is what happens in a *mashup*. Some credit the term to a slang version of the term 'match-up', as we have seen earlier referring to matching samples to be used by their tempo relationship. Let's dwell on the difference between a remix and a mashup for a moment. They are both on the same creative continuum of borrowing, yet they differ, on the one hand, in that the remix is oriented to give prominence to an original piece through musical recontextualisation. The mashup, on the other hand, gives equal prominence to the component pieces that are being 'matched-up' together or 'smashed up' (take your pick). In film director Brett Gaylor's 2008 documentary *RIP! A remix manifesto*, we follow the creative issues of sampling vis-à-vis copyright in the work of Girltalk

(Gregg Michael Gillis); his mashups are so democratically interwoven with musical chunks, hits, breakbeats and spoken word that if he were to clear all the samples he uses he would actually need to pay a fortune (in the millions!). This would make his music commercially non-viable; plus we could argue that no particular sampled artist has prominence in his pieces and that he is simply riffing from a common pool of popular music culture. This music is virtuoso collage and well worth the listen. Should it not exist because the law is not ready for this kind of creativity? Should we retrospectively ban Hip-Hop and all sampling musics until the legal problem can be solved?[14]

. . . intellectual property

So, what is the way forward if you want to work with samples in a remix, mashup or collage style, and you are interested in the micro-soundworlds that samples bring and how combining them creates a rich tapestry with so many creative possibilities?

One approach is to process your samples to a point where they are no longer recognisable as the original yet they retain elements of the groove; to quote the Chemical Brothers, 'You start with a sound that you generally know, and think is cool, and then you move it somewhere else . . . You know, someone took it that far, and now you're taking it somewhere completely different.'[15]

The other approach is to seek clearance for your use of samples or simply to create your own, as many producers do. Clearance is then the only way to sample legally unless you are sampling from a composer who has licensed their work through *Creative Commons* (CC). This is an organisation founded in 2001 to promote interaction and exchange of ideas and artistic material by providing legal tools that allow artists, scientists and researchers in general to share and protect their work in specific ways.[16] These legal tools are contracts: termed licences that the user declares to any interested party. The licences are written by a group of intellectual property and cyberlaw (in essence, internet law) experts and made available for free over the internet to anybody who wants to use them. It is led by a board of directors that includes, among its experts and specialists, Professor Lawrence Lessig, who wrote *Remix: Making Art and Commerce Thrive in the Hybrid Economy*, a book very appropriate to this discussion which, true to the spirit of CC, is free to download.[17] In 2002, CC released a set of copyright licences, free to the public. They were partly inspired by a pre-existing licence designed for collaboration amongst users of open-source software, the Free Software Foundation's GNU General Public License (GNU GPL).

The licences cover four basic aspects:

- Attribution: how the use of your work, or parts of it, must be credited to you.
- Sharing: that others must share their work in the same way you have shared with them.
- Commercialism: whether you want to stipulate that if others use your work they cannot then profit from it.
- Derivation: whether you want to stipulate that if others use your work they can not make derivative works, i.e. no remixes allowed.

The CC website provides what it calls 'human readable' versions of the licence and legal code. They are explained in plain language and their website even offers an online questionnaire that, after a few key questions, recommends the licence you are most likely to need. Well-known users of CC licences include: Nine Inch Nails, Beastie Boys, Youssou N'Dour, Tone, David Byrne, Radiohead and Snoop Dogg. Finally, the website also includes a search engine that allows you to locate works that have been licensed under Creative Commons.

Creative Commons Licences

Attribution
abbreviated as: **cc by**
This licence lets others distribute, remix, tweak and build upon your work, even commercially, as long as they credit you for the original creation. This is the most accommodating of licences offered, in terms of what others can do with your works licensed under Attribution.

Attribution Share Alike
abbreviated as: **cc by-sa**
This licence lets others remix, tweak and build upon your work even for commercial reasons, as long as they credit you and license their new creations under the identical terms. This licence is often compared to open-source software licences. All new works based on yours will carry the same licence, so any derivatives will also allow commercial use.

Attribution No Derivatives
abbreviated as: **cc by-nd**
This licence allows for redistribution, commercial and non-commercial, as long as it is passed along unchanged and in whole, with credit to you.

Attribution Non-Commercial
abbreviated as: **cc by-nc**
This licence lets others remix, tweak and build upon your work non-commercially, and although their new works must also acknowledge you and be non-commercial, they don't have to license their derivative works on the same terms.

Attribution Non-Commercial Share Alike

abbreviated as: **cc by-nc-sa**

This licence lets others remix, tweak and build upon your work non-commercially, as long as they credit you and license their new creations under the identical terms. Others can download and redistribute your work just like the by-nc-nd licence, but they can also translate, make remixes, and produce new stories based on your work. All new work based on yours will carry the same licence, so any derivatives will also be non-commercial in nature.

Attribution Non-Commercial No Derivatives

abbreviated as: **cc by-nc-nd**

This licence is the most restrictive of the six main licences, allowing redistribution. This licence is often called the 'free advertising' licence because it allows others to download your works and share them with others as long as they mention you and link back to you, but they can't change them in any way or use them commercially.

More information and links available at http://creativecommons.org/about/licenses/

Chapter 6

The producer

Nobody seems to be exactly sure what a producer does or what their job description actually entails. Yet we know a producer when we see one: George Martin for the Beatles, Teo Macero for Miles Davis, Brian Wilson for the Beach Boys, Phil Spector for Tina Turner or Quincy Jones for Michael Jackson. At the very least, we assume they do something that makes them worthy of mentioning in the same breath as the artist, but few people actually know what that 'something' is. In this chapter we will explore how the producer's role has changed from the early days of sound recording to our day, and what we can learn from that. As audio technology (the technology of accurately handling the audio signal) becomes music technology (the creative application of audio technology to musical ends), the producer becomes arranger and composer, and eventually performing musician.[1]

The role of the producer

The term 'producer' covers many possible roles. These can include that of the entrepreneur trying to get a song to become number one; the financier putting down the money for a first CD by an up-and-coming band; the 'overseer' of the recording process; arbiter of the quality of the finished mix; or the engineer looking after every aspect of his recording project.

Mark Cunningham, in his book *Good Vibrations*,[2] tells the story of Bill Haley recording 'Rock Around the Clock' for record label DECCA on 12 April 1954, with ten minutes to go in the recording session. Producer Milton Gabler asked the band to play on the studio stage as if live and using the natural acoustics of the room. This instruction alone was responsible for a gritty sound which we later would associate with rock & roll. The decision to go for a sound with character as opposed to the cleanest possible sound (very much the practice at the time) is typical of what we have come to know as 'production'. Further, even if originally producers started as managers of the recording process, there is no doubt that for many years they have been, in a sense, the representative of the eventual audience;[3] the first listener, as it were, and with powers to shape the final mix.

Producer, songwriter, composer, performer?

In a world dominated by the broadcast of popular music, the word 'songwriter' seems to be used far more than the word 'composer'. The latter seems to be reserved for 'classical music' (whatever that broadest of terms means to people today!). In dance music, however, the term 'producer' tends to be used instead of 'songwriter'. It is not uncommon to hear young popular musicians refer to themselves as producers, even when they are only talking about their own music, as opposed to working with a band. This change in the use of the word gives us an idea of how the role of producer has become creative enough that it may actually encompass both technical and artistic responsibilities. Virgil Moorefield in his book *The Producer as Composer: Shaping the Sounds of Popular Music*, argues in his conclusion that production skills are today as important as keyboard skills,[4] and, going even further, describes how being in charge of a technology that does away with the need for manual dexterity places the producer, as performer, on the concert stage and their imagination above traditional music skills. I agree with this to an extent, but would add that Moorefield doesn't seem to take into account the rise in recent years of producer's controller virtuosity or controllerism as coined by performing artist Moldover.[5]

The studio as composition and arrangement tool

When producer and composer Brian Eno delivered his lecture, 'The studio as compositional tool',[6] during *New Music New York* in 1979, he celebrated the idea that recording had become more than a documentation tool, but also a creative one.[7] In recounting his personal experience of the studio as a place for sonic exploration and composition, he was summarising what he perceived as recording practice at the time.[8]

Eno was essentially saying that not only had recording/playback devices become musical instruments, but that recording in itself had become a musical act; that musical decisions were being taken during the process of recording that affected the music through modifying the recording itself as opposed to adding any new instrumental parts. Although I will present ideas on the studio as experimental laboratory in Chapter 8, I thought I could mention the idea here, and show evidence of how this tendency has grown.

Think about it: recording is in principle a form of documentation. Historically, its earliest objective was to preserve audio in a way that could be reproduced as faithfully as possible: a re-creation of the original music-making or captured sound event. Because of this, listeners assumed for a long time that what they heard was the precise register of a performance:[9] frozen in time as it were. Popular music gradually changed this. As early as the 1930s, guitarist and producer Les Paul was experimenting creatively with recording in the studio. At that time, he began layering his own guitar playing to create several musical voices.[10] Les Paul would record onto one acetate disc machine and then play his guitar alongside it while feeding the result to a second machine. This is today a standard resource for electric guitarists who use digital 'loop stations', but when Les Paul made use of it, not only was it an unknown resource but most musicians could not see any use for the technique!

This idea of sound on sound would also be increasingly used in film around this time. As sound developed for picture, it became necessary to have 'composite' recordings: a film needed to have not only the actor's speech but also sound effects and music. Because film was something to be played back, it made sense to think of its sound as something to be constructed or assembled. From the early Vitaphone shorts of the mid 1920s,[11] through *The Jazz Singer* (1927) and other musical films, recording sound on sound became a necessity. In the film industry this process has been (and is still) known as re-recording.[12]

Later, by the early '50s, Les Paul had developed multitrack recording on tape. This time the performer could substitute any previously recorded layer. Still, few people could see how this would be useful to anybody other than Les Paul and Mary Ford. A useful example of their overdubbing art can be seen and heard on their *Listerine Presents* TV 'performances'.[13] Their recordings of 'How High the Moon', 'Alabamy Bound' or 'The World is Waiting for Sunrise', among many others, are full of detailed layered guitar and vocal parts. Previously only possible with a very competent musical ensemble, now two musicians could gradually construct a rich and complex performance by overlaying musical parts. Another important, if subtle, Les Paul contribution consisted of close-miking Mary Ford's voice and recording her voice in unison with itself singing the melody.[14] Rather than wanting to record something that sounded 'natural' when played back, this capturing of every vocal nuance produced a 'hyperreal' effect that further made the recording much more than the document of a performance. It is also a very early instance of the double-tracking effect that would later be used by The Beatles in *Revolver* in 1965.

Creativity in production took flight in the 1950s. In 1952, Elvis's producer Sam Phillips began to experiment with reverb and slap delay. In the late 1950s, Norman Petty blended different layers of Buddy Holly's guitar to achieve the final recorded sound in hits like 'Peggy Sue' (1957).

Joe Meek, in 1960s London, created the first 'concept album', *I Hear a New World*, by studio crafting an entire disc with one thematic set of pieces intended as a compositional whole. In 1962, Mexican composer and producer Juan García Esquivel used impossible-to-perform techniques like extreme panning effects, wild changes in reverberation from one instrumental part to the next, and recording two orchestras in separate studios at the same time through one control room as heard in *Latinesque* (1962), an album that was tellingly subtitled: 'Stereo Action: the sound your eyes can follow'.

From 1963, Phil Spector (who preferred working in mono although stereo was already widely available) would essentially rearrange music by adding multiple instrumentalists to parts traditionally assigned to one player (drum kits, basses and pianos, for instance). As early as 1965 in California, Frank Zappa was using editing as a compositional tool, taking recorded segments from other songs and inserting them in the one he was working on (a technique he called *Xenochrony*,[15] or *strange synchronisations*). At the same time, George Martin in London was introducing tape-manipulation techniques into the Beatles's work as heard in *Revolver* (as well as using Abbey Road engineer Ken Townsend's Artificial/Automatic Double Tracking).[16]

Concept albums and creative collaboration

The seed sown by Joe Meek with *I Hear a New World* (1960) would flower (no pun intended!) in the late 1960s. The experimentation with music during the record-production stage encouraged collaborative work between composing/improvising musicians, producers and engineers. The Beatles's *Sgt. Pepper's Lonely Hearts Club Band* of 1967 is a well-known example, but there were many more. A whole trend of concept albums followed, and musicians became so involved creatively in the production process that they would also (as in the case of Pink Floyd's *Dark Side of The Moon* (1973)) credit themselves as producers. Concept albums of the late 1960s and early 1970s further include: The Moody Blues's *Days of Future Past* (1967), The Pretty Things' *S. F. Sorrow* (1968), The Who's *Tommy* (1969), Emerson, Lake and Palmer's *Tarkus* (1971), Pink Floyd's *Dark Side of the Moon* (1973) and Genesis's *The Lamb Lies Down on Broadway* (1974), among many others.[17]

Although not a concept album, The Beatles's *White Album* (1968) also benefitted from this spirit of open collaboration.[18] A nice example is the piece 'Revolution 9'. Made mainly by John Lennon, Yoko Ono and George Harrison, it is a true collage of sound, instrumental and choral music, speech, applause and reversed sound.[19] This collaboration (if not style of music!) was typical of the way many bands approached studio work. Witness to this is the fact that in the ensuing 'prog rock' era so many pieces were authored collectively (for example in *Dark Side*, the song 'Time' credits Mason, Waters, Wright and Gilmour – in 1970s prog rock this was far from rare).

Creative collaboration between a composer and a lyricist is very common in music in general, but that between two or more composers developing the musical elements of a song or an instrumental work seems almost exclusively confined to popular musics. It may well be that this collaboration has been enabled by the development of creativity in production.

Post-production

So far we have considered production during the recording process, but not so much discussed how producers continue to mould the music after it has been recorded. Although not a term much in use in popular music, we can borrow it from the audiovisual industry since, in a way, our production techniques in music have shadowed theirs. Film has always been an 'edited' art form, and so from the very start it has been possible in film to create a final product that goes beyond the actual filming thanks to the way it is put (edited) together.

As we have moved from acetate to tape and later to hard disk, studio work has become ever more creative and less 'documentary'. Simply put, editing has become easier, so we do more of it: there is much we can fix after recording, and even become creative, when all the other musicians have left the studio. But editing has not always been considered a respectable alternative. To some, the use of recording techniques like editing and splicing was close to cheating. When Miles Davis and producer Teo Macero released the album *In a Silent Way* in 1969, it was a statement of sorts, saying that an edited work was as much an 'ideal' performance as the real one.[20] Jazz critics and fans were scandalised to discover that thirty-three minutes of recording had actually been edited into a forty-five-minute album (by repeating takes or placing them in a different order, in fact not much different to how a film is put together!).[21]

The ability to edit as well as multitrack audio was compounded by the later appearance of digital sampling music instruments. In the early 1980s, the appearance of devices like the Fairlight Computer Musical Instrument or the Synclavier by New England Digital (both expensive sampler/synthesiser systems) gave producers even more power to augment the recorded performance. Yet these instruments were out of reach for ordinary musicians. In commercial music-making, only artists like Peter Gabriel, Kate Bush, Chick Corea, Herbie Hancock or Frank Zappa could afford them. In the academic world, resources like these were mainly available at universities or research institutions, like the Institut de Recherche et Coordination Acoustique/Musique (IRCAM) in Paris or City University London in the 1980s. It wouldn't take long, however, before advances in digital technology became accessible. The rise of portable sampler units from the classic EMU Emulator of the early 1980s to the AKAI S900 in the late 1980s made advanced production tools available to all. Samplers not only allowed us to emulate acoustic instruments, but they also allowed us to apply principles of tape editing to digital samples. This made it possible to 'fly in' a vocal take many times in a song without using up tape or real audio tracks, to play segments backwards by simply changing a parameter, and to loop drums, percussion or, well, anything!

Table 6.1 *Technical milestones in popular music production, 1930–1990*[a]

Year	Producer	Technique milestones
1930	Les Paul	Sound on sound using acetate disc[b]
1949	Les Paul	Adds a 4th head to the Ampex tape machine, paving the way for multitracking[c]
1951	Les Paul	Vocal close miking for an unrealistic but detailed recording of the voice [listen: 'How High the Moon' (with Mary Ford) – 1951][d]
1952	Sam Phillips	Use of 'hollow booth-like object' to reverberate Johnny London's saxophone against an uneffected ensemble for Sun Records[e] [listen: 'Drivin' Slow' – 1952]
1953	Raymond Scott	First use of electronic sound effects in a commercial jingle in 'Good Air' (Take 7); continued to innovate with his own design of drum machines, synthesisers and **algorithmic music** generators right up to the late 1960s[f]
1953	Mike Stoller and Jerry Leiber	In founding Spark Records, songwriters become 'record writers' for the first time[g] [listen: 'Down in Mexico' – 1956, The Coasters]
1954	Sam Phillips	Slapback delay sound is introduced at Elvis Presley's debut recording for Sun Records[h] [listen: 'Blue Moon of Kentucky' – 1954]
1957	Norman Petty	Records Jerry Allison (Holly's drummer) playing the drum part by slapping his knees[i] [listen: 'Everyday' – Buddy Holly]
1957	Norman Petty	Records Buddy Holly's guitar at the amp and also the unamplified strumming, blending the two for a 'natural' electric guitar sound[j] [listen: 'Peggy Sue' – 1957]
1960	Joe Meek	Extreme close-miking techniques: stuffing kick drums with blankets, miking piano from the inside, covering the guitar amp and microphone with blankets to isolate the sound[k]
1960	Joe Meek	*I Hear a New World* becomes the first concept album.[l] [listen: 'Valley of No Return'; 'Magnetic Field' – 1960]
1962	Juan Garcia Esquivel	For his album *Latinesque* experiments by placing two orchestras in separate studios coordinated from one control room.[m] He makes extreme use of stereo and arranges the music to make extensive use of panning and 'hard' left/right positions [listen: *Latinesque* – 1962]
1963	Delia Derbyshire	Realises and produces Ron Grainer's *Dr Who* theme on synthesisers

(cont.)

Table 6.1 (*cont.*)

Year	Producer	Technique milestones
1963	Phil Spector	Begins to develop his wall of sound by recording all musicians in the same room with no acoustic separation and multiple instrumentalists to a part[n] [listen: 'Da do ron ron' – 1963, The Crystals]
1965	George Martin	Brings his experience of producing radio shows to recording The Beatles. Introduces them to tape techniques. [listen: *Revolver*: 'Tomorrow Never Knows' – 1965]
1965	Frank Zappa	Starts developing his Xenochrony, by which he took segments from one recording and overlayed them on others, in later works, eventually creating a completely different piece. He also uses *Musique concrète* techniques in his albums. Editing becomes a compositional tool[o] [listen: *Freak Out!* – 1965]
1966	Phil Spector	Records 'River Deep' with Tina Turner, arguably his best achieved 'wall of sound'[p] [listen: 'River Deep, Mountain High' – 1966]
1966	Brian Wilson	Produces the Beach Boys' *Pet Sounds* album (with lush arrangements, exotic percussion and even bicycle bells). Later introduces theremin and cello in a rock context. Assembles a complete song by recording and editing completely separate sections recorded in different studios[q] [listen: 'Good Vibrations' – 1966]
1967	George Martin	Produces the *Sgt. Pepper* album for the Beatles. The Mellotron, an early sampler, is used in 'Strawberry Fields Forever' and synchronising tape decks, echo sends and re-recording techniques are applied extensively
1967	Tony Clarke	Sends the echo returns of one instrument channel to the opposite channel (stereo) for an impression of width and separation[r] [listen: 'Nights in White Satin' – 1967, original version from *Days of Future Passed*]
1967	Glynn Johns/George Chiantz	Best-known early use of phasing by using three tape machines playing simultaneously with slightly varying speeds[s] [listen: 'Itchycoo Park' – Small Faces 1967]
1968	George Martin	The Beatles's *White Album*, especially Lennon, Ono and Harrison's piece 'Revolution 9', that uses *Musique concrète* techniques extensively
1971	Genesis	Essentially self-produce their album *Nursery Cryme* with complex theatrical arrangements. Sound placement and treatment is integral to the contributions of the band members, mostly obviating the need for a producer in the traditional sense.

(*cont.*)

Table 6.1 (*cont.*)

Year	Producer	Technique milestones
1972	Stevie Wonder with Malcolm Cecil and Robert Margouleff	Outstanding synthesiser production using the TONTO multitimbral polyphonic synthesiser on *Music of My Mind*
1973	Pink Floyd	Release *Dark Side of The Moon*. Self-produced by the band and engineered by Alan Parsons.
1975	Arif Mardin	Produces the Bee Gees's *Main Course*. The prominence of the Moog mono/portamento bass line in 'Nights on Broadway' is a precursor of much later dance music
1977	Giorgio Moroder	Completely electronic production for Donna Summer's hit 'I Feel Love', foreshadowing techno and dance music of the '80s
1979	Trevor Horn	Writes and produces 'Video Killed the Radio Star' (The Buggles) exploring how to make drums sound machine-like and pushing sound production to stylistic extremes for uniqueness within the music industry. He is still productive and his work has included ABC, YES, Frankie Goes to Hollywood, Seal, Robbie Williams, Pet Shop Boys, The Art of Noise and many others. His style is characterised by rhythmic precision, carefully crafted sound and impeccable production. You can 'hear' his production come through in the music of the artists he works with. He used the Fairlight CMI extensively in his productions when sampling was relatively new.
1980	Richard James Burgess	Extensively programmes the Fairlight CMI for Kate Bush's *Never for Ever*
1981	Hugh Padgham	Produced the classic gated drum sound of Phil Collins in 'In the Air Tonight'
1981	Phil Ramone	First digital recording of a live album: Billy Joel's *Songs from the Attic*
1983	Bill Laswell	Very early use of DJ techniques (turntablism), especially featuring scratching by GrandMixer D.ST on Herbie Hancock's 'Rockit'
1984	Brian Eno	Works with U2 on *The Unforgettable Fire*. Brings his ambient approach to commercial production. His unorthodox techniques draw as much from an experimental approach to studio work as to his 'oblique strategies' philosophy.
1985	Paul Hardcastle	Makes use of the stuttering sampler effect on his anti-war No.1 Dance Chart hit '19'

(*cont.*)

Table 6.1 (*cont.*)

Year	Producer	Technique milestones
1985–9	Stock, Aitken and Waterman	Songwriters and producers of a veritable hit factory. A technique used by Peter Waterman to increase perceived loudness of their songs on radio and fool the limiting devices was to carefully roll off bass frequencies in the final mix. Their work epitomises the classic Eurobeat/Hi-NRG sound and the British Synthpop of the late 1980s

[a] I stop at 1990 because I believe these are the seminal ones. There is much still to cover in the 1990s and 2000s, especially in electronic music production, so let's call this table a work in progress.
[b] Cunningham, 1998, p. 25.
[c] *Ibid.*, p. 28.
[d] *Ibid.*, p. 30.
[e] *Ibid.*, p. 37.
[f] See Chusid, 2000.
[g] Covach, 2009, p. 124.
[h] *Ibid.*, p. 38.
[i] *Ibid.*, p. 43.
[j] *Ibid.*, p. 42.
[k] *Ibid.*, pp. 91–5.
[l] *Ibid.*, p. 89.
[m] www.spaceagepop.com/esquivel.htm.
[n] Covach, 2009, p. 131.
[o] Michie, 2003; Slaven, 2003.
[p] In my opinion! But see (and listen to): Covach, 2009, p. 130; Cunningham, 1998, p. 60.
[q] Massey, 2000, p. 82; Cunningham, 1998, p. 42.
[r] Cunningham, 1998, p. 124.
[s] Cunningham, 1998, p. 114.
[t] *Ibid.*, p. 282.

Aside from the development of DJ turntable virtuosity in the late 1970s, it is no wonder that the Hip-Hop movement gathered such momentum in the 1980s with the advent of the sampler.[22]

The studio as performance tool

It's no secret that the studio is not a fixed place anymore. The portability of studio gear today allows us to put on stage equipment that in previous years could only be used inside a purpose-built facility. It is not uncommon to watch performing computer musicians lugging laptops and even desktop computers to their gigs so they can reproduce their music faithfully on stage. In the least sophisticated cases, the gear is used for simple playback of pre-recorded accompaniments. In more interesting scenarios, producers (of Hip-Hop, dance and experimental electronica in particular) create studio-like environments on stage which allow them to edit, remix, transform audio and essentially (re)compose 'on the fly' (see Figure 4.3 for a typical laptop stage setup). Brian Eno's *Studio as Compositional Tool* has become the 'Studio as Performance Tool'.

Learning from the avant-garde

Although the average music technology student is more likely to have heard of Massive Attack than of Schaeffer or Stockhausen, there is much evidence that they can find a wealth of inspiration in the work of the electronic music pioneers. In the end, today's producer in commercial music has much more in common with experimental musicians than they may realise, and by being aware of experimental trends they can simply do a better job.

There are already plenty of examples of the beneficial crossover of avant-garde techniques into commercial music:

- The soundtrack for the Sci-Fi film *THX1138* by George Lucas and sound designer Walter Murch was influenced by Murch's knowledge of Pierre Schaeffer's *Musique concrète*, as Murch acknowledges in his *Conversations* with Michael Ondaatje.[23] In *THX1138*, Murch uses sound-looping techniques and reversed recordings, among other unusual treatments, as actual musical elements in the way Schaeffer may well have done. Although sampling and looping has become pervasive in popular music since the late 1970s (especially in Hip-Hop), it had its origins in the late 1940s and early 1950s work of Schaeffer and Pierre Henry in France. Murch was a sound experimentalist from an early age, and his exposure to Schaeffer helped give him a creative edge by enriching his artistic palette.
- In The Beatles's *White Album* (1968), the piece 'Revolution 9' could be easily listened to as an avant-garde piece quite out of place among the other straightforward songs that constitute the double album. Clear influences of *Musique concrète* are heard in this piece, and some argue it owes a lot to Stockhausen's *Hymnen*.[24]
- Frank Zappa, the great songwriter, composer, bandleader and electric guitarist whose name is synonymous with musical innovation, was fascinated by the music of French avant-garde composer Edgard Varèse and frequently acknowledged his influence.

Chapter 7

Music, sound and visual media

In this chapter we will explore the advantages of using music technology for the creation of sound and music for film, games and similar new media. We will look briefly at some of the theories of how music and sound sync to visuals. We will look at the workflow of the creative music technologist working in this area and suggest some tips for working effectively. We will also consider surround playback and applications beyond film and games.

Music technology in multimedia

The application of music technology to multimedia is an exciting field for collaboration with game designers, film-makers, TV/video producers, web developers and others. Music technology owes more to film than it may seem at first. From the drawn-sound experiments (actually drawing directly on film then playing that back through an optical sensor) of the Russian experimental composers Evgenii Sholpo and Arsenii Avraamov to the investigations of Rudolf Pfenninger and Oskar Fischinger, the synthesis of sound through drawing on film is probably the first creative attempt to treat music as a *plastic* art;[1] this is to say that once 'moulded', its shape will not change. Think about this for a moment: up until these experiments with optical sound, musical composition was essentially a 'symbolic' art. Music notation stood in for sound, but now sound is able to represent itself. For sound artists drawing on film, electronic-music composers cutting and splicing tape, and performers documenting their playing, sound itself is an object.

When they work in film, video or any internet media, sound designers and composers have to be part of a team. This presents new challenges to them, as their art has to be shaped by common objectives and agreed aesthetic goals. Further than say, traditional Western opera, where the composer is the driving creative source, composers of music for media are simply part of a team.

In the past, creating music for film required the composer to write out the music, not just compose it. Effectively this barred (or at least made it very difficult for) composers who could not read or write music. Music technology has changed this.

Thanks to sequencers and notation programs, composers without a formal musical education can effectively create film scores and music for games, for instance, by using visual representations and MIDI recording. And, thanks to the ease with which modern audio sequencers can translate MIDI information into notation, musically illiterate composers can communicate with orchestrators and arrangers. This calls into question the importance of reading and writing music: it would seem not to be so crucial nowadays.

Traditional musical education is always an advantage, but not having it is much less of an obstacle than it ever was. The use of loops, whether rhythmic breakbeats, orchestral phrases or instrumental techniques (trills, tremolandi and various pre-recorded ornaments common as part of orchestral sample sets), allow composers to effectively mock-up performances that in some cases are good enough to be used 'as is' for the soundtrack in progress. The growth of the music-sample libraries attests to this and has shifted musical creation to a sort of collage and remix approach that puts electronic musicians at an advantage. They can now turn around a film score in record time as well as being able to quickly amend and rearrange the music as requested by directors, producers or editors.

In being able to work at the level of single pitches and rhythms, as well as orchestral phrases or horn riffs, the music technologist is in control of all the time-scales of music: the music at the *micro time-scale* as well as at the *macro time-scale*.[2] Together with this level of control of the music itself, through music technology we also control synchrony with the moving image.

Further than being able to write individual notes and rhythms, composers now are able to deal with the following musical 'objects':

- Sample 'construction kits': these place the composer at a mid-level of decision-making by providing them with rhythmic phrases, orchestral or selected instrumental passages, instrumental riffs, synthesised textures. The low-level questions of pitches, rhythm and range are preset so the bulk of the work is in reorganising these to produce convincing compositions. This is probably one of the developments in music technology that has most accelerated the production process.
- Mood music: mood-music samples place the composer at a high level, where decisions mostly concern the broad synchrony of the music's emotional rendering to picture. Whether originally composed or supplied by another musician as 'production music', the deploying and matching of mood music to picture (fixed or interactively) requires a sense of the overall structure of the projected score.
- Sound effects: from steps to explosions via birdsong, the presence of these elements will have a bearing and potential interference or collaboration with the music. Now the composer can easily incorporate these into their score.

- Atmospheres: environmental sounds and their layering are often used as incidental music in film (A very good example is Eduard Artemyev's music for *Solaris* (1972), directed by Andrei Tarkovski.)

Theorising on music and visuals

As a composer or sound designer, there are questions you will have to ask yourself at some stage. They involve deciding on how incidental music and sound will relate to film. The most basic concept is that of the role of music in relation to the film narrative. When music is part of the story (it is seen to be played on screen in some form) we say it is **diegetic**. When music helps the telling of the story as an accompaniment to the film, we say it is **non-diegetic**.

Much material has been written in this field and great insights can be derived from being familiar with texts on music, sound and image in terms of synchrony or interaction. Nicholas Cook, in his *Analysing Musical Multimedia*, proposes three basic models of multimedia by looking at how the different elements relate to each other.[3] Do the images and sound suggest similarity between them or not? Or do they suggest difference? If they are similar are they consistent or coherent? And if they are consistent, how do they conform to each other?

These questions are posed and examined by Cook from the point of view of analysis, but it is fair to assume that composers and sound designers have these at the back of their minds or have even explicitly agreed on how to answer them in practice with film/game directors and sound editors. Before creating a new cue (the music for a particular visual sequence) they must all agree on which strategy will better render the emotion and help communicate the plot (or the game-state, in the case of games).

Let's pause on this for a moment. When viewing a film, exploring a presentation or playing a game, the audience is creating a subset of their total audiovisual experience: within the broader context of where they are (a living room, a theatre or a sound studio), there is a subset of audiovisual events which for whatever time they are engaged with, the audience can pretend they are the sum total of their present experience. This is what Michel Chion calls the 'audiovisual contract' in his, now classic, book *Audio-Vision*.[4] We, as an audience, feel afraid or elated, anticipate disaster or relax with pleasure as we witness the film. We agree to pretend it is real and our reactions are at times undistinguishable from experiencing the same events in reality.

When we talk about film music (and by extension similar media) we are actually discussing what Chion calls **empathetic** and **anempathetic** relationships between sound and image; this is probably a simpler distinction than Cook's more rigorous distinctions in analysing musical multimedia mentioned above. Empathetic in this context means that we perceive the sound as reinforcing the image, or 'going in the same perceived direction' as the image. As Cook states in his book reinforcing the notion of film-music empathy, 'multimedia depends heavily on quasi-synaesthetic correspondences' (meaning that one sensation seems equivalent to another);[5] he explains that the roles of music, and I would add this holds for sound design also, range from literally representing the image through to enhancing it by connotation. In this way, the sound of a double bass can effectively accompany the image of an elephant, while a piccolo flute can accompany that of a mouse. Or, in sound design, an authentic phonograph recording will lend to the image a connotation of age or times gone by.

Anempathetic music or sound is when we perceive them as being indifferent to the image. This creates a sort of cognitive dissonance (roughly, you seem to perceive one thing but feel another). A classic example of this is the cliché thriller film that opens with a scene in a suburban house, in the middle of the night, and the music is a lullaby. We hear the otherwise comforting sound of the music at the same time as we see the killer lurking in the shadows. The music is anempathetic in one sense, as it does not represent the imminent danger, yet it also reinforces the sense of danger by representing the innocence of the child unaware of impending evil.

Some empathetic tasks that can be accomplished by music and sound

- Unification: audio can bridge the gaps between scenes: even when the scene has changed, the sound spills over into the next one creating a sense of continuity. This is also achieved by a persistent sound that tells us that a certain action is taking place even when we don't see it. We find an example of this in *Star Wars* when Luke Skywalker is practising with the lightsaber while Hans Solo plays chess with Obi Wan Kenobi: the camera moves away from Luke for quite a while but all throughout the scene we hear the buzzing lightsaber telling us that Luke is still practising off screen and unifying the whole sequence.
- Punctuation: a well-placed audio cue helps to heighten the importance of something on screen. Sound can also separate narrative sections as if they were grammatical sentences in language. In TV, for instance, 'stings' are used to round up scenes or to end a shot before going to commercials or to introduce the audience back to the story after a commercial, or to separate different sections of the story. In film this is less grammatical and more subtle, as the action flows through the movie without external interruptions.
- Symbolic punctuation: instead of using a literal sound for the image, the cue may represent a certain character, for instance the sound effect that accompanies each sighting of the creature in *Predator* (1987), or the themes used by composer John

Williams to illustrate the characters in his collaborations with Steven Spielberg (*Star Wars*, *E.T.*, *Indiana Jones*, etc.). This technique is an inheritance from opera, Wagner in particular, but used by many others and also called 'leitmotif'.

- Auditory setting: sounds that help emphasise location, like crickets at night, dog barks or the sound of the sea.
- Anticipation: sounds or music that lead us to believe that something will happen. Imagine a crescendo drum-roll that ends in a loud hit and then imagine the same crescendo drum-roll suddenly stopping without reaching a conclusive hit. These coupled with image could emphasise either something inevitable or a surprise, depending on which is used. Similar effects can be achieved through chord progressions and our expectation of harmonic resolution. In his book *Audio-Vision*, Chion calls them convergence (as the audio helps satisfy your expectation) and divergence (as it sets up an expectation that does not resolve).
- Silence: Chion comments on how since sound appeared on film it is now possible to have actual silence! (In silent movies, musical accompaniment was continuous.)
- Synchronisation: we could see this as punctuation in a broader sense, or music closely following the action. Depending on how loose or tight the sync is, we perceive softer or harsher effects. Contrary to what many beginners in film scoring believe, it is not enough to make the loudest transient of a sound coincide with a precise film frame: the degree of looseness or tightness of sync will nuance different emotions.
- Synchresis: a term invented by Chion to name the welding of sound and image by emphasising their synchrony. In the *Predator* example above, the predator sound is a punctuation to begin with, but as the film evolves it becomes impregnated with the sense of danger that the creature implies. This is achieved by bringing image and sound together repeatedly.

When the above roles are entrusted to audio, they help the audience understand the film better by shadowing the narrative: where events or sequences of events might begin and end; what events are important; what expectations to derive from those events, and so on.

In music video, even when the visuals seem far removed from the lyrics, rhythmic and harmonic groupings within the music will seem to link whole sections together. Take Radiohead's official promo video for 'Knives Out' from *Amnesiac* (2001). The lyrics are already fairly cryptic, although, paired with the visuals, the meaning seems to narrow down at times. The visual narrative is surreal and only vaguely related by the themes of love/loss/fight, yet the structure of the song functions as a blueprint from which the visual sequences and sub-sequences are erected. We are led to expect changes to coincide with the fulfilment of chord progressions and their cadences. The music is effectively 'breaking down' the dream-like visual sequence and giving it meaning.

Music can also appear to be located in space by coincidences with the image; we know this from older monaural film, where, regardless of all sound coming from a single speaker, the audience perceives the different sound effects as coming from wherever in the screen they are represented.[6] In discussing this in *Audio-Vision*, Chion calls it the spatial magnetisation of sound and goes on to speculate on the conditions that make the psychological placement effective.[7] A corollary of this is that sound/music directs our attention: it allows us to be somewhat manipulated by the director or game designer. Further, it creates a sonic world that seems to spill out of the screen and promotes a more immersive environment.

All the issues discussed in this section point to the importance of music in rendering emotion and can be well summarised by a well-used quote from the classical Hollywood film composer Bernard Herrmann:

> I feel that music on the screen can seek out and intensify the inner thoughts of the characters. It can invest a scene with terror, grandeur, gaiety or misery. It can propel narrative swiftly forward or slow it down. It often lifts mere dialogue into the realm of poetry. Finally, it is the communicating link between the screen and the audience, reaching out and enveloping all into one single experience.[8]

How much music theory do we need to know?

Sequencers allow us easily to record/program melodies and their accompaniments, and quickly orchestrate them, eventually separating musical elements into reusable patterns. They enable us through the use of templates and preset patterns, loops and musical textures to put together what, in another age, would have been considered quite complex compositional constructs. So, the question is: how much music theory does a music technologist actually need to know to compose for film, if they can work 'by ear'?

The greater music literacy one has, the better. Texts have been appearing recently aimed at helping computer musicians to grasp music theory, but the main prob lem that may be encountered is that the theory is too simple compared with the practical musical skills of music technologists. We may be able to play complex chords and create advanced harmonic progressions just because they sound good, and there is nothing wrong with that! However, the limitations come when we want to arrange music and involve other instruments. At that point, we encounter issues of instrumental range, harmony and counterpoint, which bring us back to theory. Arrangements can be done by ear, of course, but in the end a little theory will save us much trial and error.

Assuming that some basic instruction in how to shape chord progressions and modulations has been undertaken, and that we are familiar with using rhythm to drive the music forward and punctuate important moments, understanding pace in music is the main issue in scoring for media. We can define pace in this context as being the speed of musical change that is perceived by the audience. This does not lie simply in how many notes per second are heard, but in how much change is evident to the audience and how fast it is. Is it a steady rate of change? Does the rate of change vary throughout (slow to fast or fast to slow)? Does the rate of change vary unpredictably? The question is not whether there is change, but how fast that change is introduced.

Visual time is different from musical time, and they influence each other. A scene in which nothing happens, for instance an establishing shot of the city where the action will next take place, can work as a kind of visual silence. Yet if that same shot is accompanied by a chord progression that begins to modulate as the tempo increases, a sense of expectation is introduced telling the audience that this shot is some kind of build-up. This is being communicated by the music and not by the visuals, and the rate of change in the music will also tell the audience when to expect the change to the next scene. The changes in harmony have given the audience an aural measuring stick by which to understand the length of the visual sequence.

As rhythm measures the passage of time in music, it emphasises time divisions in the images it accompanies. Once a musical pattern is established for the listener, perception can be manipulated by where in the pattern the visual changes happen. Changes that coincide with strong (main) beats will create a strong audiovisual momentum, introducing changes on weak beats or upbeats can then help surprise the audience, and so on.

At this point it is useful to differentiate between music for fixed visuals (film or TV) and music for video games (or any other multimedia that needs adaptive audio).[9] Karen Collins discusses this in *Game Sound* (2008). She quotes quite a few authors to support the idea that all the functions of film or television sound apply to game sound,[10] and it is easy to agree with her, even without the multiple references. Collins explains, then, that because of the nature of games, synchrony cannot be as close in games as it is on film. This is because games are played in real time and so visual elements will change unpredictably. However, we could ask ourselves whether this is a question of simply developing better machine listening or artificial intelligence for music computing. If we had all the computing power necessary, could the music be also generated in real time to the point where scoring the game is as precise as scoring a film?

Recently publicised attempts in this direction have happened in the work of Troels B. Folmann for two games of the Lara Croft series: *Tomb Raider: Legend* and *Tomb Raider: Anniversary*. In an interview for the video-game music website Gsoundtracks in 2010, Folmann describes his technique as micro-scoring:

Micro-scoring is essentially about breaking the score into a variety of small components that are assembled in real-time according to player action and/or interaction. The micro-scores are made in such a way that they adapt to player action or interaction. You have to imagine that there are thousands of things going on in the game environment – the idea behind micro-scoring is to support the major elements in the environment. An example can be a 3-second score for breaking pillars or falling stones, which is scored in the same key as the main ambient background score. We also have more detailed types of micro-scores which are based on slices samples like REX and other sliced sample formats. This allows us to fully adjust pitch and timing based on player interaction with the game. An example of this is adjusting beat to footsteps and increasing tempo when she starts running. A good example of micro-scoring application relates to chopping up a score in multiple components. So essentially composing a score in 15 different steps and cutting each step up, so it can seemingly integrate into any of the other 15 steps. The system then blends the steps in real-time and you have a much more varied and versatile score – made from micro-scores. This allows you to adjust mood in music with using basic cross-fades, but actually have adaptive types of compositions.[11]

Commercial forerunners

Although new to video games, the idea of micro-scoring is far from new. Companies like Yamaha were working on the creation of intelligent auto-accompaniment keyboards in the mid '80s.[12] These instruments brought a number of musical styles that offered instant arrangements by reacting to trigger keys. These keys would activate patterns that corresponded to the harmonies selected by the user (depending on combinations of keys). Introduction patterns, endings and breaks could be selected on the fly, and levels of complexity in the arrangement (dynamic adding of arrangement stems), were activated by the player's MIDI velocity average or by density of notes played. The keyboard's programming worked on the assumption that if the player wanted to play louder, then the arrangement should grow in response, or that if many notes were played, as in a solo improvisation, the arrangement should also react to that. Given the development of game audio engines like FMOD Designer, from FMOD interactive audio middleware, and Wwise© (WaveWorks Interactive Sound Engine©) from Audiokinetics, composers and sound designers can capture the game state with great precision and streamline their creative workflow by allowing them to test the effectiveness of their cues against real-time game situations.

Workflow

Originally, the work of composition for film was a team effort relying heavily on a number of people undertaking very specific roles. In his *Complete Guide to Film Scoring*,[13] Richard Davies details an ideal music workflow:

1. The post-production stage of the film where the locked picture is sent to the composer (meaning that the visual edits are final by this stage);
2. The spotting session or the creation of timing notes together with a music editor;
3. The composition of the music;
4. The orchestration;
5. The copying of parts;
6. The seeking of appropriate music clearances (if third-party songs or compositions are used); the recording of the music and its mixing;
7. The mixing of the music together with the rest of the sound in sync to picture.

And an ideal sound-design flow:

1. The creation of sound effects;
2. The recording of Foley (live recording of effects to picture) is added;
3. The dubbing of any necessary dialogue lines;
4. The final mix of all the audio elements.[14]

This is all very well, and serves as a useful guideline, but reality is far more messy! Depending on the budget of your film, you may be showing musical sketches to the director before a final cut is produced; segments of visuals may be cut to your cues and you may not require traditional orchestration; or you will work on it at the same time as the composition takes place. In the worst-case scenario you may end up having to imitate a **temp track** put together by the music editor and which the director has become overly fond of. Furthermore, sometimes you will simply be recording cues to picture in an improvisatory way!

There is no perfect method. Whatever sounds good and gets you to the deadline is valid. The same can be said of games; although their ideal music/sound workflow is quite similar, there is the added complication of interactivity, as mentioned earlier.

Delivering the music

Audio/MIDI sequencers, notation packages and game audio engines enable composers and sound designers to create their audio content and check it as they go along. This significantly reduces the time of execution. It also allows the cycle of creation and directorial approval to go faster, although in the end the process may be slower since the director may ask for many more scoring alternatives, simply because they can!

Music technology allows, in not uncommon cases, for one composer to complete the whole scoring process with little outside help. A telling example is that of Mark Snow, writer of the music for the science-fiction television series *The X Files*. In an interview by Greg Rule for the March 1996 edition of *Keyboard* magazine we find the following exchange:

> [K.] Walk us through a typical *X-Files* week in the life of Mark Snow.
>
> [M.S.] The first thing that'll happen is they'll send me a VHS rough-cut of the show, and I'll get to view it and get a sense of what it's about. No note taking, no nothing. Just watching. Then next the locked 3/4″ [videotape] is sent to me along with spotting notes from our musical editor, Jeff Charbonneau. Jeff is fantastic... he spots the show completely by himself ...] and he sends me the notes... I get the notes, and what I usually like to do is start with the biggest cue first: either the longest or most involved, which is usually in the last act.
>
> [K.] What day of the week is this?
>
> [M.S.] It changes. But let's just say, for example, over the weekend I've watched the rough cut. On Monday I get the 3/4″ tape and the spotting notes, and I can start. I'll do the writing Monday, Tuesday, Wednesday, and maybe a little bit on Thursday. On Friday, they'll come over like they did today, and we mix it, send it out, and get ready for the next one.

In the case of Mark Snow, his sequencer of choice in the mid '90s was the Synclavier, an expensive sequencing and sampling instrument. In the 2010s a state-of-the-art laptop can provide similar computing power for a very small portion of the price of a 1990s Synclavier.

Where do you start when scoring music for video?

Make sure you ask for a QuickTime Movie if you are working on a Mac, or an AVI if on a PC. Request that it be rendered at the correct frame-rate for your project (this will depend on where you are working, but for TV standards PAL or SECAM[15] you will need this to be 25 frames-per-second (fps); for NTSC it will be 29.97 fps;[16] and if you are working on film, you will need 24 fps. Don't ask for a full-resolution copy as your sequencer will run much more smoothly if the video is small in memory size. Try the following activities to start your scoring process:

- When given a copy of the video load it into your sequencer software and watch it while playing the metronome.
- Listen to the default tempo settings, usually 120 beats per minute, and see if the video looks 'faster' or 'slower' than the click. Then adjust accordingly until the speed looks right and you have as many main visual events coinciding with main beats of the bar (one or three in a 4/4 bar). There is a catch here, as the faster the tempo, the more things will fall on a click! So you need to balance hit-points against accelerating or slowing down the audiovisual feel. Don't worry if things don't fall exactly on the

musical beat: a few frames either way may be fine. Plus, you can always insert tempo changes later.

- Bear in mind that a lot of animators and video editors are working against a timeline which is divided in minutes and seconds, so they are usually tempted to land on whole divisions of time; this is not a rule, but by no means a rare occurrence.
- Experiment with different time signatures. The most common is 4/4, but alternative ones may work well: try 6/8 and 9/8 for a triple feel that can easily subdivide, or 12/8 for a metre that is at once 'square', since you can divide the bar into four groups of 3/8, and sprightly as the subdivision into three is less stable than the feel of 1/16 or 1/8 in a 4/4. Try compound signatures like 7/8 or 5/8 for a slightly unpredictable but energising feel.
- Once you have set the tempo and time signature, mark the frames you have been instructed to support/hit using the sequencer markers. Ensure that you build up to these points in the music, because even if they will be synced to a sound effect, the music may need to prepare the audience for this.
- If you are writing an atmospheric or ambient-like cue, all you may need is judicious deployment of pads and textures, but if you are working in a more traditional rhythmic/melodic/harmonic idiom, knowing how many bars you have is invaluable. Map out your general structure (accounting for the hit points): intro, outro, main sections and transitions in between. Once this is done, your creativity is ready to flow!

Surround and immersion

Although most music is still listened to in stereo, and mobile players and smartphones work in this format, films and games feel more realistic when audio is in surround. A surround system by itself doesn't guarantee a feeling of immersion; the soundtrack (music, dialogue and sound design) must be mixed with this in mind. Surround can be confusing as there seem to be so many systems, and the first impression we have is that delivery formats are changing all the time. While it is true that there is a relentless pace in audio innovation, it is also true that formats take time to get established commercially. Also, once established, they can take a long time to be replaced. For instance, stereo has been commercially with us roughly since the late '50s, and, despite all the myriad speaker systems that are available, it is still the prime way we listen to audio. That is already a good sixty years! Yet both the film and game industries are promoting new surround systems actively. Movie-theatre chains can afford to try new and even proprietary systems, but in the end, the mass market depends on what people consume at home. The most popular commercial systems at present are based on 5.1, that is: five speakers and a subwoofer.[17] These speakers account for left, centre, right, left surround and right surround, as well as a low-frequency effects channel. The low-frequency effects channel can be addressed directly (an audio track with this information) or it can contain the low frequencies from other channels syphoned off by means of a cross-over filter.[18] This can cause difficulties in semi-pro sequencing environments, as audio sequencers may simply offer you the surround format as discrete tracks filled with information resulting from surround panning. If you want to control what is on the '.1' channel, you may need to direct the low frequencies there yourself.[19] In general, though, the trend is for even larger speaker arrays like 6.1 and 7.1.

Immersion is difficult to measure and its relationship to sound is also a fairly mysterious area, yet many scholars are working on this, especially in games.[20] Although our work in music technology needs to be aware of this research to ensure greater integration, our craft depends heavily on our command of the relevant surround technologies.

Dolby Laboratories, leaders in surround sound, have been researching for many years how to marry the convenience of stereo with the immersiveness of surround for consumer systems; in a sense they are an industry standard. In the late 1990s the Dolby Pro Logic system used a stereo signal to encode three front channels and a mono surround. This was a convenient way to pipe surround sound as part of the TV signal. Software plugins were made available so that users could encode into this format without a specific hardware unit. Successors to this format today are Dolby Pro Logic II, IIx and IIz, and they cater for increasing number of channels (IIx) and channels for height placement of effects (IIz); but again, despite this wealth of innovation, it is still an open question to see which surround format settles into consumer culture. Dolby are by no means the only ones innovating in surround and trying to establish themselves as the standard. DTS Systems is strongly promoting their brand of **codecs** and making them available for audio production software so users can encode for Blu-Ray DVD, a growing segment of the market at present.

On a less commercial vein, the Ambisonics standard (see Chapter 2), developed in the '70s (and also less well known and marketed), is a very interesting approach that seeks to reproduce the field of sound independently of the number of speakers in the array. Unfortunately this system does not, yet, have any major endorsement from the big industry players. There is also the question of using binaural audio recordings which are achieved by using special microphones placed inside a dummy head, as explained in Chapter 2. With the growth of personal players, smartphones and mobile playing devices, it is rather wise to be aware of new systems that can deliver surround (and thus greater sound immersion) through headphones.

Applications

We have mentioned film and video games as they are the most obvious areas of work for the music technologist to develop content, i.e. for creative music technology. Yet there are many more areas that can be explored:

- Dramatic/theatrical: film, video games, music theatre, theatre;
- Broadcasting: TV programmes: musical elements (themes, stings, underscores, programme credits), documentaries;
- Marketing and promotion: commercials, branding audio elements and film trailers;
- Production services: music, sound effects and loop libraries;
- Corporate Communications: audiovisual presentations, interactive information media (consoles or touch screens for exhibitions or museums).

Market forces

As video games compete solidly with Hollywood films and DVD releases in the entertainment market, their music/sound production values become increasingly similar. In *Star Wars: The Force Unleashed* (2008), an action video game based on the *Star Wars* film series, the score by Mark Griskey (with two themes by Jesse Harlin) is not only in the style of John Williams, who composed the original Hollywood scores, but the orchestral sound is comparable to the film soundtracks. To get an idea of the kind of budgets that video games may be commanding let's compare figures from late 2009 of initial-day launch of a videogame vs. first weekend sales of films. In its first day, according to the Reuters News Agency,[21] *Call of Duty: Modern Warfare* for the Xbox 360/PS3 projected sales of $300 to $340 million dollars. Meanwhile, *Harry Potter and the Half-Blood Prince*, released by Warner Bros., grossed $394 million in its opening weekend. The video game grossed in one day almost three-quarters of what it took the film to make in a weekend. Video games are a force to be reckoned with; however, one can also argue that their commercial impetus is helped by the many games that are derived from blockbuster films.

Final tips

- You should become familiar in detail with the surround formats you are likely to encounter in your chosen area. You must also follow innovation and trends within your field, be it film, commercials, games or interaction.

- Music and sound for digital media will be synchronised to the image and embedded into an appropriate delivery format (some type of MPEG, most probably). You need to be clear with the video/film/game editor about what processes of compression or further post-production will be applied to the audio. This will determine what kind of audio mastering is appropriate. Your tracks will rarely sound the same after they have been embedded in the film, and it is worth gaining experience in this area to be able to best prepare your mixes.
- Audio for video applications is usually delivered at a sampling rate of 48 kHz. Remember that for most audio production you may be working at 44.1 kHz. Since commercial CDs are still mastered at 44.1 kHz and 16-bit, you may want to do the rate conversion yourself at the end of your production, as well as the dithering if you have been recording at 24-bit. The rule of thumb is to work at the highest resolution your system will allow and then convert and dither as appropriate.

Chapter 8

The studio as experimental lab

Throughout this book, we have been looking at different aspects of the sound studio. I feel that a particular approach mentioned in the chapter on production (Chapter 6) should be examined here in more detail: the recording studio as a place for creation and experimentation, beyond recording instrumental performance. In this chapter we look at the implications of this, and consider more closely the issue of creativity in the studio.

We know that once we have captured sound we can do all sorts of interesting things with it beyond playback. The idea of the studio as a music laboratory, a place (or virtual environment) for testing, experimentation and synthesis, is well established today. And, thanks to laptops, smartphones and tablet computers, quite sophisticated recording, editing and synthesis facilities are portable as well.

Earlier, in Chapter 6, when discussing music production we touched on this topic lightly, but I think it is worth exploring it some more. Are we 'cheating' when we present music that has been made by editing choice recordings? For example, when we take the best of four guitar solos and keep that as our recorded 'performance', are we misrepresenting ourselves as players? Is it any different if the music is based largely on sounds not made by musical instruments (and so, not expected to be 'live' anyway)? Maybe some of the answers are obvious to you, maybe not, but these questions keep coming up among young musicians and are worth considering if we are prepared to view recording as a creative tool.[1] Let's now outline a brief overview of how the studio evolved as a place for experimentation.

Sounds from scratch (literally, sound produced from scratching)

The origins of studio creativity can be traced back to the early twentieth century and the development of film technology. Notice I did not write 'the origins of the studio', but specifically 'studio creativity'. Remember, we are discussing 'the studio as lab'. It so happens that although the earliest recordings date from the late 1870s, as exemplified by Thomas Edison, using a recording medium for creating sounds rather than just recording sounds only began to happen with the development of sound on film. And so, in the late 1920s, at the time when films were acquiring a fixed soundtrack, artists were already experimenting with sound through film technology and, in particular, 'optical sound'.[2]

When optical sound was developed, recordings could be represented either by a variable area on the strip allowing light through or by variable density of the film itself (degrees of opacity of the film). By shining light through this part of the film through to a photo sensor, differing voltages could be produced (not dissimilar to the transduction allowed by running the needle of a turntable through vinyl grooves). It was not long before somebody noticed that you didn't have to record anything but simply scratch the film itself and so 'etch the sound' onto the celluloid directly! In this way, and using the variable density method mentioned earlier, when you shone a bright light through the strip and focused it onto the photo cell, different sounds could be obtained.

As we have mentioned before, the Russians were pioneers in this area, even establishing a studio for drawing sound onto film. In Leningrad in 1929, Arsenii Avraamov and Evgenii Sholpo drew directly onto film with a pin and Indian ink.[3] As this work was rather difficult, given the available film width on which to draw, they started photographing individual drawings with the film camera and produced their first drawn sound films in 1930.

In 1932–3, Avraamov directed, in Moscow, what must have been the first music laboratory. This studio lab was intended for experimenting with drawn sound and was called the Laboratoriya Risovannogo Zvuka.[4]

Roughly at the same time, Norman McLaren, then a student at the Glasgow School of Art, experimented in a similar way to the Russians by drawing and painting onto the celluloid film strip.[5] While in Switzerland, Rudolf Pfenninger also experimented with drawn sound and photographing shapes to create sound waves, and Oskar Fischinger, in Germany and then in the USA, worked with similar techniques and proposed music as a visual experience.

The experiments in drawn sound are, aptly, the beginnings of music as a plastic art: music created directly on a medium that would retain the music itself, not a representation of it.[6] More clearly, scores can be said to contain recipes for re-creating music, but recorded music and in this case drawn sound, when played back, is the music itself.

Early sound labs

In 1937, in Seattle, John Cage delivered a lecture entitled 'The Future of Music: Credo'.[7] In it he goes further than the Futurist artists (see Chapter 10) had in their manifestos earlier in the century regarding the use of any and all sounds for music. In particular, Cage makes several references to film sound and the optical soundtrack, even to the film frame as a unit of time, and talks about composers being able to create any rhythm they can imagine. Cage himself did not run any studio as such, but he did experiment with turntables in pieces like *Imaginary Landscape No. 1* (1939). He used the variable speed of the turntables to produce sweeping pitch changes. A simple act, yet an important one in that he was employing a reproduction machine for synthesis or creation.

Quite unrelated to Cage's experiments in the early '40s, a band leader, jazz musician and radio/TV jingles composer by the name of Raymond Scott had been building his own electronic music studio for commercial use near New York City. Scott clearly saw his studio as a lab. Open for business in 1946, Manhattan Research Inc. offered 'classic and original devices for sound generation and processing . . . [including] the Martenot, Ondioline and a special modification of the Hammond organ . . . [and] nine recording channels on four tape machines'.[8] Among the innovations in his studio, Scott filed for a patent for an 'orchestral machine' (which seems to describe a modern-day playback sampler), invented the sequencer and several synthesis instruments, including one that could generate music automatically: the Electronium. Scott's was certainly one of the earliest electronic music studios, maybe even the first private one, and certainly the first experimental studio open for commercial business (he later advertised, as a commercial selling point, that one could create *Musique concrète* in his studio), and in his work we can see a prototype for the kind of studio setups composers enjoy today. Scott was self-financed through his jingles and by commercialising his studio. He was also a forerunner of the contemporary popular music composer/arranger/producer.

In the late '40s, similar ideas to those of Cage began to take shape in France. In 1948, with the definition of *Musique concrète*, Pierre Schaeffer proposed a music of everyday sounds or *sound-based music* where sounds could become sonic building-blocks in preference to pitch and harmony.[9] Closer in spirit perhaps to the Russian lab for drawn sound, in that they were virtually ring-fenced from the need to succeed commercially, Schaeffer's Groupe de Recherches Musicales, or GRM, and was hosted (and still is) at the installations of Radio France.

By the early '50s, in America, Louis and Bebe Barron, perhaps best known for their 'electronic tonalities' for the 1956 film *Forbidden Planet*, had also set up a studio. They had no institutional funding like the GRM or later European studios and had to finance themselves through commissions. Yet they were clearly linked to the avant-garde crowd as we know from their studio work for Cage in *Williams Mix* (1952–3) and their electronic music for *Bells of Atlantis* (1952), and, interestingly, they also experimented with creating sounds through electrical circuit building/manipulation, known today as circuit bending or hardware hacking (see Chapter 10). It is interesting that they effectively created a business model that allowed them to be productive and artistically challenging at the same time.

Contemporary with the Barrons, but institutionally funded, West German Broadcasting (Westdeutscher Rundfunk, or WDR) opened its now famous electronic music studio, thanks to the efforts of Werner Meyer-Eppler, Robert Beyer and Herbert Eimert.[10] This studio attracted a variety of famous composers (including Karlheinz Stockhausen and Pierre Boulez).

By the late '50s and early '60s, the studio as an experimental lab became effectively a worldwide phenomenon. Studios sprang up everywhere sponsored by broadcasting organisations, universities and at least one manufacturer (Philips, in The Netherlands). From Santiago de Chile to Tokyo, via Buenos Aires, Mexico, New York, Toronto, London, Warsaw, and many other places, electronic music and thus studio experimentation was well under way. However, it is arguable whether this growth in practice actually had much impact on the general public. It was not really until the use of synthesisers (particularly the Moog) in popular music became widespread in the '60s and '70s that electronic music, and so studio experimentation, reached its tipping point.

Creativity in the studio

Recording musicians and sound artists develop their own tricks and methods for dealing with audio; while some may be genuine discoveries, there is a lot of creative studio practice that has not been thoroughly documented. Although we can't do that comprehensively here, at least we can show some interesting samples of creative approaches in the studio.

Accidents

A golden rule of the studio is never to erase accidental recordings before listening to them first! Audio accidents can be a rich source of inspiration; anybody working with audio has experienced this, but it would be interesting if more artists documented these accidents. Let's look at an interesting anecdote. In 1961, Raymond Scott believed that electronic music was unfamiliar enough to audiences at the time that associations between music and words could be arbitrarily seeded in people's minds.[11] He thought there was such great potential in this that he actually set up a company called *Audio Logos Inc.* especially for applying this to advertising, creating short electronic music melodies (musical logos) that could be used to identify a product. The accident that inspired this happened because Scott wanted to test for what sorts of words would come into a professional voice-over artist's head if electronic music logos were randomly played and they were asked to improvise a commercial announcement on the spot. In his first session, Scott set up the system and recorded all the spontaneous announcements; but before he was able to sync the edited voice with the musical logos for play back, the tape machines were run by accident at the same time and out of sync. Scott recounts that he was amazed by the effect as words matched up to logos in unintended places creating new and convincing associations. Scott then recorded the 'accident' and quickly concluded that electronic music logos were unexpectedly flexible in a way acoustic music was not. He felt that, given their short history, electronic sounds did not evoke any moods in particular and so could illustrate any given words. Scott did not run a comparative experiment to see if the same would actually happen with acoustic music! However, the point I would like to make is that Scott set up a creative environment, in the first place, that involved improvisation. This provided a playground for the voice-over artist which was then further and happily complicated by an accidental playback. Our workflow in the studio should perhaps follow this example and always look to create fertile grounds for musical intuition to flourish.

> Keep your recording software or equipment running as much as possible and be prepared to mix and match your takes just to experiment. You might be pleasantly surprised.

Re-recording

The practice of re-recording started in film. Being able to record the voices of actors to improve a spoken line or substitute for a cleaner take is very useful, but Hollywood sound designer Walter Murch took it a step further in the direction of creativity. Perhaps taking a page out of the book of audio producers from the late '50s and early '60s like Joe Meek in London, who would feed a sound into a reverberant space and record the result, Murch applied the same technique to his sound effects. By playing a recorded sound in a given environment and then recording the playback, he obtained a sound that was flavoured with the acoustic characteristics of the playback space. For the film *THX1138* (1971), to create background radio transmission vocals that would sound futuristic, he had a voice-over artist broadcasting through radio equipment and then picked up the transmission on a radio receiver while playing with the frequency tuning. In this way he found he could add new partials to the sound by simply receiving slightly off frequency and slowly tuning in. In general, Murch aimed to get clean studio-recorded sounds to belong to real acoustic environments by re-recording them in those environments; he called this sort of process *worldizing*.[12]

In a variation of this technique, producers have often re-recorded instruments and vocals while playing them back through guitar amplifiers to achieve a certain band-passed distorted sound.

Try 'worldizing' your loop samples by playing them back through different speakers; don't worry about the quality of the speaker, every choice will give you a different sound colour, which you can then combine with a clean recording.

Re-recording is excellent for creating a sense of space, but this can also be achieved by changing the release envelopes of your samples and loops. Reverb is essentially a prolongation of the sound and this is what adding time to the release envelope does. If you create two different sample slots or key-groups in your sampler and you assign the same sample but with different release values, you will get an automatic panning movement for that sample alone (in a sample keyboard setup you will only be able to set each sample's panning or move the panning of the patch as a whole; this allows you to create individual, albeit fixed, panning trajectories for your separate samples). We used this technique in the late 1980s to create a sense of stereo with mono samplers like the AKAI S900.

Reversing

Reversing recordings used to be a favourite of anybody beginning to use a tape machine as it was quite easy to try out and intriguing to listen to. Given something of a psychological and spiritual connotation by the listening public, reversed recording has been considered as a way of conveying subliminal messages as well as playing with Satanism.[13] The Beatles put the effect to good use, though, in the song 'Rain' from *Revolver* (1966). Thanks to the breadth of the musical education of producer George Martin, The Beatles were exposed to many techniques only really practised by the avant-garde at the time, and this included tape-manipulation techniques.

Gating

The process of opening or closing an audio signal path when a certain amplitude threshold has been met has been used widely in the analogue studio. Gates are more often used for controlling the *noise floor* of a signal: as soon as the intended signal goes below a certain loudness threshold, the signal is suppressed. In this way, if the noise floor in a recording competes with the quietest moments of the intended signal, the whole thing can be silenced with a fade-out when the threshold is met.

An emblematic use of this effect, which would dominate '80s drum pop production, can be appreciated in Phil Collins's 'I can feel it coming in the air tonight' (1981). Engineer Hugh Padgham used the compression and gating capabilities available per track on the then new SSL mixing desk, to process (gate) the drum sound played through a reverse talkback mic to achieve the emblematic 1980s gated sound.[14] In simple terms, gating is a way of triggering something else. In general, to achieve 1980s snare drum sounds, the snare would be routed to a reverb with a large hall setting (or something similar), but you could not hear the effect as the gate was active unless the drum was struck. Once this happened, the gate would open and let the reverberant snare through, giving the impression of a large space only to be cut out quickly by the release time. The aural contradiction between the large space of the snare against a sudden dampening of the sound gives it an unnatural feel which inspired much electronica-oriented pop of the '80s and beyond.

Another creative use of gating is to link two sounds that must be in tight unison. One use is to 'fatten' a kick drum sound by having it trigger a low sine wave signal previously tuned to the key of the song. You can also let the kick drum control the bass guitar signal in styles like funk or Hip-Hop where 'locking' them improves the rhythmic feel of the song.

> In the Phil Collins example, the gated sound was the ambience of a studio control room applied to the drums; take a cue from this and put your own sounds through any DSP effect like a delay or heavy flanging, or even pitch changing, and try gating it to achieve unusual colours or to enhance the 'energy' of the sound whenever your set amplitude threshold is met.

Sound effects

Sound effects in the studio, or 'SFX', have been created since radio dramas began to develop in the 1920s, some argue even as early as 1914.[15] To accompany the drama, sounds had to be used that illustrated the words and helped transmit a feeling or realism to the listener. In *The Stuff of Radio* (1934),[16] early BBC radio drama producer Lance Sieveking defined certain rules of sound production for radio drama which are a good starting point for understanding the role of sound effects:[17]

- The realistic, confirmatory effect (a sound that confirms what is being said by reinforcing a sense of place or an event);
- The realistic, evocative effect (a sound that although realistic is only meant to evoke what is alluded to in the dialogue);
- The symbolic, evocative effect (a sound symbol of mind state);
- The conventionalised effect (an easily identifiable sound);
- Impressionistic effect (maybe better understood as surreal, effects which represent dream-states like delays or reverbs on the voice);
- Music as an effect (using music for its cliché associations).

I have taken the trouble to quote Sieveking's categories for sound effects to show that from the earliest days of broadcast media the work of studio sound production was conceived beyond the merely technical. To choose, combine and treat sounds for the different types mentioned requires more than technical dexterity, but demands technical dexterity nevertheless. In this sense, the studio is a laboratory where art meets science.

Together with radio, film studios are also forerunners for the studio as lab. In an issue from the early 1930s of *Popular Mechanics*, John Draper attests to the applied creativity of sound crews, writing: 'The talkies are filled with sound tricks. Many are more faithful reproductions than the noises created during the scenes you witness . . . Not a telephone bell tinkles in a drawing room scene, not a door slams, until the sound experts have placed their approval on the effect.'[18] In another magazine of the same period, *Modern Mechanix*, Earl Theisen writes:

> By playing on the aural nerves with symbolic sounds and noises the psychological reaction of the audience is controlled and varied according to the dramatic and emotional needs of the cartoon story. If Donald Duck falls, for example, it is not enough for the sound man to hit a drum for the noise, but an additional sound characteristic must be added to convey a certain kind of fall . . . When a sympathetic attitude is desired, the 'fall' sound is hollow and devoid of jarring characteristics, while a harsh sound which shocks the aural nerves is created for that effect . . . Through study and experimentation Walt Disney and his engineers have found that by introducing music or various sounds and noise frequencies into the cartoon, the response of the audience is varied and controlled. By combining noises of certain pitches or tempos the psychological values of the cartoon music is emphasised in keeping with the story requirements.[19]

The BBC Radiophonic Workshop

The creation of sound effects is further evidence of the studio as a laboratory for sound experimentation. Along with the well-known institutions where experimentation flourished and was institutionally encouraged, like the WDR-Cologne and RTF-Paris, many lesser known studios have contributed to the history of audiovisual creation. Their work is and has been more utilitarian, but not less creative. In particular, the BBC pioneered the studio as lab with its Radiophonic Workshop.

Started in 1958 by Daphne Oram and Desmond Briscoe at the BBC Maida Vale studios, the Radiophonic Workshop was dedicated to providing sound effects and music for BBC programmes until 1998 when it was shut down.[20] The early years of the Radiophonic Workshop are now famous for the creation of the music and sound effects for the British TV sci-fi series *Dr Who*, among many other contributions. In the beginning, they were limited to a few oscillators, tape machines and reverb chambers (re-recorded ambience, as discussed earlier), yet the Radiophonic Workshop created a wealth of effects for radio and TV programming, creativity thriving regardless of means.

Oram was at the workshop for less than a year, and when she finally left the BBC in 1959 she set up her own studio. As an independent composer, she made music intended for the concert hall as well as film music and music for drama. Oram, as well as being a musician, was trained in audio engineering and acoustics.[21] Further, she was an innovative electronic instrument-builder, creating her own synthesiser controlled by drawing envelopes on clear 35 mm film to be read by photoelectric cells.

Among the many talented members of the Radiophonic Workshop, Delia Derbyshire merits particular mention. Her work at the BBC went beyond sound effects and, in fact, Derbyshire's earlier musical contributions were done under the workshop's creative umbrella credit, but later works are more clearly attributed and have received attention in recent years from electronica bands (Chemical Brothers, Aphex Twin and others) that either recognise her as an inspiration or actually have covered her music.[22] Derbyshire famously realised and recorded the *Dr Who* theme (written by Ron Grainer), and this is perhaps what most people will remember her for, yet, together with Oram, she became one of the earliest female electronic music composers in Britain.

The Radiophonic Workshop, with its do-it-yourself beginnings, was a true laboratory of sound; for instance, since they did not have a synth at the time when the instruments were just becoming available, they made a keyboard from piano keys and used them to control the electronics that could drive twelve individual oscillators (of the kind used for audio testing). They also had a pre-FM synth in the form of the Wobbulator, 'a sine-wave oscillator that could be frequency modulated. It consisted of a very large metal box, with a few switches and one very large knob in the middle that could sweep the entire frequency range in one revolution. They were used in the BBC for "calibrating reverb times in studios" apparently.'[23]

In the late '60s the Radiophonic Workshop acquired British synthesisers like the EMS VCS3 and the Synthi 100 modular system (known as The Delaware)[24] to aid them further in their sound inventions. During this same period, both Delia Derbyshire and Brian Hodgson teamed up with Peter Zinoviev (founder of EMS) to take electronic sounds outside the studio with their band Unit Delta Plus. They later formed, with David Vorhaus, a band called White Noise. After many organisational redirections imposed by the BBC, the Radiophonic Workshop was finally (and sadly) closed in 1998.

Future studios?

It seems that electronic music studios are increasingly now audiovisual studios as well; this is due in part to work in electronic music becoming ever more cross-disciplinary and music software being extended to incorporate visuals (from movies in audio sequencers like Logic Pro, Cubase or Pro-Tools to visual extensions like Jitter to the MaxMSP programming environment, among others). The availability of electronic hardware and know-how is fuelling a new generation of musicians with an interest in human/computer interaction (HCI) and its applications through the creative use of sensors. At the same time, the idea of a physical space where sound artists work as a group is increasingly rare.[25] The studio/lab has mutated into a network of home computer setups linked by the internet. There are a growing number of web-based studio facilities now creating virtual points of contact for composers and sound artists,[26] not to mention the hundreds of smartphone and tablet apps that allow you to create on-the-go and share your work instantly across the world thanks to the internet. Portable music production is probably the next wave.

The portable studio is a portable sound lab

Roughly forty years after the blossoming of institutionally sponsored studios, the studio has become portable and personal. Both recording and synthesis can be performed with no more than a good laptop (or even a smartphone or tablet, as mentioned earlier) and there are plenty of available programming languages and software for experimentation. So if the laptop can be a mobile sound lab, what tools can we expect to use for experimental work to keep the 'lab spirit' alive?

Ordinary audio sequencers on computers aim to replicate the traditional recording studio. They contain software equivalents of everything we need — mixer, synthesisers, effects processors — and attached to a sound card they can record and process audio from microphone or line inputs. Chances are that if you are interested in music technology you will already own one of these sequencer programs (Cubase, Garage Band, FL Studio, etc.). What you may not have thought about is that they are designed for you to make music within a narrow stylistic window. So, for instance, the default time signature will be 4/4, as most popular Western music is in that metre. In most cases you can change it, but creating more complex time signatures like 7/4 or 5/8 or compounded ones like 3/4 | 1/8 will be difficult if not impossible within most sequencers. Changing time signature every other bar-line, for instance, as is common in much classical contemporary music, will usually be troublesome if at all possible. Similarly, your suggested workflow will be basically like that of a studio: record all tracks and then mixdown. Rarely will audio sequencers provide tools to generate music automatically (**algorithmic music**) and if they do, it will probably be limited to arpeggiation patterns and some MIDI-delay processing. For these reasons, it is very useful for a music technologist to be acquainted with programs that extend the functionality of the laptop in different ways and help it become a sound laboratory. In the paragraphs that follow I would like to review some key software tools you should explore.

Studio software: representing the studio on your computer

We can group the ways that music software designers represent the sound studio or sound lab into four main categories.[27]

(1) Linear sequencers
Similar to the analogue studio production model, these are based on graphic interfaces depicting a tape studio environment, with pre-set procedures for managing and transforming audio, and visual ordering of musical events on screen at specific timings with immediate auditioning. Their application is quite generic but tends to be favoured by song writers and more traditional composers and arrangers.

(2) Sample and loop triggers
Based on the DJ performance model (and inspired by drum machines and hardware workstations like the AKAI MPC-60 from the late '80s), they offer graphic interfaces depicting recording and performance situations mostly related to DJ practice, although these have also been used extensively in experimental and ambient electronica. Pre-set procedures are available, as in linear sequencers. Immediate auditioning of musical material and placement of events in time or in easily accessible slots is possible for live performance. Although this kind of software lends itself quite well to pattern-based music, it has also found much use in live experimental electronic music and even as trigger software for electroacoustic music.

(3) Music visual programming
Although the interface is graphic, as in the two types described above, the emphasis here is on programming, thus the user is presented with a blank canvas on which to arrange visual representations of audio processes and signal flow. These softwares are typically harder to use than (1) and (2), but the user can construct custom applications for greater specificity than in linear sequencing or sample/loop triggering.

(4) Textual language music tools
These are programming languages with 'music commands' specified as part of the language. They have a steep learning curve and are typically (but not exclusively) popular with academics and users with a greater interest in tool development than in musical composition. They are very general purpose and in a sense are the basis of all the above.

Table 8.1 *Types of music software and well-known examples*

Type of music software	Popularly known examples
Linear sequencers	Logic Pro, Cubase, ProTools
Sample and loop triggers	Ableton Live, Sony's Acid Pro
Music visual programming	MaxMSP, Reaktor
Text languages	SuperCollider, C-Sound

Of interest here, perhaps because they allow us to look at the studio more as an inventor's laboratory, are the programming languages. As described earlier, one kind is based on visual representations of audio elements that can be chained together and the other is based on the more traditional command-line programming languages. Visual programming languages in music/audio tend to be quite user-friendly, as they allow you to 'see' the flow of data. Yet both visual and textual approaches have their advantages, when it comes to experimenting with sound, over traditional sequencer software. Although they inevitably also impose some stylistic biases, you will find it easier to experiment as you can literally start with a blank slate and nothing pre-set. Let's look at them in more detail.

The graphic approach

Graphic programming environments for music enable you to build software synthesisers, or audio processors or even algorithmic music-making programs.[28] They allow you to experiment by connecting different graphic objects with virtual cables to control or process audio. Some of these modules, also called objects, represent your hardware units (delays, reverbs, compressors, amplifiers, etc.), others represent MIDI processors and computer control, and in environments like MaxMSP/Jitter or PD, they can represent video processing and playback units.

MaxMSP/Jitter and PD

Key languages in this category are *Max* (Max-MSP-Jitter), *Pure Data* (PD), *Reaktor*, *AudioMulch* and *OpenMusic*. They all work in a similar fashion, so perhaps by looking at one which is representative, we can get a better idea of how they work. Max is possibly the best-known visual programming language for music, but I will also comment on PD for reasons that will become clear later on.

Max 5, marketed by Cycling '74,[29] is a set of software objects conceived by Miller Puckette in 1988 at the *Institut de Recherche et Coordination Acoustique/Musique* (IRCAM), in Paris, and later significantly rewritten and improved by David

Zicarelli,[30] who runs Cycling '74. Max was given its name as a homage to computer music pioneer Max Mathews, who created the first computer music programming languages named MUSIC-N ('N' being the version number); Max is said to descend from MUSIC-V due to its similar modular approach.[31] Puckette intended it as a way of describing or visualising control and signal flow in a unified graphic environment.[32] Because Max was first developed at IRCAM in the mid to late '80s, it initially became useful as a tool for controlling their *4X* signal-processing engine via MIDI from a Mac computer (it was the only way they could control the audio processor from the Mac at the time).

Max was first called 'Patcher', after the visual representation of modules connected together by virtual patchcords I mentioned earlier, reminiscent of the way analogue modular synthesisers were programmed. A new Max document is still called a 'patcher'. It is a blank page to which you can add and connect objects like sliders, number boxes, buttons and even graphics (see Figure 8.1). Some objects perform functions (which means they 'do things') like sound processing or data control. Sound-processing objects carry a tilde at the end of their name, to indicate to the user that they process audio: delay~, fft~, dac~, etc. Control or data objects have names like 'counter', 'select', 'abs', 'random', etc., which also tend to be descriptive of what they do. Objects have data inlets and outlets through which they can be interconnected. Apart from data, Max sends *bangs* from one object to another. A bang is an instruction that prompts an object to perform the function it is programmed to do. For example, sending a bang to the object called 'random' causes it to generate a random integer between 0 and a set number (excluding that number); i.e. 'Random 5', when a bang is received, will generate any number from 0 to 4.

Although Max started purely as a means of controlling data, it soon developed beyond that. Audio was added by David Zicarelli in the '90s as a set of externals called *MSP*,[33] and video was added in 2003 as another set called *Jitter*. Today, Max includes both, and it presents the user with a very comprehensive package of objects as well as independently created libraries of externals that can be further added by the user if they wish to. There is a very active community contributing to Max and a multitude of freely exchanged patches (known as *abstractions*) that allow novices to experiment easily by modifying parameters or adding more objects. Thanks to its excellent helpfiles, tutorials and manuals, Max is very popular at universities and with independent artists. In Figure 8.2 we see a Max 5 patch; observe how the objects double up as interface widgets.

The open source alternative to Max is Pure Data or PD.[34] This language is also very popular and is open source software. This means that anyone can contribute to the source code to improve it and that when *builds* are made (source code made into executable versions of the software), they are distributed freely. Miller Puckette, the

MAX OBJECTS FOR CONTROL OF DATA, AUDIO AND MUSIC

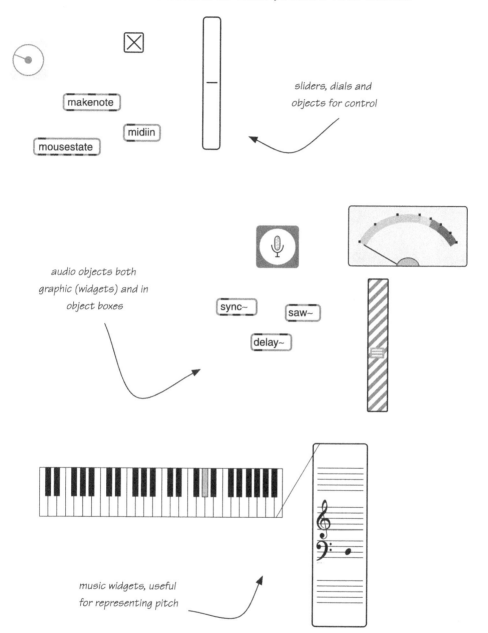

*sliders, dials and
objects for control*

*audio objects both
graphic (widgets) and in
object boxes*

*music widgets, useful
for representing pitch*

Figure 8.1 A variety of Max objects. Courtesy of Cycling '74

A TYPICAL **MAX 5** PATCH

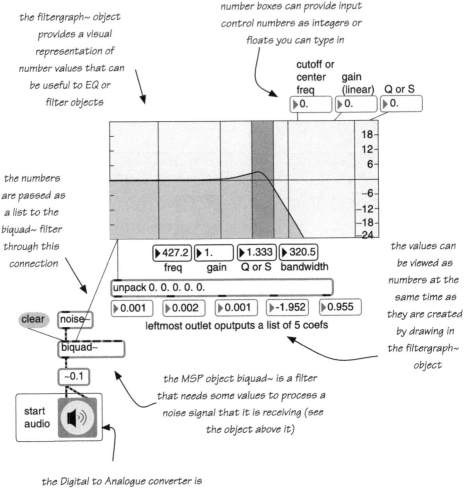

Figure 8.2 A typical Max 5 patch. Courtesy of Cycling '74

original author of Max, is also the author of PD, and this explains the great similarity to Max. PD also deals with audio and video as well as control data and is free to download. Originally, Puckette developed PD to improve on Max data structures at the time, as well as adding non-audio signals like video.[35] To the end user, in spite of the different underlying programming approaches, they are very similar and it is fairly easy to learn one if you know the other.

More commercially oriented graphic programming environments like Reaktor and AudioMulch have appeared in the wake of Max and PD. In particular, Reaktor (developed by Native Instruments) seems to have a strong following and places great importance on the visual beauty of the programming widgets. The company has also been savvy in marketing its product by providing, from the start, impressive sounding and looking examples (although sometimes at the expense of processing speed). Native Instruments also markets a number of popular software products for DJs and guitarists, which arguably gives them a greater potential clientele.

Finally, an interesting graphic programming environment to mention is Open-Music (OM) because it uses musical notation objects, allowing for a more traditional treatment of pitch and rhythm.[36] OM is based on the computer language Common Lisp and the Common Lisp Object System (CLOS). OpenMusic was developed at IRCAM in the early '90s with composers in mind and deals with music notation objects as well as audio.

The text approach: coding

Chances are that as a music producer, film composer or musical director you will never have to program computer music at the code level. However, if you are serious about music technology, chances are you will. Code, or writing instructions for a computer to do things, is where it all starts. The thinking required to code as compared to graphic programming environments is not really that different. Coding computers for sound requires a logical flow of instructions telling the computer what to do with the audio signal. If you would like to become a serious developer you probably need to explore the C programming language in one of its varieties (C++, C#, etc.), but you can still do quite a lot with computer music languages for composition and improvisation. Having learned both graphic programming environments and traditional code, I think that you need a good working knowledge of both if you want to practise digital music to any degree. It is hard, but so is playing the cello!

Not all computer languages are created the same. Some require you to code absolutely everything from very basic instructions: this is what we call 'low level'. Computer music programming languages like *Csound, SuperCollider, Common Music, ChucK* or *Impromptu*, on the other hand, work at a higher level. This means that some instructions actually contain many low-level commands, yet to the user they look like a simple word. For instance, in SuperCollider, writing:

```
{SinOsc.ar}.play
```

results in the playback of a sine wave at 440 Hz (which is the default pitch in this case); the word 'SinOsc' tells the computer to perform a function and create a sine wave through building a specific type of synth. This is complicated, but is actually made to look easy by encapsulating the process in a word or a short command. There is no point in reinventing the wheel every time you want to ride your bike, so high-level languages are usually a good thing!

The main difficulty with programming languages for music is that before you can make a sound there may already be a steep learning curve to be experienced. For this reason, it is worthwhile choosing languages that can give instant feedback to the user. For the computer to interpret text instructions, these need to be *compiled*. If the language you are using allows you to compile instructions within its own environment, as you go along, then you will learn faster because you can try things out quickly. In this sense, a language like SuperCollider is ideal as you can type your instructions and compile each line separately if you wish.

SuperCollider was presented by James McCartney at the International Computer Music Conference in 1996;[37] since then, the language has had a major rewrite in the early 2000s and become open source.[38] It has a very active community that ensures the language continues to grow. SuperCollider is ideal for experimentation with audio, for it was designed for musical creativity. In McCartney's own words, his motivations behind designing SuperCollider were 'the ability to realize sound processes that were different every time they are played, to write pieces in a way that describes a range of possibilities rather than a fixed entity, and to facilitate live improvisation by a composer/performer'.[39]

Another important computer music language is Csound. A descendant of the MUSIC-N series by Max Mathews, Csound was originally created by Barry Vercoe in 1986 while at the MIT Media Lab. This language requires you to create code to define your instruments and a score for them to play. It is a venerable language to say the least and has an abundance of resources available for synthesis. There are also fine resources for learning it, including *The Csound Book* edited by Richard Boulanger, which covers synthesis techniques in depth in a number of articles covering synthesis, processing and programming including topics like granular synthesis and mathematical modelling.[40]

There are many more languages as well as extension libraries for computer music.[41] Two more are worth mentioning. ChucK was developed by Ge Wang and Perry Cook and presented in 2003 and is used by the Princeton Laptop Orchestra (PLOrk) and the Stanford Laptop Orchestra (SLOrk).[42] It is designed to be easily used in live-coding situations and for quickly prototyping compositions.[43] *Impromptu* is also intended for live-coding performance; created by Andrew Sorensen and presented in 2005, it aims to allow the artist programmer to create, modify, distribute and evaluate their code on-the-fly.[44] Finally, *Wiring* is a programming environment coupled with an electronics input/output board which is intended, beyond music, for 'teaching and learning computer programming and prototyping with electronics', introducing users to the world of hardware and allowing those interested to extend their musical ideas beyond software experimentation.[45]

More tools you should know about

As we have discussed earlier, tools influence the way you use them. The way they are presented, how accessible their various capabilities are, how fast they are to learn — all these things determine what you will do with any given tool, up to a point. We have commented on some graphic environments and command-line interfaces, and I would like to end this chapter by mentioning some software programs that present the musician with unusual interfaces that can aid you in experimenting with sound. *Metasynth*, a commercial program by U&I Software,[46] provides the user with a series of environments where sound can be drawn on screen to be synthesised, or its spectrum analysed and reshuffled. *Usine*,[47] another commercial application, allows live sampling, effects processing, sound design and sequencing, again using a novel graphic interface where the user can draw sound. *IxiQuarks*, an open source program built on SuperCollider by Thor Magnusson, provides a set of innovative tools for sound design and manipulation as well as live performance, including a predator–prey game-like interface for triggering sounds among many original and compelling GUIs.

In terms of mobile platforms (smartphones and tablets), software like Jan Trutzschler's GLISS or Nick Collins's TOPLAP and iGendyn make use of the touch surface to further use drawing gestures for sound control and synthesis. Brian Eno's *BLOOM* and *Aura Flux* by Hige Five use touch and the visual arrangement of shapes to create generative ambient music.

With the arrival of multi-touch surfaces for smartphones and the impending tablet 'boom',[48] the list of applications allowing people to experiment with sound by touch and drawing gestures is actually endless! Related to these are tangible user interfaces like the ReacTable,[49] which have helped inspire modes of control now found on mobile devices (having started as a bulky table top interface, there is now even a mobile ReacTable). The present trend seems to be towards creating playful experimentation interfaces on mobile devices as these have brought multi-touch surfaces to the masses. Regardless of the lifespan of any of these tools, the opportunities for creating and experimenting with sound are truly democratic and the future seems to be pointing towards increasingly open participation in music and a constellation of networked studio labs.

Chapter 9

Controllers: new creative possibilities in performance

New performance scenarios

> *Playing traditional musical instruments presents us with a straightforward model*
> *of performance: some effort is invested in plucking, hitting, rubbing or blowing and*
> *some sound is produced with more or less control. That is: physical effort causes*
> *and affects sound, and so, musical output. Computer music seems to have destroyed*
> *this model. Press a button – which takes minimum effort – and you can hear a*
> *nuclear explosion, or whale-song, or a landslide or the interior perspective of a 747*
> *airplane! Minimal effort can produce maximal sound, or so it seems. For this reason*
> *alone, we can safely say that digital music has brought us unique models of musical*
> *performance. In this chapter we discuss the topic of controllers for performing with*
> *computer music based instruments.*

The appearance of digital musical instruments, like keyboard synthesisers, drum machines, customised electronic instruments or even music performance software (for DJing or manipulating sound files on stage) has required us to develop new skills. And so, in musical performance, we often find ourselves wanting to do one or more of the following:

- Triggering ready-made audio files (samples or loops);
- Creating sounds through synthesis and manipulating them on-the-fly;
- Processing or extending electrically or mechanically produced sound (made by traditional musical instruments, including electric guitars, pianos and basses or anything that produces an interesting sound when beaten, rubbed or blown).

The first two of these options remain quite independent from traditional instrumental playing skills. To perform music with a game controller or trigger samples by hand gestures aimed at a video camera linked to a computer it is not necessary to have any real musical instrument skills, just to be musical. The third option is more dependent on traditional skills, because it may involve having to play an instrument or coaxing sound out of an object with the same kind of playing skills you would use, say, as a percussionist. But then, depending on how involved the processing of sound is, the player may be limited to very simple actions. You can easily (and perhaps often) find yourself in a performance scenario where you are doing all of the above. For this reason alone, musical performance and notions of virtuosity in playing are being redefined. This chapter, then, provides an introduction to new instruments or control devices for music generated or aided by computer music software.

Controlling digital music

Computer-based musical instruments or digital musical instruments are different from traditional ones in that the parts of the instruments do not make a unified acoustic whole: they don't vibrate together.[1] Digital musical instruments receive an input which has to be interpreted as control instructions to make a sound, while the source of sound (the computer or microchip) is separate from this input (or control surface). This separation became apparent when we started controlling synthesisers with computers in the early 1980s. The MIDI spec allowed, as mentioned in Chapter 2, for a 'LOCAL ON/OFF' message that allowed the user to disengage the physical music keyboard from the digital synthesis engine within an instrument. The practical use of this was to avoid the synth playing the current sound preset when the user was trying to access a different timbre inside a multichannel instrument, or indeed to stop the keyboard from sounding, say, a piano when the user was trying to sequence a string arrangement. With LOCAL OFF, the user could make sure that the music keyboard was just a controller, not playing any sound unless expressly channelled by the sequencer to do so.

In traditional instruments, the player has some sort of tactile feedback when playing. For instance, the tension of a guitar string will let you know how far you are 'bending' a note with your left hand and you can adjust accordingly to produce the desired intonation. Since the decoupling of source and playing surface in digital musical instruments mentioned above has become more usual (as evidenced by the growth in the controller keyboards market), the player has a new problem: there is no longer much tactile feedback from their actions – a synthesiser keyboard will feel much the same no matter how deeply you depress the key, unless the instrument programmer has routed the MIDI aftertouch messages to a significant aspect of the sound. Even then, what is an intuitive effect for a programmer might not be so for the player, so we cannot take for granted that the feedback will feel correct even if it has been pre-mapped.

The good news is that, thanks to our games consoles and other electronic controllers used in daily life, we are accustomed to interacting remotely with digital devices. This inadvertently prepares us for digital musical instruments.[2] In fact, we

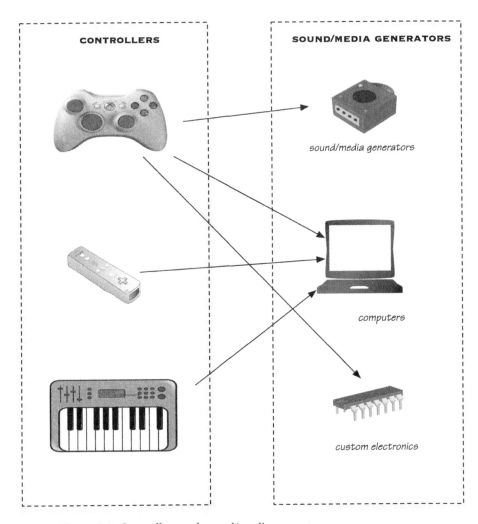

Figure 9.1 Controllers and sound/media generators

can create our own digital musical instruments by repurposing devices used in daily life and connecting them with the right communication standards; see Figure 9.1.

By using various protocols, including MIDI, and a network communication standard called OSC (Open Sound Control)[3] almost any controller whose data we can capture can be used to input data for sound synthesis or playback control of audio software.

There are many unconventional controller surfaces appearing on the market and providing an interesting panorama of options for digital musicians. Up to now, we have been accustomed to using keyboards for controlling synths and knobs and dials for changing the sound, but handheld devices like videogame joysticks and remote game controllers are becoming ever more sophisticated and widely available.

Advances in computer vision are making it possible to produce commercial game systems that work by natural human gestures (hand signals, waving, body movement, etc.), but it remains to be seen how successful these systems will be in the long run.[4] It is also important to note that the development of multitouch surfaces in smartphones and tablet computers is inspiring the creation of many innovative music and creative audio applications quite separate from games. Yet regardless of whether you use physical controllers or capture the waving of hands in the air, you will, in the end, be faced with very similar issues. Namely, to work out what kind of input from you as a performer will change which aspect of the sound the computer is producing. This is what we call 'mapping', and I would call 'the mapping conundrum', as it is not an easy task at all.

Mapping?

The need for thinking about mapping is clear when you consider how a human may interact with a computer (which is essentially what a synth does nowadays). In the work on physical interfaces in the electronic arts by Bert Bongers, we see how the idea of human–computer interaction can be applied to a digital musical instrument.[5] Put simply, the human is capable of acting upon the instrument by using their body to effect sensors (a keyboard, a sensor strip, a light sensor, ultrasound, etc.). These are, in effect, inputs processed by the computer and evaluated according to software, which then generates some actions, like making a sound to be amplified and played through a speaker. The human, in turn, senses the result of their actions and adjusts their playing accordingly. All this means that we may program our digital musical instrument to change the sound dynamically in response to our input, so we can perform it expressively. This can be done by carefully assigning controller actions to different synthesis parameters. For instance, with a straightforward MIDI keyboard controller one can map aftertouch to filter cut-off (to get a sound to brighten as you 'dig' into the keyboard), use the modulation wheel to control filter resonance (to change the brightness of the sound as you play) and map velocity to amplitude envelope release (to make louder sounds have a longer release time, for an impression of reverberation). Things become less intuitive when you use general purpose controllers like a Wiimote or a standard Xbox-type controller. Just remember that mapping is very important: it determines the playability and expressiveness of your digital musical instrument.

Feedback

Once you have chosen your mapping strategies, you need to decide on how to communicate to the player that those strategies are successful *as they play*. We become aware of our instrument's response through our senses. Different communication channels will carry the feedback we need as players:[6] seeing where our hands are positioned, feeling the playing surface through touch and, most importantly, hearing the result of our actions. Depending on how sophisticated your sensors are, you could also involve the sense of smell, resistance to touch, the feeling of a surface texture, and so on. And, since we are dealing with music software systems, the computer can also behave with intelligence (remembering players' actions and executing set actions according to sensor input) and interact with the player for an even more complex relationship.[7]

The amount of feedback you can give to a player will depend on specific controllers. You may have a controller which feels 'precise' simply because the buttons are very responsive (for example, they don't stick when pressed) or because the device vibrates in your hands as an immediate response to an action (the Wiimote and other game controllers have this feature and it is often coupled with rumbling sound effects in game; it can provide the user with a sensation of effort).

Finally, remember that the effectiveness of feedback will depend on how controller and sound generator are mapped. For instance, if your device works on accelerometers (like many smartphones have and which, together with their multitouch surface, gyroscopes and other sensors, makes them interesting for sound control), you need to map the accelerometer values properly so that waving the device will feel like the user has great control over the audio feature that you decide waving will affect. If you are controlling pitch-bending and a strong shake of the device produces very little change in the sound, your feedback is poor as you are expending more effort for less result. You get the idea . . . imagine a whammy bar on an electric guitar that hardly bends the sound even when you push it as far as it will go! Figure 9.2 illustrates the idea of controls mapped to selected sound parameters for musical performance.

Where do you start?

Armed with the knowledge that you can (a) construct, hack or redirect the data of a controlling device like a game pad, smartphone or midi fader-board; (b) work out some strategies for mapping its controls to changes in the sound generation; and (c) create as much feedback as possible for the player, how would you start creating your own digital musical instruments?

Scenario 1: You can use commercial MIDI controllers. Although you could, of course, simply hook them up to the virtual instruments bundled with your digital audio sequencer, which would be no more than the same sort of thing we normally do when sequencing. However, if you try linking all the faders on a USB fader board to parameters of a soft-synth, you will get a taste of what a digital musical instrument

CONTROLS   **SOUND GENERATION**

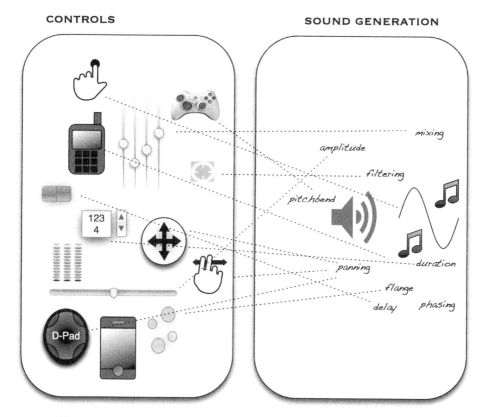

Figure 9.2 Control mapping for performance

is with a negligible investment of time and equipment. You will be actually using an external control – that makes no sound on its own – and you will be controlling your sound-generating software residing in the computer. All you need to do is to sustain a note and start playing with the assigned faders. This simple exercise already presents you with mapping challenges: what order should you assign the faders in so they are intuitive to use? What parameters will you target so that the sound can be changed noticeably? How will you organise the controller assignments so that the sound is playable expressively in real time?

Scenario 2: You can control synths you create using music programming languages. The most popular music computing languages for this would be PD, Super-Collider or ChucK, which are open source and thus free, or MaxMSP, which, although not initially free, relies on an active and collaborative community of programmers who freely exchange patches. All of these will have facilities to read the USB port of your computer and can then work with MIDI; further flexibility is given by other externals that allow you to access specific network ports for transmission and reception of OSC messages. Although MIDI and OSC are the easiest choices for

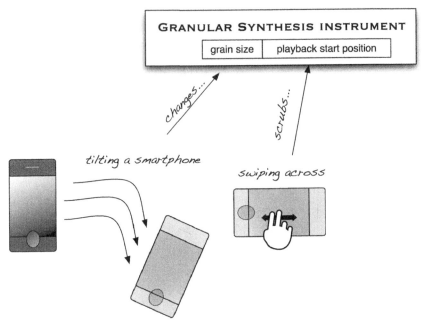

Figure 9.3 Tilt and swipe actions can control an instrument
Controlling a granular synth from a smartphone, you could assign tilt to grain size (more tilt → larger grain) and swiping across the screen to sample playback position.

non-programmers, reading the input of your controllers through a computer's serial port allows you to use arbitrary protocols. You can also talk to any device plugged into a USB port via messages from your computer's operating system (known as operating-system calls).

In this scenario, your efforts go into creating a custom software synth or sampler that can be musically controlled by data input from a remote device. This will allow you to enable data input for sound parameters that may not usually be found on commercial synths. The simplest choice may be to use controllers that already contain rotary knobs and faders and send MIDI. But unusual game controllers, smartphones, touch surfaces and general computing devices can also provide you with effective control over your synth via OSC. In any case, it is relatively easy to use any USB-compatible controller, as there are plenty of utility applications for translating the information arriving through the USB port into OSC or MIDI, as well as many software extensions to programming environments that will give you access to OSC directly, as mentioned earlier.

Scenario 3: Build it yourself. As mentioned earlier, with a little more preparation than using a standard USB game controller or routing sensors that have a USB

Table 9.1 *Some common sensors*

Sensor	What it does
Accelerometer	Measures the acceleration it is subjected to; it can be bought as a separate component but is commonly found on smartphones
Gyroscope	Measures orientation
Inclinometer	Measures inclination; it tells you if it is being tilted and in what direction
Photoelectric sensor	Detects the proximity of an object by means of light
Photoresister	Changes the resistance in an electric circuit depending on how much light it is exposed to
Pressure sensor	Measures how much force is applied on it
Torque sensor	Measures torque of rotation
Heat sensor	Measures the flow of heat
Ultrasonic sensor	Measures the proximity of an object in a similar way to a sonar

connection into your computer, you can assemble your own controllers from separate electronic sensors. These are relatively inexpensive and a great variety is available to buy online or even at your local electronics shop.[8] Table 9.1 shows a representative list of sensors you can easily find.

Typically, once you have chosen your sensors, you will need a digital interface to capture their data and send it to the computer. This is done by using electronic prototyping boards of which, among many options and depending on your project, perhaps the most popular is the Arduino.[9] You will also need to create some kind of support for your sensors and your circuit board so it can be used in performance; this can border on hardware hacking (of which more in Chapter 10). The beauty of this approach is that your control over both the sensor system and the synthesis engine is limited only by your own creativity.

More on communication between devices

We discussed MIDI in Chapter 2, but we have not really discussed OSC, so perhaps this is a good opportunity for a brief discussion. If you read the note to my first mention of 'OSC' (note 3) you will already know that it is a protocol for communicating computer music devices. This means that it is a set of conventions on how to format data so it can be shared, i.e. one device (like a videogame controller) can send messages to computer music software (like SuperCollider) in a way that it can understand. As we saw with MIDI in Chapter 2, messages can be formatted so that data can be sent efficiently. Yet, in the case of OSC, the limitations of MIDI don't apply. For instance, MIDI only allows pitch to be represented by the numbers 0–127, yet in OSC we can decide what set of numbers will represent pitch and how precisely it will do so, thus we can send OSC messages for pitch with as much precision as necessary.

The key difference between OSC and MIDI is that the latter presupposes what messages can be sent and, in doing so, is already determining what the recipient will (should) be like. This is to say that by sending Note-On and Note-Off, MIDI assumes the recipient will respond to triggers of this kind. MIDI also assumes that the device may understand Pitchbend and to what resolution (because in MIDI that is fixed to −8k to 8k roughly), that it has a limited set of possible controller numbers to be used, and so on. OSC, on the other hand, assumes nothing: you can make up your OSC message name and what types of data it will carry. This makes it very flexible.

OSC functions on a network, so it benefits from higher speeds than MIDI and from being able to be sent through the same ports you would use for the internet. In fact, every OSC message needs a basic address to where it is sent. The 'name tags' you make up for your messages will be sent relative to that address; again, this is supremely flexible! For instance, you create a synthesiser that is connected through the network to an address (like you see for internet settings) named 127.0.0.1 and you use a given port, let's say 57120.[10] OSC allows you to send messages to different parts of your synth 'living' at that address,[11] so if you send something like '/pitch, 2000', it works out this is an address relative to 127.0.0.1. If you were to change the base address, everything relative to it will change automatically.

OSC is so flexible you can even send text, which as a data type is known as a 'string', so you could create a chat window within the interface for a software synth you design; this could allow you to communicate with other users of your synth during a performance, for example.

To do all this, OSC is based on the computer sciences concept of a *client–server* architecture. In this scheme, the message sender is known as the client and the message receiver is known as the server. You may be thinking ahead and realising that this could allow for several clients to send the same type of messages to the same server containing a software synth, which is another advantage over MIDI.[12] Provided your software instantiates the synth on command, you could even have many musicians sending OSC to the same synthesiser.

For a plus on the MIDI side: it's important to note that MIDI can be used with relatively simple setups; so, for instance, you can connect a videogame controller through a USB to your computer and, by using the right extensions for your software, you can read the control data and translate it into MIDI. Popular applications like *osculator* bridge the gap between controllers and software using OSC, but then send MIDI.

Sources of information about new interfaces

When you hook up controllers or sensors to your synths or music software in a customised way, you are creating new interfaces for your musical instruments. In doing so you are, in effect, looking for the most efficient way to control digital sound for musical purposes. Since the late 1990s this has become a strong trend in the music technology community. In computer science, this field is known as HCI or human–computer interaction (also dealing with human–technology interaction more generally). In 2001, the *Special Interest Group on Computer–Human Interaction* (SIGCHI) held a workshop at their *Conference on Human Factors in Computing Systems* that dealt with new interfaces for musical expression. From this event, a new group was born that has gathered enough momentum to establish an important annual meeting in the music technology calendar: the International Conference on New Interfaces for Musical Expression, or NIME.[13] Every year, researchers, students and inventors gather to share their latest practical innovations in musical HCI, as well as to present academic papers on the subject.

If you visit the NIME website and search for the proceedings you will find literature covering a fantastic variety of inventions and improvements in digital music instruments. Areas covered include controllers and interfaces (as we have been discussing in this chapter). They also look at new software tools and design issues, mapping arbitrarily selected sets of data to sound as a way of representing those data (sonifications), the use of mobile technologies (including, but not restricted to, smartphones), computational issues, mapping strategies, robotic music, collaborative tools for performance, innovations in sensor technology and interactive computer systems with artificial intelligence.

In the music industry there are also annual and biannual conferences that showcase the newest technologies available for music-making as well as audio recording; not as innovative as NIME, but at least tried and tested and (mostly) ready to be shipped to consumers. The more important ones are the National Association of Music Merchants (NAMM)[14] and the Frankfurt Musikmesse.[15] Although NAMM was originally an American association, it represents music merchants worldwide as well as running the well-known biannual trade show. They also lead many educational initiatives and provide grants that encourage music-making and some degree of research. Musikmesse is a similar initiative to the NAMM trade show, but held in Europe. Last, but by no means least, the Audio Engineering Society (AES) is an international organisation where innovation in music technology is showcased.[16] Although their meetings function in a similar way to a trade fair (providing an exhibition area, etc.), their conferences provide a meeting ground for research and industry. Their electronic library is a key source for audio studies and they run valuable educational sessions and workshops.

Final thoughts

The use of custom controllers allows musicians to go 'beyond the grid', creating opportunities for novel ways to affect sound in performance. OSC and MIDI are protocols you should be conversant with as a professional music technologist: the more you know about them, the better. If you happen to be a computer programmer you should delve even deeper into technical aspects of communication protocols used for music; yet for most practitioners OSC and MIDI will suffice!

Electronic prototyping boards are quite inexpensive: take the time to build your own instrument controller – this 'learning by doing' is essential for music technologists. Remember the importance of mapping, discussed earlier. Always ask yourself: will the audience be able to tell how you are affecting the sound? Are the movements and gestures mapped for control commensurate with the sound being produced in some way? In general, make sure that your tinkering happens as preparation in the studio and not on stage, as you risk alienating your audience.

Chapter 10

Hacking electronics for music

Hardware hacking and circuit bending are the art of customising electronic circuits for sound production. This chapter aims to provide a historical overview and some practical tips for those who are seriously interested in tinkering with electronics for musical purposes!

Precedents

Hardware hacking involves intervening in or tampering with electronic hardware, as well as introducing transducers or found objects into the audio chain for unexpected filtering effects. Some hardware hackers have also acquired a taste for eavesdropping on the sounds of electromagnetism as picked up by transducers placed on unsuspecting hardware and use this in their artistic production (bringing observation into performance!).

To an extent, it could be said that all (historically) early electronic musicians were hardware hackers: early sound-production technologies were frail, and connecting several electric sound sources was always an exercise in customisation. This was aesthetically enhanced by the sound-hunting spirit of John Cage, along with Christian Wolf, Earle Brown and Morton Feldman in the early '50s. Their contact with Louis and Bebe Barron, who had already begun their music-making journey with their privately owned studio, marked the start of Louis Barron's experiments with circuit bending.

The Barrons' circuit manipulations for their film soundtrack work of the '50s represented a new approach to electronic music-making. The activity of electronic circuit design and building, amplification and harvesting of electronic sound became a compositional process in itself. They were influenced by the cybernetics theories of American mathematician Norbert Wiener (1894–1964). Wiener coined this term to denote the study of self-regulation systems, by means of feedback, both in animals and machines.[1] Louis Barron believed his circuits were, in a sense, self-regulating, and recorded onto tape the sound resulting from their feedback processes while experimenting with filtering and the balance between input and output of electricity.

The Barron's circuits did not actually constitute musical instruments for them but rather instances of electronic experimentation with organic 'living electronics';[2] in this sense they uniquely paved the way for today's hardware hackers and circuit benders.

Trying to find out how a trend starts is a tricky business, but hindsight is an invaluable tool. What is essentially tinkering with electricity in the quest for musical results is also an art form. Some of the early electronic music instruments came about unexpectedly. They resulted from customising circuits with the intention of producing, transmitting (as in telecommunications) or controlling sound, and sometimes as a by-product of other experiments. Examples of this are seen in many instruments developed in the late nineteenth and early twentieth centuries, like Elisha Gray's Musical Telegraph (1874), Cahill's Telharmonium (1898) or, later, Léon Theremin's 'Theremin' (1919). In the case of Gray's Musical Telegraph (1874–6) the instrument results from experiments (or perhaps hacking?) with telegraphy and what later became telephony. Gray transmitted and received Morse code over a single line using a pair of reeds tuned to different pitches. But it didn't end there: although unsuccessful in patenting a telephonic device (Alexander Graham Bell beat him to the patent office by one hour!) this led him to use the reeds connected to a loudspeaker so the pitches could be heard.[3]

To put it all in context, consider that later instruments like the Theremin were developed for music-making in the traditional sense. If we listen to music for the Theremin (for instance, Bernard Herrmann's score for *The Day the Earth Stood Still*, 1951) for all its novel electronic sound, it functioned much like a string instrument in articulation and expression. The earlier Musical Telegraph, in similar traditional spirit, had a piano-like keyboard with a two-octave range. What I want to highlight is that the thinking behind them was traditionally musical, even if the use of technology was innovative. So where can we find true precedents for hardware hacking? Enter the *futurist* musician's noise-making machines. The futurists were an artistic movement spanning poetry, art and music of the early twentieth century. They advocated a fascination with noise, movement, speed and strength as found in automobiles, airplanes, or even the activity and energy of city life. Such obsession with force, and even violence, is clear in artist Filippo Tommaso Marinetti's manifesto of 1909 (in fact, I dare you to read the manifesto and not be slightly scandalised by its political incorrectness! Try it: read article no. 9).[4] Yet one positive outcome of futurist theorising was a document by proto-sound-artist Luigi Russolo published in 1913. In *The Art of Noises*, a document seemingly written in response to a concert of music by fellow futurist musician Balilla Pratella, Russolo expounds his ideas on music and noise in his time and the role of machines in making it. He argues that in the acceptance of noise 'our hearing has already been educated by modern life'.[5] He goes further, advocating that we go beyond the noise that can be made with conventional instruments and actually build instruments that will make noise. He proposes six basic families of noises for a futurist orchestra and went so far as to build the instruments to make those noises: they were called *Intonarumori*. Even though these were mechanical instruments (although apparently some used electricity to power their motors), the spirit of hacking is obvious in the Intonarumori and arguably set an important precedent for an art of electric sound where the noise to be obtained is the result of instrument-building experiments.

Although John Cage (1912–92) made use of everyday objects for music-making and thus paid homage to the futurists, it was his fascination with chance and noise that helped set the scene for live electronic music and electronic music experimentation. Cage has been an inspiration for hardware hackers and circuit benders, even if some have not heard of him. I suspect it is no coincidence that after his association with Louis and Bebe Barron in the early 1950s, they would become interested in the cybernetics theories of Norbert Wiener. One could argue that Louis Barron's consideration of circuits as *organic* or gifted with the possibility to self-regulate is similar to Cage's view of silence as music (insofar as silence can be seen as the result of sounds coexisting without dominance of any one in particular and forming perhaps a balanced 'acoustic eco-system').[6] Apparently Cage was not overtly interested in cybernetics, but Bebe Barron considered Cage and Wiener were related through their interest in probability.[7] She also made the connection between probability, chance and entropy in the way electric circuits could be made to function and 'die'.

The Barrons built, and tampered with, electrical circuits in their studio with the intention of eliciting novel sounds, but never developed an actual instrument. They would create much of their electronic sound world by bridging between sections of circuits to redirect the current from one place to another even, as mentioned earlier, at the expense of the circuit burning out and then recording the result – including the burnout. The aim was to obtain interesting sounds at any cost. I would think this was probably the first instance of music being made at the expense of an instrument! These were, then, the first hardware hackers.

The synth explosion

The late 1960s and the 1970s saw the rise of the synthesiser as the core instrument of the electronic music studio; yet, as Collins points out in *Handmade Electronic Music*,[8] while hardly anyone could afford one, integrated circuits used 'under the hood' to power the synths were themselves getting cheaper. This represented, then, an obvious alternative to bold 'proto music technologists' who were looking to explore sound without corporate sponsorship. In the United States, with fewer traditional musical institutions in the European sense, the ground was fertile for this kind of experimentation to prosper. This helps explain how the creative hacking found in the work of David Tudor, or Alvin Lucier, for instance, would come to happen in that country. From an aesthetic point of view we could also say that hardware hackers have been, in a way, sponsored by the influence of John Cage, both in America and abroad.

To understand the significance of independent artistic experimentation out-with institutions, consider that in the late '70s, 'serious' sonic experimentation was reserved for the select few with cultural connections. Institutionally financed studios functioned as exclusive music research centres. This was in keeping with the European tradition, mentioned earlier, which was started in the late '40s and early '50s by *Radiodiffusion-Télévision Française* (French public radio and television) where Schaeffer would host his Groupe de Recherches Musicales or the correspond-ing patronage of *Elektronische Musik* by the *Westdeutscher Rundfunk* (WDR or West German Broadcasting, in Cologne) where Stockhausen and Boulez took their first steps in electronic music. A more recent institution like the famous Institut de Recherche et Coordination Acoustique/Musique (IRCAM), founded in Paris by Pierre Boulez and opened in 1977, was in line with its European predecessors in terms of exclusivity. Access to its resources was (and still is!) carefully guarded by a strict process of selection weighted by social connections between composers, audio engineers and 'contemporary music tsars'. In the face of this exclusiveness, the audio experimentation pioneered by the Barrons with no institutional backing or by Cage's later disciples like Tudor and in turn his younger associates like Nicolas Collins, Paul De Marinis, Ron Kuivila, Linda Fisher, Paul Edelstein and others, was truly revolutionary. Not to mention, even further afield, efforts like those of Reed Ghazala's circuit bending started in the 1960s. At that time, artists were showing that to be innovative in sound no institutional support was actually necessary; anybody who could solder a wire to a motherboard could potentially find a new sound.

Few institutions recognised this practice, but some understood the vision of the hacker and this is why we cannot fail to mention STEIM.[9] In the '70s, amidst so much institutional support for accepted electroacoustic music practice, STEIM fostered a different approach to electronic music, much more in tune with the hacking spirit. The *STudio for Electro Instrumental Music* in Amsterdam started in 1969 and was traditionally more open that its establishment counterparts. STEIM fostered a culture of innovation in electronic instrument-building, development of controllers, and software for live electronics performance that survives to this day, particularly emphasising the use of human touch to control electronic instruments.[10] Having welcomed hackers and electronic instrument-builders for many years, some interesting hack-instruments have been developed at STEIM including: the *Crackle Box*, *Crackle Synth* (a hack of the VCS-3 synthesiser) and *The Hands* by Michel Waisvisz; the *Open Terrarium*, designed by Laetitia Sonami ('A glass terrarium measuring 1×0.5 metres is filled with rubber gloves that sway like sea anemones. Each glove contains a little electric motor whose operation is controlled by sound');[11] the *Electronic Baby Mirror* by Dorothée Meddens and Michel Waisvisz, which consists of a doll studded with electronic sensors, connected up to a computer, which shows your image holding the baby and alters it and makes sounds according to how nice you are to the baby; the *Animal Symphony web*; the *Bebop Table*; and the *Office Organ*. These are just a few among many other unusual and exciting instruments developed through hacking at STEIM.

Benders and hackers

'Circuit bending' and 'hardware hacking' are terms that ultimately describe the 'intervention' of electronic machines whose original purpose in many cases may not be musical *per se*. As you can guess from my use of the word, this is closer to art *intervention* practice than it is to instrument-building (*lutherie*).

Art intervention (in one of its accepted meanings) is the practice of modifying a pre-existent work of art to create a new one. Part of the charm of an intervention is that the viewer is able to recognise the original work and appreciate the modifications introduced by the second artist. There is also another sense to the term 'art intervention', referring to a group of artists taking over a space with the purpose of making an artistic statement, but this is not the sense I am focusing on, although some hardware hacking can also be an intervention in this sense as performance art.

A classic example of hardware hacking (in both senses of the term) is *Rainforest IV* (1968) by David Tudor (1926–96), in which the performing/hacking team plays sounds through transducers affixed to solid objects which are then captured by contact mics subsequently amplified.[12] The intermediation of the objects transforms the sounds, effectively filtering them according to their characteristics. The result is then amplified over normal loudspeakers. We could say that *Rainforest IV* is not only the performance of the composition, but the actual process of building and installing the transduction systems.

As explained earlier, the hardware hacker often makes music out of found sounds by short-circuiting or, let's say, recircuiting electricity. In *Handmade Electronic Music: The Art of Hardware Hacking*, Nicolas Collins illustrates the search for sound 'intrinsic' to objects by quoting David Tudor: 'I try to find out what's there – not to make it do what I want, but to release what's there. The object should teach you what it wants to hear.'[13] Reed Ghazala expresses a related idea:

> At first, this free-for-all we're having with circuitry might seem out of place. Fact is, earthlings *musicalize* things. A coconut washed up on the shore could be

struck like the wood block of a percussion set. It could become the shell of a drum, the vessel of a flute, or the resonator of a fiddle. Idiophone, membranophone, aerophone, or chordophone, the simple coconut can be modified to fit all the major instrument groups of the orchestra. Add steel strings and magnetic pickup to the coconut fiddle and you've got the electronic group covered, too . . . [14]

Practical matters

At the time of writing, we see different expressions of the hacking spirit: combining analogue and digital technology, musical-toy modifications, circuit building and many more. This could seem a bit confusing, but there are two excellent sources for getting you started. One source is the book and related work to 'Hardware Hacking', a term used by Nicolas Collins of the Art Institute of Chicago. In *Handmade Electronic Music*, Collins takes us through the basics, all the while contextualising the practice of hacking within the work of the experimental electronic musicians of the mid twentieth century. This is, in my opinion, crucial as it provides the student with an aesthetic perspective as well as practical information. Collins was a former pupil of David Tudor and a member of the ensemble for the original *Rainforest IV*.[15] He has given numerous international workshops and also published widely on the subject, helping many to explore sound through electronic hardware modification. The other source for students is *Circuit-Bending: Build Your Own Alien Instruments* by Reed Ghazala.[16] Significantly less contextualised than Collins, but nevertheless offering some excellent practical advice for the rookie 'bender', Ghazala has offered his ideas in the form of articles and books and through his website.[17] Some of his instruments have been endorsed by famous artists of popular music like Tom Waits and Peter Gabriel.[18] Ghazala and Collins are by no means the only ones, but, as mentioned above, they have both been especially consistent at divulging the techniques and inspiring others in this field. Both sources, *hacking* and bending, are well worth investigating further if you are interested in making or modifying your own instruments (non-mains powered, please!).

Very basic knowledge

So, what do you need to know, in practice, about electrical circuits? In his hardware hacking workshops and in his books, Nicolas Collins emphasises that to be a music hardware hacker you don't need to know much at all about electricity: 'No previous electronic experience is assumed, and the aim is to get you making sounds as soon as possible'.[19] Reed Ghazalas tells us similarly: 'That's the beauty of circuit bending;

anyone can do it. You don't need to be an electronics guru or a [work]shop genius. All you need is the ability to solder and think outside the box.'[20]

The above idea sounds a little crazy, but is given sense for two reasons. Firstly, both authors demand that *all* hacking be done *only* with battery-operated devices or circuits. Secondly, that the hardware hacker is after the sound produced, not any utilitarian function of the circuit: so, if it sounds good, the wiring is correct (however long it takes for your design to burn down!).

But surely – you ask yourself – I need to know something about electricity? In practice, the answer is that you will learn as you go along. For a starter you need to remember that electronic devices do their work as a result of circuits that make use of electricity in various ways but mainly from resisting its flow (which includes storing it) and from changing its course.

Where to start

The recommended books by Collins and Ghazala will give you a very good guide into experimenting with circuits for sound production, but we can give you a few spoilers here to start you off.

Collins opens his hacking explorations with a simple exercise in electromagnetic voyeurism: *circuit sniffing*. He recommends to the apprentice hacker to find a cheap AM radio, switch it on, tune it to a spot where no stations can be heard and explore the electromagnetic emissions of other electrical hardware by putting the radio close to them.[21] By doing this you become familiar with the hidden sounds of computer hardware, portable audio equipment, phones and anything you can find.

Another easy experiment for beginners is recommended by Ghazala. It goes something like this:

1. Find a battery operated sound-making toy. It could be a talking doll or a baby driver's set (the one with an accelerator pedal, horn and steering wheel) or literally any toy that is meant to produce sound. This means it will have a speaker and some more or less complicated electronics.
2. Open it so you can see the electronics. You will see many components soldered to a common board, known as the circuit board.
3. Observe the components carefully and you will see different shapes and sizes and how they are connected in a very complicated circuit.
4. Switch the toy on.
5. Take a piece of wire and try making a contact between any given point on the circuit board and any other.
6. Listen to what happens to the normal sound the toy is meant to make.

A BASIC CIRCUIT

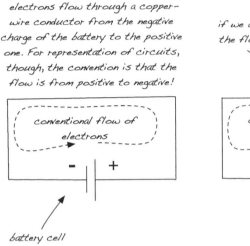

electrons flow through a copper-
wire conductor from the negative
charge of the battery to the positive
one. For representation of circuits,
though, the convention is that the
flow is from positive to negative!

conventional flow of

electrons

− +

battery cell

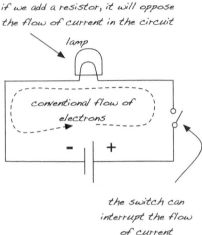

if we add a resistor, it will oppose
the flow of current in the circuit

lamp

conventional flow of

electrons

− +

the switch can
interrupt the flow
of current

Figure 10.1 The flow of electricity

7. Once you stumble upon an interesting sound, get a soldering iron and make it permanent.
8. You have now hacked/bent your first instrument!

In case this sounds less exciting than it is, you must try it out. Unexpected squeals, noises, glitches and even tones can be obtained this way. After soldering your wire you may then want to interrupt it with some sort of switch so you can turn the hack on and off at will.

By connecting the wire to different arbitrary points you are essentially redirecting the flow of current and, if the circuit is not 'shorted', the sound production can be stable.

Electricity flows through a circuit, and by convention we say it flows from the positive end to the negative. As it trickles down the circuit, it finds different obstacles that change its properties. Resistors make it harder for the current to flow and energy may be released as a consequence. Capacitors can store the current until it exceeds a certain amount that will allow it to continue flowing. Transformers can change the current from one voltage into another, and so on. The interesting thing for us is how, by including elements like resistors of various kinds (simple resistors, capacitors and inductors), we can get different sounds. In the example above, interrupting our new wire with a potentiometer would allow us to control how much of the 'found sound' we can produce. The potentiometer is a variable resistor and as we open it and let the current through, the sound changes. When we turn the potentiometer to zero, no current flows through the hack and the original sound remains unchanged. Following the sort of process described above, we could find several useful sounds in one device and turn them on and off at will through the use of switches and potentiometers to create a palette of sounds we could use in performance.

So, what does what?

In terms of getting started, it is useful to become familiar with the electrical components you are likely to find easily and can use for modifying your devices. Figure 10.2 shows a basic set that you will find useful in your hacking experiments.

In the Ghazala experiment described above, you could incorporate any of the components from Figure 10.2. The most immediately useful would be the switch, as mentioned above, but the photo cell would allow you to control the flow of current by waving your hand to block it from the light. In this way you could control the amplitude of the sound or the timbre, depending on where your cable is connected. The potentiometer will do a similar job, with the advantage that once you find the right amount of resistance, you can leave it dialled to the position you found. Connecting the LED will allow you to help visualise where the current is flowing. Capacitors are useful for filtering sound: this is their net effect on a sound signal, especially if combined with a resistor. If you place one along your selected connection, depending on the spec of the component you will get different filtering results, i.e. changes in timbre. 'Alligator clips' are very useful for this sort of experimentation because you can explore the circuit board for sound without having to solder things down, until you are sure of the usefulness of your connection. Finally, an assortment of mini-jacks and plugs will always come in handy, as will battery holders for your source of direct current (I cannot stress this enough, do not use power from the mains!).

Laying of hands?

This is an amusing expression that Collins uses to describe creating or modifying connections with your hands directly on the circuit board of a radio. This will work with other devices, not just the radio, but, as Collins explains, the radio contains most of the parts you would find in an analogue synth, including oscillators, noise generators, filters, amplifiers, ring modulation and access to live broadcast sound.[22] Ghazala also makes use of the body to help modulate circuit boards and often suggests you leave a contact exposed by soldering a piece of metal to a point where you know you can cause an effect just by touching and making your body part of

ELECTRICAL COMPONENTS

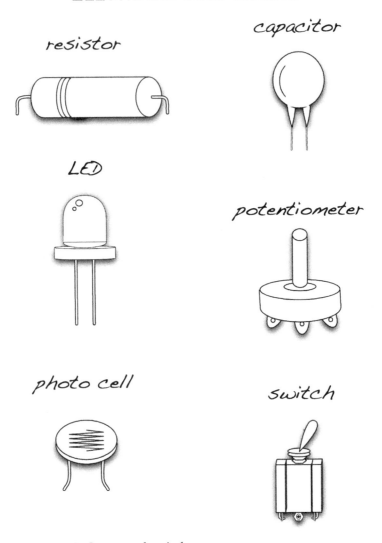

Figure 10.2 Common electrical components

the circuitry. This kind of mod allows you to have access to the circuit board after you place your hacked instrument in a custom case.

Finally . . .

The field of hardware hacking/bending is a rich and creative area. Some positively interesting and musical devices can be made with humble materials and an open mind. Any toy that makes sound patterns or speech will have an internal clock that you may also hack; this can lead to very interesting results. You will find that cheap microphones and speakers provide rich material for hacking and that even credit cards can make music if you can find an old tape playhead. Collins provides twenty-five rules of hacking in his book; they are all extremely useful even when they look merely entertaining. Here are my favourites:

Rule #1: Fear not!

Rule #2: Don't take apart anything that plugs directly into the wall.

. . .

Rule #14: Kick me off if I stick (Zummo's rule).

. . .

Rule #17: If it sounds good and doesn't smoke, don't worry if you don't understand it.

. . . [23]

Further avenues for exploration

Feeling adventurous?

I believe it is useful for a student to be aware of research relating to concepts explained in this book. The papers listed below are beyond the level of an introduction, but even if you just read their abstracts you will have an idea of what sorts of things you may be able to do in the future as a music technologist and what diverse areas can be covered. I have also included some 'classics' that are well worth a read even though technology may have moved on. Some of these papers are available for free on the internet by searching through sites like *scholar.google.com*;[1] for others you may have to check the digital library or journal collections of your educational institutions. So, here are some suggestions:

Audio

- If you are interested in the whole business of machine listening: 'Musical Genre Classification of Audio Signals' by George Tzanetakis and Perry Cook of the Computer Science Department of the University of Princeton. Published in the *IEEE Transactions on Speech and Audio Processing*, 10, 5 (2002), 293–302.
- For academic sound engineers: 'Engineering the Performance: Recording Engineers, Tacit Knowledge and the Art of Controlling Sound' by Susan Schmidt Horning in *Social Studies of Science*, 34, 5, Special Issue on Sound Studies: New Technologies and Music (Oct. 2004), pp. 703–31.
- If you want to check for the most detailed database of sound levels ever, go to: nhca.affiniscape.com/associations/10915/files/Noise%5FNav%2Exls.
  E. H. Berger, R. Neitzel and C. A. Kladden, 2008. 'Noise Navigator® Sound Level Database with Over 1700 Measurement Values'. E•A•R / Aearo Company and Univ. of Washington, Dept. of Environmental and Occupational Health Sciences, Seattle, WA.

- A historically important paper, since we always quote Nyquist when talking about sampling, is: H. Nyquist, 'Certain Topics in Telegraph Transmission Theory', trans. AIEE (American Institute of Electrical Engineers), 47 (April 1928), 617–44, from *Proceedings of the IEEE*, 90, 2 (2002). Available at: www.loe.ee.upatras.gr/Comes/Notes/Nyquist.pdf.
- A great all-round book on audio technology with some down-to-earth introductions to aesthetics on audio technology and including a brief discussion of how semiotics relates to sound design is: Gary Gottlieb, *Shaping Sound in the Studio and Beyond: Audio Aesthetics and Technology* (Boston, MA: Thomson Course Technology PTR, 2007).
- A great sampling primer: C. Roads and J. Strawn, *The Computer Music Tutorial* (Cambridge, MA, and London: MIT Press, 1996), 30–8.

Computer music

- On SuperCollider: J. McCartney, 'Rethinking the Computer Music Language: SuperCollider', *Computer Music Journal*, 26, 4 (2002), 61–8.
- On PD: M. Puckette, 'Pure Data: Another Integrated Computer Music Environment', in *Proceedings: Second Intercollege Computer Music Concerts* (Tachikawa) (1997), 37–41.

Human–computer interaction

- An introduction to digital music instruments: N. Schnell and M. Battier, 'Introducing Composed Instruments, Technical and Musicological Implications', in *Proceedings of the 2002 Conference on New Instruments for Musical Expression* (NIME-02, Dublin).
- On sequencers: M. Duignan, J. Noble and R. Biddle, 'A Taxonomy of Sequencer User-interfaces' (2005). Available at: www.music.mcgill.ca/~ich/research/misc/papers/cr1260.pdf.
- On laptop performance: M. Zadel and G. Scavone, 'Laptop Performance: Techniques, Tools, and a New Interface Design' (n.d.). Available at: http://citeseerx.ist.psu.edu/viewdoc/download?doi=10.1.1.118.9000&rep=rep1&type=pdf.
- On musical instruments: T. Magnusson and E. Hurtado, 'The Acoustic, the Digital and the Body: A Survey on Musical Instruments', in *Proceedings of the 2007 Conference on New Interfaces for Musical Expression* (NIME-07, New York).

Music and media

- If you are interested in sound effects in media: D. Miller and J. Marks, 'Mental Imagery and Sound Effects in Radio Commercials', *Journal of Advertising*, 21, 4 (1992).
- On sound effects for film and TV: J. Rose, 'Reality (Sound)bites: Audio Tricks from the Film and TV Studio', in *Proceedings of the 2003 International Conference on Auditory Display*, Boston, MA.
- On representing electroacoustic music: J. B. Thiebout, P. Healey and N. Kinns, 'Drawing Electroacoustic Music', in *Proceedings of the International Computer Music Conference* (ICMC-08, Belfast). International Computer Music Association.

Psychology

- An introduction to psychology of music with reference to electronic music: P. Toiviainen, 'The Psychology of Electronic Music', in *The Cambridge Companion to Electronic Music*, ed. N. Collins and J. d'Escriván. Cambridge: Cambridge University Press, 2007.
- Scientific discussion of music and emotion based on evidence presented by mirror neurons: Istvan Molnar-Szakacs and Katie Overy, 'Music and Mirror Neurons: From Motion to "e"motion', *Social Cognitive and Affective Neuroscience*, 1, 3 (2006), 235–41.

THE LEARNING CENTRE
TOWER HAMLETS COLLEGE
ARBOUR SQUARE
LONDON E1 0PS

Notes

1 Representing and storing sound

1 Named after German scientist Heinrich Hertz. To express frequencies above 1000 Hz we use kilo-Hertz or $1000 \times$ Hertz: thus 1000 Hz = 1 kHz.

2 Noise has many definitions depending on your angle. Musically, it will be any sound in which pitch cannot be perceived properly: slapping the piano lid, picking behind the nut of the electric guitar, etc. Acoustically, it will be the result of all frequencies present at the same time with random amplitudes at any given moment. For media theorists, it may be any unwanted element in communication. Culturally, it will be one thing for classical music lovers and another for Japanese *Glitch* enthusiasts. And so on!

3 Depending on manufacturer, middle C can be either MIDI note C3 or C4 depending on where they start from in identifying the MIDI range: if it is C-2 to G8, then it should be C3. Some define the range as being C-1 to G9, thus middle C will be C4. Independently of how we label the octave, the MIDI note number for middle C is always 60.

4 I was inspired by the explanation in Collins, 2009, p. 10.

5 Berger, Neitzel and Kladden, 2008.

6 You will find many charts comparing SPL on the internet; here is a good one: www. engineeringtoolbox.com/sound-power-level-d_58.html.

7 Without rounding them up, the numbers would be 0, 29.9, 60, 89.9, 109.9, 129.9, 140.

8 For an in-depth discussion of the sampling process, see Roads, 1996, p. 30.

9 Nyquist, 1928.

10 Loy, 2007, p. 13.

11 Roads, 1996, p. 13.

12 Collins, 2009, p. 16.

13 A good introduction to the perception of timbre and pitch can be found in Toiviainen, 2007, p. 226.

14 Collins, 2009.

15 Pronounced 'tahmbrah' – I am often amazed at how many people don't know this!

16 Loy, 2007b, p. 103.

17 Freely available at: www.klingbeil.com/spear/.

18 For further information, see www.informal.org/projects.htm.

19 Moore, 2000, pp. 213–44, includes a thorough discussion of this.

20 Suzuki *et al.*, 2003.

21 See Collins 2007, pp. 91–9, for more detailed information on this topic.

22 Although arguably all audio encoding systems are lossy!

23 More specific information is available at the Microsoft Developers Network, http: //msdn.microsoft.com/en-us/library/ms713497(VS.85).aspx.

24 In-depth information is available through the US Library of Congress: www. digitalpreservation.gov/formats/fdd/fdd000005.shtml (do follow the links at the end of the page for extensive information about chunks).

25 We will be covering MIDI properly in Chapter 2. At this stage in the history of music technology it would be very strange if somebody wasn't familiar with the term, but more later!

26 Rumsey and McCormick, 2009, p. 305.

27 For more information, see www.id3.org/.

28 There is an excellent and well-documented entry for AAC at http://en.wikipedia.org/ wiki/Advanced_Audio_Coding.

29 Rumsey and McCormick, 2009, p. 307.

30 www.aes.org/standards/about/.

2   A studio overview

1 The word is relatively new as it has only been in use since the twentieth century, referring to broadcast spoken word, reproduced sound or indeed the sound signal. Check the *Oxford English Dictionary* for more details on etymology.

2 At the moment there are some serious shareware low-cost alternatives, which allow you to do full productions, including Reaper (www.reaper.fm) and Ardour (www.ardour. org).

3 www.studer.ch/news/glance.aspx, also corroborated by many online resources.

4 Be aware that mixing desks are also known as mixing boards, or mixing consoles or just mixers.

5 For electroacoustic music in the tradition of the French multi-speaker 'orchestra', such as the Acousmonium of the Groupe de Recherches Musicales in Paris.

6 Roads, 1996.

7 On an analogue mixer you would not normally have the record enable buttons on the channel strip, as recording functionality is part of the actual recording device. This distinction is completely blurred in the software mixer of an audio sequencer.

8 Typically, your computer will allow you to create more than one instance of the same plugin so you can insert completely different settings in different tracks.

9 Sidechain inputs can also be found in dynamic processors (that deal with signal amplitude) like gates, expanders and compressors.

10 Also known as panning potentiometer, or pan knob, in hardware mixing desks.

11 This is because as the dB is the logarithm of a ratio between two measurements of power, or voltage or sound pressure level, when the measurements are equal, the ratio will be equal to 1 (1:1) and the logarithm of 1 is 0. Thus OdB but Unity (meaning '1') gain.

12 Rumsey and McCormick, 2009.

13 You will find many sources for this; these figures are taken from Davies and Jones, 1989.

14 Consulted at www.genelec.com/1036a/specs/.

15 Toiviainen, 2007, p. 221.

16 Moore, 2001, p. 250.

17 For a good simulation of tinnitus you can consult this recording at the British Tinnitus Association: www.tinnitus.org.uk/files/representation%20of%20tinnitus%20sounds%2032b.mp3.

18 d'Escriván, 2009.

19 Moore, 2001, p. 250.

20 Or... 'typically calculated as a power average across a uniformly distributed set of incident locations... [with] minimum phase' (Gardner, 1998, p. 28).

21 www.asha.org/Publications/leader/2009/090526/090526e.htm.

22 He might have been singing through headphones for all I could see, but I just want to illustrate that choosing a mic can define your sound quite markedly.

23 See Owsinski, 2009 for an accessible and more extended discussion of mic types and specifications.

24 See Rumsey and McCormick 2009, p. 37, for comprehensive explanations.

25 Which we will call $0°$ – remember that decibels are a measure of relativity between two values.

26 Huber and Runstein, 2010.

27 Rumsey and McCormick, 2009, p. 43.

28 Information on ambisonics can be found at www.ambisonic.net/, as well as at www.ambisonia.com/wiki/index.php/Main_Page and, finally, a reliable article exists at http://en.wikipedia.org/wiki/Ambisonics. I would strongly encourage the reader to find out more in these and other specialised sources.

29 www.aes.org/e-lib/browse.cfm?elib=11909.

30 http://tecfoundation.com/hof/05techof.html#13.

31 Abstract at http://www.aes.org/e-lib/browse.cfm?elib=11909.

32 '++' is a common symbol in computer music to denote chaining things together; also known as 'concatenation', from the Latin 'catena', which means chain.

33 www.midi.org.

34 There are exceptions to this structure like the bank select control that needs a most significant byte, or MSB, and a least significant byte, or LSB; this allows one instruction to give a coarse value and a second to give a fine value so instead of having just 127 values you can have 127 values for each of the 127 values of the MSB, yet this specialised use is mostly applied to hardware synths and unusual for most beginning music technologists. It's not rocket science, though, so the most advanced of you probably have learnt all you need to know just from reading this footnote.

35 Schmeder *et al.*, 2010.

36 Nick's software tools can be downloaded from: www.informatics.sussex.ac.uk/users/nc81/code.html.

37 http://mdsp.smartelectronix.com/livecut/.

3 Synthesisers, samplers and drum machines

1 For much greater detail and some variation in the classification headings, see Tolonen, Välimäki and Karjalainen, 1998, and Smith, 1991, these are both freely available online; also Reck-Miranda, 2002.

2 A friendly account of the early days of (computer) synthesis is offered by Serafin (2007, p. 203).

3 An interesting synthesis method of this kind, implemented in SuperCollider, is the dynamic stochastic synthesis generator by Iannis Xenakis and described in his book *Formalized Music* (Xenakis, 1992); refer to the SuperCollider helpfiles for the Gendy class for more information and sound examples.

4 Chusid, 2000.

5 Although not present in the Linn LM-1 Drum Computer, an expensive first effort in digital percussion sampling made by Roger Linn, its sound pervades the pop music of the 1980s and was key in making drum machines fashionable (Devo, The Cars, The Human League – a quick listen to 'The Things That Dreams Are Made Of' from *Dare* of 1981 with its Linn Drum introduction is an excellent example if you are not familiar with the sound).

6 The early sequencers were not much use in the GUI department; efforts by Yamaha with the QX1 or Roland with the MC-4 looked more like giant calculators than anything musical.

4 Live music technology (the FAQs)

1 Harrison, 2000.

2 *Ibid.*

3 Standard operating levels are described in many audio engineering textbooks. I have condensed the discussion you find here from the *Yamaha Sound Reinforcement Handbook* (Davies and Jones, 1989).

4 See Davies and Jones, 1989, p. 331.

5 See *ibid.*, p. 344.

5 Select, remix, mashup

1 Rosen, 2006.

2 It is probably not a coincidence, then, that as radio stations exercised more control on their music programming on marketing grounds, that DJs began to emerge as performers. I base this opinion on the fact that as radio stations diminished the 'musical curation' role of the DJ, they forced them out of the station and onto the dance floor, as it were.

3 Which is not to preclude instances of original radio artistry, it is simply to say that the time of the DJ as musician had not come. There is an interesting note on Wikipedia's 'mashup' entry that tells of a kind of mashup of songs created by Billie Buchanan and

Dickie Goodman in 1956. There may well be more experiments like this and even earlier, but I am taking the view that this only becomes significant when it starts to become accessible to all, as it did with the birth of Hip-Hop.

4 Dacks, 2007.

5 Gross, 1998.

6 That in turn gave rise to many other loudspeaker orchestras all over the academic world, with the most impressive and venerable today being the Birmingham Electroacoustic Sound Theatre, or BEAST, from Birmingham University, UK.

7 The AKAI MPC-0 had sixteen soft pads for performance input. They were sensitive to MIDI velocity as well as aftertouch, which meant that they could not only provide a MIDI trigger (by which pad is played) but also its velocity (thus yielding dynamics and expression) as well as aftertouch (MIDI information on the physical pressure on the pad before it is released, for controlling sounds before their release).

8 www.arduino.cc.

9 Although at the time of writing the process of licensing other artists' music is cumbersome in general, I have no doubt this process will become streamlined in the future as publishing/recording companies understand better the dynamics of contemporary music creation and can harness it to their advantage. Remixes tend to extend the useful life of songs that may have become archive material already or to revive forgotten hits, or serve as an advertisement for listeners to find the original piece.

10 Rosen, 2006.

11 You can read more widely on Afrika Bambataa and his importance in Hip-Hop in Toop, 2000.

12 Oswald, 2006, p. 137.

13 Cooper, 2001.

14 See Lethem, 2007 for a very informative article on plagiarism, borrowing, etc.

15 Preve, 2006, p. 87.

16 Creative Commons, 2010.

17 www.archive.org/details/LawrenceLessigRemix.

6 The producer

1 In looking at the role of the producer, many authors have contributed 'must read' texts: Mark Cunningham's (1998) history of record production goes through the details of how the role evolved with many insightful first-hand accounts; Virgil Moorefield (2005) takes a more analytical approach, and tries to identify trends that show the emergence of the producer and their possible obsolescence today (Moorefield shows, in the end, how anybody involved in music recording today is in fact (or *de facto*) a producer); and Howard Massey (2000) has compiled a useful selection of interviews with top producers in *Behind the Glass*. Trade journals often contain interviews and non-academic (but very useful) articles on the music production process. Part of the excitement in this field is due to its youth and the speed at which things have changed, and continue to do so.

2 Cunningham, 1998, p. 34.

3 Blake, 2009, p. 36.

4 Moorefield, 2005, p. 110.

5 www.youtube.com/watch?v=L2McDeSKiOU. Where turntablism is closer to instrumental practice, I would say controllerism is closer to production.

6 http://music.hyperreal.org/artists/brian_eno/interviews/downbeat79.htm.

7 Eno, 1983.

8 If you check the original article (Eno, 1983) you will notice that his knowledge of recording technology history is quite sketchy, but his theoretical grasp of the impact of the studio on music creation is insightful nevertheless.

9 Brock-Nannestad, 2009, p. 149.

10 Cunningham, 1998, p. 25.

11 These were short films to demonstrate the effectiveness of Warner Bros. sound-film technology named 'Vitaphone', which was based on synchronising acetate discs with the projected film to provide a soundtrack.

12 Murch tells the story of how they re-recorded speech transmitted and then picked up by radio for the backing 'telecommunication' speech tracks in *THX1138* (Ondaatje, 2002). It is interesting how re-recording can add ambience information to the result; this is often used to situate sound in a certain context (Murch calls it 'worldizing').

13 Widely available on youtube.com.

14 Cunningham, 1998, p. 30.

15 Slaven, 2003, p. 231.

16 See the liner notes of the *Revolver* EMI digital remaster of 2009.

17 The sleeve notes to *Dark Side* say clearly 'Produced by PINK FLOYD' (Pink Floyd, 1994), sadly not acknowledging the contribution of engineer Alan Parsons, who later became a well-known producer in his own right.

18 Everett, 2001, p. 174.

19 'Revolution 9' is essentially *Musique concrète* as practised by Pierre Schaeffer and Pierre Henry in *Symphonie pour un homme seul*, for instance (among other avant-garde predecessors known to Lennon possibly thanks to the influence of Yoko Ono).

20 Recorded from 24 September 1968 to 20 February 1969.

21 Blake, 2009.

22 George, 2004.

23 Ondaatje, 2002, p. 8.

24 http://web.archive.org/web/20031217063601/www.stockhausen.org/stockhausen+_by_david_paul.html.

7 Music, sound and visual media

1 Not as common in English as in other languages, the term plastic arts refer to painting and sculpture and any art form where you make an object that 'stays'. Music, by its very nature, disappears when it stops sounding, but recording allows us to capture it and treat it like sculpture.

2 Or the 'micro time scale' and 'macro time scale' as discussed by Curtis Roads in *Microsound* (Roads, 2004).

3 Cook, 2000, p. 98.

4 Chion, 1994.

5 Cook, 2000, p. 75.

6 Although this is both personal anecdotal evidence, supported by Chion's observations, it seems to me to be common sense.

7 Chion, 1994, p. 69.

8 *Ibid.*, p. 66.

9 Audio that can change as the media runs; film music cannot do this, but game music can.

10 Collins, 2008, p. 128.

11 www.gsoundtracks.com/interviews/folmann.htm.

12 I was a freelance consultant for Yamaha in the late '80s and worked creating styles (essentially programming stems) for these keyboards as well as creating original sounds (voicing) synthesisers for what was known then as the SY division.

13 Davies, 2010.

14 Davies, 1999, p. 78.

15 These two formats are used in Europe, Asia and Africa, with PAL also being used in Brazil and Argentina.

16 Used in the Americas and the Pacific coast of Asia, including Japan and Taiwan.

17 We discussed some of this earlier in the book, in Chapter 2, but I think there is no harm in reviewing it here.

18 Where frequencies below a set threshold will be directed to the subwoofer.

19 Needless to say, you will need to check with the video or game editor.

20 Sweetser and Wyeth, 2005; Grimshaw, Lindley and Nacke, 2008.

21 www.reuters.com/article/idUSN1032711620091110.

8 The studio as experimental lab

1 In the *Cambridge Companion to Recorded Music* (Cook *et al.*, 2009) there are several interesting contributions on this subject that I recommend highly, especially 'Recording Practices and the Role of the Producer' by Andrew Blake and other shorter texts by Michael Haas, Albin Zak and others.

2 In a nutshell: printing a representation of the recorded sound onto film so it could be played back by projecting light through it. To us, this imprint onto 35 mm film can look very much like an amplitude vs. time representation as found in any computer audio sequencer.

3 Davies, 2010.

4 *Ibid.*

5 Jordan, 1953.

6 I may be a bit generous here with the expression 'music itself', as strictly speaking we retain a transduction of the music, which is still a representation of its effect on another medium.

7 Cage, 2009.

8 Chusid, 2000, p. 59.

9 Landy, 2007.

10 Holmes, 2002.

11 Scott discussed this in a lecture on electronic music in radio and television at the Advertising Age convention in Chicago on 31 July 1962 (Chusid, 2000, pp. 111 and 131).

12 Ondaatje, 2002.

13 See Sullivan, 1987, for more.

14 Flans, 2005.

15 Crook, 1999, p. 4.

16 Sieveking, 1934.

17 Crook, 1999, p. 70. If you are interested in the original see Sieveking, 1934, pp. 64–8.

18 Draper, 1931.

19 Theisen, 1937.

20 Marshall, 2008. Radiophonic workshop members would later include Dick Mills, Brian Hodgson, Delia Derbyshire, Roger Limb, Peter Howell, Paddy Kingsland, Mark Ayres, Ray White and many others.

21 Hutton, 2003.

22 www.delia-derbyshire.org.

23 Marshall, 2008.

24 *Ibid.* Named for the road outside the Maida Vale studios, Marshall claims it was the biggest in the world at the time in 1970. As it boasted sixteen oscillators, it probably was one of the largest, at least.

25 For a thorough discussion on the evolution of the recording studio, see Schedel, 2007.

26 Like indabamusic.com or looplabs.com, among many others.

27 Duignan, Noble and Biddle, 2005. Although their classification is very useful, I have reinterpreted it broadly here since there is so much crossover between categories.

28 Also known as Visual Programming Languages, but Miller Puckette refers to Max as a Graphical Programming Environment, which I find more accurate. Puckette, 1991.

29 http://cycling74.com/.

30 As acknowledged by Puckette in his 1997 paper on PD (Puckette, 1997).

31 This is stated by Ge Wang in the *Cambridge Companion to Electronic Music* (Wang, 2007), but he specifies 'similar modular approach to synthesis', and this may be due to the fact that it was conceived to describe not only control but also signal flow, although signal processing only came later when added by David Zicarelli in the form of MSP.

32 Puckette, 1991.

33 *Ibid.*

34 http://puredata.info/.

35 Puckette, 1997.
36 http://recherche.ircam.fr/equipes/repmus/OpenMusic/.
37 McCartney, 1996.
38 McCartney, 2002.
39 *Ibid.*
40 Boulanger, 2000.
41 Wang, 2007, has a comprehensive account of the history of computer music languages.
42 Wang and Cook, 2003.
43 *Ibid.*
44 Sorensen, 2005.
45 http://wiring.org.co/.
46 www.uisoftware.com.
47 www.sensomusic.com/usine/.
48 At the time of writing, late 2010, the market is filling with tablet computing alter-natives to the Apple iPad, developed on Google software (Android and perhaps ChromeOS).
49 www.reactable.com.

9 Controllers: new creative possibilities in performance

1 In academic papers, the term 'digital musical instruments' has been used by Wanderley and Depalle (2004): '[input] devices and sound synthesis methods can be combined to create new computer-based musical instruments, or digital musical instruments (DMI)'. It seems a bit misleading to me to want to make this a specialised term, though, since as working musicians we have talked about synths like the Yamaha DX7 as digital musical instruments since 1983!
 2 In the work of Bongers, 2000, there is a thorough consideration of these issues of interaction and decoupling of sound source versus control surface.
 3 Open Sound Control (OSC) is a protocol or standard for communication between computers, sound synthesisers and other multimedia devices that makes use of net-working technology (which means you can send triggers and information through internet ports). See http://opensoundcontrol.org/introduction-osc.
 4 I recommend you read 'Virtual Musical Instruments: Accessing the Sound Synthesis Universe as a Performer' from 1997 by Axel Mulder, working at the time at the School of Kinesiology, Simon Fraser University, for an interesting definition of virtual musical instruments and for a discussion of why one would want to capture gesture to control electroacoustic sound.
 5 Bongers, 2000.
 6 *Ibid.*
 7 See Collins, 2009, pp. 214–26, for more on computers as live musical agents.
 8 If you were to search in Wikipedia for 'list of sensors' you would get an impressive list sorted by type. You could also then search for the manufacturers to buy direct.

9 www.arduino.cc; but there are many compatible arduino clones like FreeduinoSB (by Solarbotics), Metaboard and Cosmo BlackSta,r among many others; a good link to compare options is: http://en.wikipedia.org/wiki/Arduino.

10 If you find these numbers familiar, you are probably a SuperCollider user!

11 To be very precise, each OSC message contains an address pattern, not an OSC address. See Wright, Freed and Momeini, 2003.

12 In MIDI you can send pitchbend from one controller to a synth and Note-on from another to the same synth, but you cannot send Note-on from two sources to the same MIDI synth without potentially wreaking havoc with the polyphony, because MIDI instruments assume just one player per synth.

13 www.nime.org.

14 www.namm.org.

15 http://musik.messefrankfurt.com.

16 www.aes.org.

10   Hacking electronics for music

1 George, 1987.

2 Wierzbicki, 2005.

3 Davies, 2010.

4 Apollonio, 1973, p. 22.

5 *Ibid.*, p. 75.

6 Wierzbicki, 2005, p. 34.

7 *Ibid.*

8 Collins, 2009, 'art & music 8'.

9 www.steim.org.

10 I can still remember a performance in the '80s by the late Michel Waisvisz, one of the earliest members of Steim and its artistic and managing director for many years, using his custom-built instrument called 'The Hands'. At the time, he used sensors and triggers to allow his hand gestures to be translated into sound manipulation very effectively, controlling a bank of eight Yamaha FM TX816 synthesisers. With later hacks he incorporated microphones and sampling controls, always guided by the importance of physicality in performance.

11 STEIM, 2010.

12 Collins, 2009.

13 *Ibid.*

14 Ghazala, 2005.

15 www.nicolascollins.com/handmade.htm.

16 Ghazala, 2005.

17 www.anti-theory.com.

18 Ghazala, 2010.

19 Collins, 2009.
20 Ghazala, 2005.
21 Collins, 2009.
22 *Ibid.*
23 *Ibid.*

Further avenues for exploration

1 If you are new to Google scholar: you can often find free pdf files of otherwise restricted access materials by clicking on 'All xx versions' below the search result.

Glossary

I have tried to define everything within the text itself, but I chose to include the following terms here as I felt they needed a little more definition and doing that within the text could have produced confusion.

Acapella
From 'a cappella', a musical term used in early music to differentiate pieces for solo voices sung as 'in chapel' from instrumental pieces to be sung in lay social settings, 'in chambers' or 'de camera'. In Hip-Hop, an 'acapella' is rap with no music under it.

Algorithmic music
In computer music, it is music generated by rules (an algorithm) programmed into the computer.

Alternating current
An electrical current that changes direction periodically.

Anempathetic
A term borrowed from psychology by Michel Chion in his book *Audio-Vision* to describe sound or music that seems to contradict what we see on film.

Artifact
An object that results from the practice of art or craftsmanship.

Band-Pass Filter
A filter in which only frequencies within a range of frequencies (the 'band') will pass untouched, while frequencies below and above it will be dampened.

Buffered (sound)
In music programming, refers to creating a temporary digital address for a sound file to be stored in RAM so it can be instantly recalled.

Capacitor
An electronic component that can store electric charge as well as impede the passage of alternating currency of a certain frequency.

Chamberlin
An early sampling instrument introduced in the 1950s, it was a precursor to the Mellotron and to our modern sampler. It worked by triggering tape loops from a keyboard (not too dissimilar from the phonogène, but designed for popular music).

Codecs

Coding-decoding refers in music technology to software that codes or decodes a signal for the purposes of processing or transmitting it digitally.

Compression

The opposite of rarefaction, with regards to a sound wave: the augmenting of density and thus pressure in the air.

Convolution

A mathematical term for the blending of two functions; in audio these functions are waveforms that produce a combined but modified version of the two original waveforms.

Cut-off point

Refers to filtering: it is the frequency threshold from which to attenuate or emphasise a sound.

Cymatics

This is a method that consists of placing plates (known as Chladni plates) filled with fluids, or covered in sand, on top of an acoustic resonator or loudspeakers. The vibrations effected on the fluids or sand create beautiful patterns that change according to frequency and amplitude content in the audio signal. See www.cymatics.org.

DAW

The term DAW appeared in the late 1980s to denote turnkey systems comprising custom-made audio hardware for digital to analogue and analogue to digital conversion and audio acceleration and software for recording, mixing and editing audio. The first working system in stereo

was the Sound Tools (1989) by Digidesign, followed by ProTools with multitracking capability. Digidesign made, and still makes, all their own hardware to complement the software. The first MIDI sequencer to incorporate audio was Opcode's Studio Vision (1990). Sometimes DAWs would be included in a truly standalone machine such as the Roland DM80 (1991). I will refer to all software DAWs and audio + midi sequencers as audio sequencers, because the distinction between them is today irrelevant for the users.

Diegetic

In discussing film, something that pertains to the narrative or 'diegesis' of a film. If we hear music playing back from a radio in a scene from a film, that music is said to be diegetic.

Domain

The word 'domain' originally means something upon which one has mastery or claim. This word is much used by computer scientists: it means an area of things, or a set of things that belong together. For example a time-domain representation of sound is when we graphically express all amplitudes in terms of when they occur (time). In programming, it refers to the area in which a variable will hold its value, so, for example, if a variable is defined within a function, then all elements inside the function can call upon that variable.

Empathetic

A term borrowed from psychology by Michel Chion in his book *Audio-Vision* to describe sound or music that seems to correspond to the film.

Envelope
The way a synthesis parameter changes over time.

Filter
A device for boosting or attenuating a range of frequencies of a sound. The boosting or attenuation is expressed in dB changes per octave of sound, i.e. how sharply the sound 'rolls off' from the cutoff point. Thus, a 24 dB per octave roll-off implies a reduction in the level of sound of 24 dB progressively between the cut-off point and its octave (which is double the frequency).

Frequency band
Used in audio when talking about ranges of frequencies; a 'band' is simply a range, for example 200 Hz to 8 kHz.

High-Pass Filter
A filter in which only frequencies above the cut-off point (frequency) will pass untouched, while frequencies below it will be dampened.

Inductor
An electrical component that can generate a magnetic field when current runs through it; it also impedes the passing of alternating high-frequency currents.

Instantiate
'Instantiating' is a term from computer science and refers to creating an 'instance' of the software object you want to work with.

ISO
International Standardization Organization is a non-governmental organisation coordinating international standards for 163 countries, with a central secretariat in Geneva, Switzerland.

Low-Pass Filter
A filter in which only frequencies below the cut-off point (frequency) will pass untouched while frequencies above it will be dampened.

Mellotron
A playback sampler successor to the Chamberlin and much used in popular music of the 1960s and 1970s, especially in Prog Rock.

Modulation
A key term in music technology, it simply means the change of a parameter. To modulate something is to change it in some way. In music it means to change from one key to another, but it can also be used to describe the change between related metres of rhythm.

Noise floor
In recording, it is the underlying ambient noise when music is not being played.

Noise
A term which adopts many meanings depending on context. In music it may mean anything that doesn't have recognisable pitch, for instance. In synthesis – which is what we use it mostly for in music technology – when we speak of noise we refer to waveforms where all frequencies are present with random amplitude at any given moment. Defining this mathematically is quite complex. There are several types of noise that we often encounter in synthesis: white noise, pink noise and brown noise. In white noise, the randomness is not weighted in

favour of any particular amplitude value, so the result is a sound that contains all frequencies with equal power across the frequency spectrum (20 Hz to 20 kHz). The resulting sound is very harsh, and, for this reason, a rich source for filtering. Pink noise is similar, but the randomness is weighted towards the lower frequencies (they will appear more often) in such a way that results in the spectrum losing power by 3 dB across the frequency spectrum every octave, starting from the lowest. Thus, as we go up the frequency spectrum, we start losing the top end and the sound is somewhat 'bassy'. Brown noise is an even more bass-heavy pink noise, as the power falls by 6 dB across the frequency spectrum every octave.

Phonogène

A machine invented in 1953 by Pierre Schaeffer and Jacques Poullin for controlling the playback speed of tape loops.

Protocol

An agreed way to do something; in the case of digital audio it refers to agreeing on standard messages and ways to construct them for communication: for instance, the MIDI protocol.

Quantisation

In signal processing it means to approximate values to a resolution grid; in sequencing it means the same but is applied to rhythm. For example, if you play a melody made up of semiquavers and you quantise to quavers, all your semiquavers will be aligned to the nearest division of the quaver grid. If you determine the smallest rhythmic subdivision that you intend to play you can use it for tightening the rhythm of your MIDI recording and usually you can set a degree of quantisation so that the result is not too mechanical.

Rarefaction

With regards to a sound wave: the diminishing of density and thus pressure in the air.

Sampling resolution

It refers to how detailed a sample has been taken, in general: more samples per second and more numbers to represent them.

Sonification

In science, it is when you map data (information) to sound parameters to obtain an aural representation of the data: the Geiger counter is an example of this for measuring radiation. In sonic arts, it is a similar process but with musical results.

Standing waves

We use this term for sound waves that get trapped by the acoustic configuration of a room and resonate, enhancing a certain frequency of the sound.

Summing

Summing means exactly that: waveforms are summed, or added together, sample by sample to create a new waveform.

Temp track

A film-music soundtrack put together temporarily by the film editor to help give an impression of how the music will interact with the visuals. If it is done too successfully, it can end up being the final music track or, worse, the composer will have to imitate the temp track!

Toslink
An optical fibre connector for digital audio.

Word clock
A signal for synchronising digital devices.

Zero-crossing
The point at which a waveform's amplitude is equal to zero.

Bibliography

Apollonio, U. 1973. *Futurist Manifestos*. London: Thames and Hudson.

Berger, E. H., Neitzel, R. and Kladden, C. A. 2008. 'Noise Navigator® Sound Level Database with Over 1700 Measurement Values. E•A•R' Aearo Company and University of Washington, Department of Environmental and Occupational Health Sciences, Seattle WA., at http://nhca.affiniscape.com/associations/10915/files/Noise%5FNav%2Exls.

Blake, A. 2009. 'Recording Practices and the Role of the Producer', in *The Cambridge Companion to Recorded Music*, ed. N. Cook, *et al*. Cambridge: Cambridge University Press.

Bongers, B. 2000. 'Physical Interfaces in the Electronic Arts: Interaction Theory and Interfacing Techniques for Real-Time Performance', in *Trends in Gestural Control of Music*, ed. M. Wanderley and M. Battier. Paris: Institut de Recherche et Coordination Acoustique Musique – Centre Pompidou.

Boulanger, R. 2000. *The Csound Book: Perspectives in Software Synthesis, Sound Design, Signal Processing and Programming*. Cambridge, MA: MIT Press.

Brock-Nannestad, G. 2009. 'The Development of Recording Techniques', in *The Cambridge Companion to Recorded Music*, ed. N. Cook, *et al*. Cambridge: Cambridge University Press.

Cage, J. 2009. *Silence*. London: Marion Boyars.

Chion, M. 1994. *Audio-Vision: Sound on Screen*. New York: Columbia University Press.

Chusid, I. 2000. *Manhattan Research Inc.: New Plastic Sounds and Electronic Abstractions. Composed and Performed by Raymond Scott*. Holland: BASTA Audiovisuals.

Collins, K. 2008. *Game Sound*. Cambridge, MA: MIT Press.

Collins, N. 2009. *Handmade Electronic Music: The Art of Hardware Hacking*, 2nd edn. New York: Routledge.

Collins, N. 2009. *Introduction to Computer Music*. Chichester: Wiley.

Cook, N. 2000. *Analysing Musical Multimedia*. Oxford: Oxford University Press.

Cook, N., Clarke, E., Leech-Wilkinson, D. and Rink D. 2009. *The Cambridge Companion to Recorded Music*. Cambridge: Cambridge University Press.

Cooper, S. 2001. 'Coldcut', in *All Music Guide to Electronica: The Definitive Guide to Electronic Music*, ed. V. Bogdanov *et al*. San Francisco: Backbeat Books.

Covach, J. 2009. *What's that Sound? An Introduction to Rock and its History*. New York: W. W. Norton & Company, Inc.

Cowie, D. F. 2009. 'Grandmaster Flash' in Conversations, at www.exclaim.ca/articles/multiarticlesub.aspx?csid1=131&csid2=946&fid1=37652.

Cunningham, M. 1998. *Good Vibrations: A History of Record Production*. London: Sanctuary Publishing Ltd.

Crab, S. 2005. 'Elisha Gray and "The Musical Telegraph" (1876)' at http://120years.net/machines/telegraph/index.html.

Creative Commons. 2010. at http://creativecommons.org/.

Crook, T. 1999. *Radio Drama: Theory and Practice*. London: Routledge.

Dacks, D. 2007. 'Dub Voyage: A Jamaican Offshoot's Journey From Studio Accident to World Power', in Research at www.exclaim.ca/articles/multiarticlesub.aspx?csid1=114&csid2=779&fid1=27342.

Davies, H. 2010. 'Electronic Instruments', *Grove Music Online* at www.oxfordmusiconline.com/subscriber/article/grove/music/08694pg1#S08694.1.

Davies, H., 2010. 'Drawn sound', *Grove Music Online* at www.oxfordmusiconline.com/subscriber/article/grove/music/47632.

Davies, G. and Jones, R. 1989. *Sound Reinforcement Handbook*, 2nd edn. Milwaukee, WI: Hal Leonard Publishing Corporation.

Davies, R. 1999. *Complete Guide to Film Scoring: The Art and Business of Writing Music for Movies and TV*. Boston, MA: Berklee Press.

Davis, R. 2010. *The Complete Guide to Film Scoring*. Boston: Berklee Press.

d'Escriván, J. 2009. 'Sound Art (?) on/in Film', *Organised Sound*, 14, 1, 65–73.

Draper, J. 1931. 'Sound Tricks in the Talkies', *Popular Mechanics*, 55, 2, 236–41.

Duignan, M., Noble, J. and Biddle, R. 2005. 'A Taxonomy of Sequencer User-Interfaces', in *Proceedings of the International Computer Music Conference* (ICMC-05, Barcelona). International Computer Music Association.

Eisenberg, E. 2005. *The Recording Angel*. New Haven and London: Yale University Press.

Eno, B. 1983. 'The Studio as Compositional Tool', *Downbeat*, 50 (July–August), 56–7 and 50–2.

Everest, F. A. and Pohlmann, K. C. 2009. *Master Handbook of Acoustics*. New York: McGraw-Hill Publishing. Retrieved 6 March 2010, from http://lib.myilibrary.com/Browse/open.asp?ID=219318&loc=329.

Everett, W. 2001. *The Beatles as Musicians: The Quarry Men through Rubber Soul*. Oxford: Oxford University Press.

Flans, R. 2005. Classic Tracks: Phil Collins' 'In the Air Tonight' at http://mixonline.com/mag/audio_phil_collins_air/index.html/.

Fligor, B. and Meinke, D. 2009. 'Safe-Listening Myths for Personal Music Players', in *The ASHA Leader* at www.asha.org/Publications/leader/2009/090526/090526e.htm.

Gallagher, M. 2008. *Music Tech Dictionary: A Glossary of Audio-Related Terms and Technologies*. Boston: Course Technology.

Games Soundtracks' Website. 2010. Interview with Troels B. Folmann, available at: www.gsoundtracks.com/interviews/folmann.htm.

Gardner, W. G. 1998. *3-D Audio Using Loudspeakers*. Norwell, MA: Kluwer Academic Publishers.

George, Frank, 1987. 'Wiener, Norbert', in *The Oxford Companion to the Mind*, ed. Richard L. Gregory. Oxford: Oxford University Press.

George, N. 2004. 'Sample This', in *That's the Joint! The Hip-Hop Studies Reader*, ed. Mark Anthony Neal and Murray Foreman. New York: Taylor & Francis. Available from: http://lib.myilibrary.com?ID=34789.

Ghazala, R. 2005. *Circuit Bending: Build Your Own Alien Instruments*. Indianapolis, IN: Wiley.

Ghazala, R. 2010. 'ghazala' at: www.anti-theory.com/bio.

Gottlieb, Gary. 2007. *Shaping Sound in the Studio and Beyond: Audio Aesthetics and Technology*. Boston, MA: Course Technology.

Grimshaw, M., Lindley, C. A. and Nacke, L. 2008. 'Sound and Immersion in the First-Person Shooter: Mixed Measurement of the Player's Sonic Experience', in *Audio Mostly*, 9–15. Piteå: Interactive Institute.

Gross, J. 1998. 'Christian Marclay Interview', in *Perfect Sound Forever* at www.furious.com/perfect/christianmarclay.html.

Harrison, J. 2000. 'Diffusion: Theories and Practices, with Particular Reference to the BEAST System', paper presented at SEAMUS Y2K Texas, USA.

Holmes, T. 2002. *Electronic and Experimental Music*. New York: Routledge.

Huber, D. M. and Runstein, R. E. 2010. *Modern Recording Techniques*. Oxford: Focal Press.

Hutton, J. 2003. 'Daphne Oram: Innovator, Writer and Composer', *Organised Sound*, 8, 1, 49–56.

Janus, S. 2004. *Audio in the 21st Century*. Hillsboro, OR: Intel Press.

Jordan, W. E. 1953. 'Norman McLaren: His Career and Techniques', *The Quarterly of Film Radio and Television*, 8, 1, 1–14.

Landy, L. 2007. *Understanding the Art of Sound Organisation*. Cambridge, MA: MIT Press.

Lethem, J. 2007. 'The Ecstasy of Influence: A Plagiarism', *Harper's Magazine* (February) at: http://harpers.org/archive/2007/02/0081387.

Levin, T. Y. 2003. '"Tones from Out of Nowhere": Rudolph Pfenninger and the Archaeology of Synthetic Sound', *Grey Room*, 12, 32–79.

Loy, G. 2006. *Musimathics: The Mathematical Foundations of Music*. Vol. 1. Cambridge, MA: MIT Press.

Loy, G. and Chowning, J. 2007. *Musimathics: The Mathematical Foundations of Music*. Vol. 2. Cambridge, MA: MIT Press.

Mandel, H. 1996. 'Joe Zawinul at 65: Interview with Joe Zawinul', *The Wire*, 149 (July).

Manning, P. 2004. *Electronic and Computer Music*. Oxford: Oxford University Press.

Marshall, S. 2008. 'The Story of The BBC Radiophonic Workshop', in *Sound on Sound* (April). Cambridge: Relative Media.

Massey, H. 2000. *Behind the Glass: Top Record Producers Tell How They Craft the Hits*. San Francisco: Backbeat Books.

McCartney, J. 1996. 'SuperCollider: A New Real Time Synthesis Language', in *Proceedings of the International Computer Music Conference* (Hong Kong, August 1996). Logroño: Universidad de La Rioja.

McCartney, J. 2002. 'Rethinking the Computer Music Language: SuperCollider', *Computer Music Journal*, 26, 4, 61–8.

Michie, C. 2003. 'We are the Mothers . . . and This Is What We Sound Like!' *Mixonline* at: http://mixonline.com/recording/business/audio_mothers_sound.

Moore, B. C. J. 2000. *An Introduction to the Psychology of Hearing*. San Diego: Academic Press.

Moorefield, Virgil. 2005. *The Producer as Composer*. Cambridge, MA: MIT Press.

Mulder, Axel G. E. 1994. 'Virtual Musical Instruments: Accessing the Sound Synthesis Universe as a Performer', in *Proceedings of the First Brazilian Symposium on Computer Music* held in Caxambu, Minas Gerais, Brazil. Belo Horizonte, M.G., Brazil: Universidade Federal de Minas Gerais.

Newell, P. 2002. *Studio Monitoring Design*. Oxford: Focal Press.

Ondaatje, M. 2002. *The Conversations: Walter Murch and the Art of Editing Film*. London: Bloomsbury Publishing.

Oswald, J. 2006. 'Bettered by the Borrower: The Ethics of Musical Debt', in *Audio Culture: Readings in Modern Music*, ed. C. Cox and D. Warner. London: The Continuum International Publishing Group.

Owsinski, B. 2009. *Recording Engineer's Handbook*, 2nd edn. Boston, MA: Course Technology.

Preve, F. 2006. *Remixer's Bible: Build Better Beats*. San Francisco: Backbeat Books.

Puckette, M. 1991. 'Combining Event and Signal Processing in the Max Graphical Programming Environment', *Computer Music Journal*, 15, 3, 68–77.

Puckette, M. 1997. 'Pure Data: Another Integrated Computer Music Environment', in *Proceedings: Second Intercollege Computer Music Concerts*, Tachikawa, pp. 37–41. Tokyo: Kunitachi College of Music.

Reck-Miranda, E. 2002. *Computer Sound Design: Synthesis Techniques and Programming*, 2nd edn. Oxford: Focal Press.

Reck-Miranda, E. and Wanderley, M. 2006. *New Digital Musical Instruments: Control and Interaction Beyond the Keyboard*. Middleton, WI: A-R Editions.

Roads, C. 1996. *The Computer Music Tutorial*. Cambridge, MA: MIT Press.

Roads, C. 2004. *Microsound*. Cambridge, MA: MIT Press.

Rosen, J. 2006. 'The Greatest Song Ever, "Good Times": An Iinterview with Nile Rodgers' in *The Guide* at: www.blender.com/guide/68321/greatest-songs-ever-good-times.html.

Rumsey, F. and McCormick, T. 2009. *Sound and Recording*. Oxford: Focal Press.

Schedel, M. 2007. 'Electronic Music and the Studio', in *The Cambridge Companion to Electronic Music*, ed. N. Collins and J. d'Escriván. Cambridge: Cambridge University Press.

Schmeder, A., Freed, A. and Wessel, D. 2010. 'Best Practices for Open Sound Control', in *Proceedings of the 2010 Linux Audio Conference*, Utrecht, Netherlands. Utrecht: Hogeschool voor de Kunsten.

Schnell, N. and Battier, M. 2002. 'Introducing Composed Instruments, Technical and Musicological Implications', in *Proceedings of the 2002 Conference on New Instruments for Musical Expression* (NIME-02, Dublin).

Serafin, S. 2004. 'Sound Design to Enhance Presence in Photorealistic Virtual Reality', in *Proceedings of the 2004 International Conference on Auditory Display*, Sidney, Australia.

Serafin, S. 2007. 'Computer Generation and Manipulation of Sounds', in *The Cambridge Companion to Electronic Music*, ed. N. Collins and J. d'Escrivân. Cambridge: Cambridge University Press.

Sieveking, L. 1934. *The Stuff of Radio*. London: Cassell.

Slaven, N. 2003. *Electric Quixote: The Definitive Story of Frank Zappa*. London: Omnibus Press.

Smith, J. O. 1991. 'Viewpoints on the History of Digital Synthesis', in *Proceedings of the International Computer Music Conference* (ICMC-91, Montreal), pp. 1–10, International Computer Music Association.

Sorensen, A. 2005. 'Impromptu: An Interactive Programming Environment for Composition and Performance', in *Proceedings of the Australasian Computer Music Conference* (2005, Brisbane). Australasian Computer Music Association, pp. 149–53.

STEIM. 'STEIM's Electro Squeek Club' at: www.steim.org/steim/piepen.html#e13 (accessed 2010).

Sullivan, M. 1987. '"More Popular than Jesus": The Beatles and the Religious Far Right', *Popular Music*, 6, 3, 313–26.

Suzuki, Y., Mellert, V., Richter, U., Møller, H., Nielsen, L., Hellman, R., Ashihara, K., Ozawa, K. and Takeshima, H. 2003. 'Precise and Full-range Determination of Two-dimensional Equal Loudness Contours', available at: http://ids-ge.ch/IMG/pdf/is-01e.pdf.

Sweetser, P. and Wyeth, P. 2005. 'GameFlow: A Model for Evaluating Player Enjoyment', *Games ACM Computers in Entertainment*, 3, 3.

Theisen, E. 1937. 'Sound Tricks of Mickey Mouse', *Modern Mechanix* (January), pp. 68–74.

Toiviainen, P. 2007. 'The Psychology of Electronic Music', in *The Cambridge Companion to Electronic Music*, ed. N. Collins and J. d'Escrivân. Cambridge: Cambridge University Press.

Tolonen, T., Välimäki, V. and Karjalainen, M. 1998. 'Evaluation of Modern Sound Synthesis Methods', in *Report No. 48 of the TKK Acoustics Lab Report Series*, Helsinki University of Technology, Department of Electrical and Communications Engineering, Laboratory of Acoustics and Audio Signal Processing, available at: www.acoustics.hut.fi/publications.

Toop, D. 2000. *Rap Attack*. Vicenza: Legoprint.

Volker, H. 1987. 'History of Cybernetics', in *The Oxford Companion to the Mind*, ed. Richard L. Gregory. Oxford: Oxford University Press.

Wanderley, M. and Depalle, P. 2004. 'Gestural Control of Sound Synthesis', in *Proceedings of the IEEE*, 92, 4, 632–44.

Wang, G. and Cook, P. 2003. 'ChucK: A Concurrent, On-the-fly, Audio Programming Language', in *Proceedings of the International Computer Music Conference* (ICMC-03, Singapore), International Computer Music Association.

Wang, G. 2007. 'A History of Programming and Music', in *The Cambridge Companion to Electronic Music*, ed. N. Collins and J. d'Escriván. Cambridge: Cambridge University Press.

Watson, B. 1996. 'Frank Zappa as Dadaist: Recording Technology and the Power to Repeat', *Contemporary Music Review*, 15, 1, 109–37.

Wierzbicki, J. 2005. *Louis and Bebe Barron's Forbidden Planet: A Film Score Guide*. Lanham, MD: Scarecrow Press.

Wright, M., Freed, A. and Momeini, A. 2003. 'OpenSound Control: State of the Art 2003', in *Proceedings of the 2003 Conference on New Interfaces for Musical Expression* (NIME-03, Montreal).

Xenakis, I. 1992. *Formalized Music*. Stuyvesant, NY: Pendragon Press.

Filmography

Crosland, Alan. 1927. *The Jazz Singer* [DVD]. Warner Bros.

Lucas, George. 1971. *THX1138* [DVD]. American Zoetrope.

Tarkovsky, Andrei. 1972. *Solaris* [DVD]. Artificial Eye.

Wise, Robert. 1951. *The Day the Earth Stood Still* [DVD]. 20th Century Fox Home Entertainment.

Spielberg, Stephen. 2005. *E.T. The Extra Terrestrial* [DVD]. Universal.

Discography

All dates correspond to the latest issue

Beatles, The. 1967. *Sgt. Pepper's Lonely Hearts Club Band* [CD]. Parlophone.
    2009. 'Tomorrow never knows' on *Revolver* [CD]. EMI Parlophone 0946 3 82417.

Bee-Gees. 1988. *Main Course* [CD]. Polydor.

Buddy Holly. 1957. 'Peggy Sue' [Vinyl single]. USA: DECCA.
    'Every Day' [Vinyl single]. USA: DECCA.

Esquivel, Juan García. 1962. *Latinesque* [CD]. USA: RCA Victor.

Genesis. 2009. *Nursery Ryme: Remastered* [CD]. Virgin.

Horn, Trevor. 2004. *Various: Produced by Trevor Horn* [CD]. ZTT.

Les Paul. 2005. *The Best of the Capitol Masters: 90th Birthday Edition* [CD]. Capitol.

London, Johnny. 2006. 'Drivin' Slow' on *Black Music Originals* [CD]. Charly Records.

Meek, Joe and the Blue Men. 1960. *Magnetic Field EP* [CD]. Sinetone AMR.

Meek, Joe. 2006. *I Hear a New World: An Outer Space Music Fantasy* [CD]. RPM.

Moody Blues. 2008. 'Nights of White Satin' on *Days of Future Passed* [Spotify]. Decca Music Group Ltd.

Pink Floyd. 1994. *Dark Side of the Moon* [CD]. EMI.

Presley, Elvis. 1954. 'Blue Moon of Kentucky' [Vinyl single]. Sun Records.

Radiohead. 2001. *Knives Out* [CD]. Parlaphone.

Schaeffer, P. and Henri, P. 1973. *Symphonie pour un homme seul* [CD]. Philips.

Small Faces. 1999. 'Itchycoo Park' [Spotify]. Sanctuary Records Group.

Spector, P. 2006. *Phil Spector Definitive Collection* [Spotify]. Universal Music TV, a division of Universal Music Operations Ltd.

Stoller, Mike and Leiber, Jerry. 1956. 'Down In Mexico' [Vinyl single]. Atco.

Stock, Aitken and Waterman. 1987. *The Hit Factory: The Best of Stock Aitken Waterman* [CD]. Stylus/PWL.

Summer, Donna. 2007. *The Dance Collection* [CD]. Spectrum.

Wilson, Brian. 2000. *Pet Sounds: Original Recording Remastered* [CD]. Capitol/EMI.

Zappa, Frank. 1999. *Freak Out* [CD]. Rykodisc.

Index

TOWER HAMLETS COLLEGE
L   e
/   s
LO   0PT
Te 020 7   7568

Lightning Source UK Ltd.
Milton Keynes UK
UKOW06f0102231014

240506UK00003B/145/P

9 780521 170420